THE COMPLETE
Fox Terrier
(Smooth and Wire)

by EVELYN L. SILVERNAIL

ILLUSTRATED

SECOND EDITION

1972

HOWELL BOOK HOUSE INC.

845 THIRD AVENUE

NEW YORK, N.Y. 10022

This book is dedicated to

PAUL,

my husband, whose encouragement
and constant help and belief in
me over all these years have made
possible the success I enjoy with
my dogs today.

"Buy a pup and your money will buy
love unflinching that cannot lie."
—RUDYARD KIPLING.

Foreword

AS I write this book on my love—the Fox Terrier—I am deeply grateful to the many people who made the book possible.

First, to my family, who over the years has also shared my enthusiasm for dogs. Second, to the many friends who not only supplied me with pictures and the incentive to write, but also had faith in my ability.

I only hope that those who have long been interested in the breed, as well as the newcomers to the breed, derive some measure of value and perhaps pleasure from the results.

I am indebted to Mr. Ernest Hart for his excellent drawings and Mr. Stephen Hodio for his photographs which appear herein. Also, to Miss Peterson, Librarian of The American Kennel Club, for her help in my research.

I think I am most deeply indebted to the little dog who made all this possible, who taught me so much, and who opened up a whole new life for me—my first "Wire"—LADY CRACK-DALE.

EVELYN L. SILVERNAIL

4

Table of Contents

PART I

By *Evelyn L. Silvernail*

THE AUTHOR
with an armful of puppies

The History of the Breed

MUCH has been said about dogs—of the different breeds and their characteristics, of their service to mankind, and always of their unselfish devotion to their owners. This book is dedicated to just one breed (one that to me personifies the good in all breeds), the Fox Terrier, Smooth and Wire. It is my desire to make this book interesting to all who read it, from the viewpoint of breeder, exhibitor, judge, and, last but not least, devoted lover of the breed.

The Fox Terrier originated in the British Isles and its ancestry can be traced back for a period of over a century and a half. We have proof of this in known paintings dated 1798 by English artists. These are indeed interesting to study, for of course they only resemble the Fox Terrier as we know him today. The improvement through the years is most apparent and has been most worthwhile.

The English author L. P. C. Astley describes this breed in his book *The Perfect Fox Terrier,* thus: "His combination of grace, beauty, gameness, utility and intuition are such as to appeal to the heart of every Englishman; they are qualities he admires in another man, 'Like master, like dog,' we say. Britain need never fear for her Empire as long as she can produce men and terriers of such a type." This shows how high the Fox Terrier rates in the esteem of the English and these same feelings are shared by all others who have owned one.

It has often been said, "Once a Fox Terrier lover, always a Fox Terrier lover," and rightly so. This little dog possesses characteristics that endear him to all who really know him—the smart looking Smooth, with his sleek coat and evenly chiseled features, and the Wire, with his dense wiry overcoat, not a hair out of place, a square-cut chin (the effect of his whiskers), and legs straight and stiff like broomsticks. Intelligence is immediately apparent in his small, clear, dark brown eyes, and one can also perceive a glimpse of the mischievousness that is part of him. One look at him when he is strolling along the avenue will show the proud bearing of this little dog. His gameness can at once be tested, let him meet a Great Dane, an elephant, or a steam engine—he meets all alike with a chip on his little shoulders and confidence in his stride! It must be remembered that the Smooth and the Wire are brothers under the coat, and that their points are identical in every way.

The Fox Terrier's evolution from the hunting fields to the homes and hearths of the gentry of England was the result of the Industrial Revolution, which made him a dog with guts and fire about him, preferable to the simpering Toys and the huge clumsy Hounds which had once held such favor. The Fox Terrier's smart appearance appealed to the woman—his companionship and ready ability to change his moods, to the man. He is truly a man's or a woman's dog, but he has also been aptly described as the "chorus girl of the dog family."

Terriers have been synonymous with England for centuries and it does not behoove us to go into their past, except to touch lightly on the facts directly concerning them after the first attempt to perfect them as distinct breeds, which began about 1860 with the Smooth Fox Terrier. But to the reader of early works on the breed, it becomes apparent that authorities differ on which breeds were crossed to bring about our Fox Terriers of today. I think that perhaps the most interesting of all that I have read is the opinion of Mr. Harding Cox, in his book *Dogs* in the volume "The Terriers," published in London in 1906.

Mr. Cox writes, "Although the origin of the Fox-Terrier is anything but remote, it is more or less mysterious, and authorities differ as to its component tap-roots. Towards the close of the eighteenth century pictorial art proclaims that there even then existed a Terrier, the predominating color of which was white, with various markings; but it was not until the next century was well advanced that the Fox-Terrier was generally recognized by that name. Some writers maintain that the 'bull' cross was one of the leading factors in that evolution, whilst others are equally emphatic when declining to recognize any such origin." Mr. Cox goes on to state further: "For my own part I have little doubt as to the primitive cross of the bulldog and the white English Terrier. At the same time the possibility must be admitted that in the early days of the breed, a strain existed which was free from 'bull' blood; being probably the result of a blend of the English Terrier aforesaid, the black-and-tan Terrier, and the beagle.

"In the early days of the Fox-Terrier bench competition, two dogs were much in evidence. These were 'Old Jock' and 'Old Tarter,'—names to conjure with, as representing the strains above alluded to. The former was an elegant gentleman, not far removed from the present-day type; but the latter obviously bore the 'bull' quarterings on his escutcheon, for he was a decidedly cobby little dog, broad chest and a shorter, chumpier head than that of his great rival. He was a hardbitten, devil-may-care character, and had a great influence on the celebrated strain possessed by the late Jack Russell. For a considerable time the two types of Fox-Terrier, as exemplified by the afore-said pillars of the 'Stud Book,' had their respective admirers and were kept tolerably distinct; but gradually they became amalgamated, so that those who maintain that the modern Fox-Terrier owes nothing to the bulldog, are probably in error."

After study of Mr. Cox's findings, one will have to admit that there is, without doubt, a lot of truth in them. However, another early writer of the breed claims that the important ancestors of the Smooth were the smooth-coated Black and Tan Terrier, the Bull Terrier, the Greyhound and the Beagle; while the same writer claims that the old rough-coated Black and Tan working Terrier of Wales, Derbyshire and Durham and the

9

Smooth Fox Terrier were the only ancestors of the Wire. (Until about 1913 the Smooth was the most popular of the two coats.)

It may be well to explain here to those who are not familiar with the derivation of the word *Terrier*, that it comes from the Latin *terra*, meaning earth, indicating a breed of dog that goes to earth after its quarry. The prefix *Fox* qualifies the work for which the breed is suited, for these dogs were used extensively in England to bring the fox to earth. The Fox Terrier was preeminently a working Terrier with a staunch heart, which also indicates one reason why size is very important.

I believe that the Wire variety was descended from the Black and Tan rough-coated Terrier, and, when these early specimens were crossed with the Smooth, produced the Wire, which took its refinement from the Smooth. And, since the Black and Tan was a larger dog, the introduction of the Smooth brought the size down. By careful mating of the best Smooths to the better types of the Black and Tan, there developed what is known today as the Wire variety of the Fox Terrier.

Early English paintings and writings show the existence of these Terriers, both the Smooth and Wire varieties, as early as 1776 and 1798. But not until about the middle of the nineteenth century was serious consideration given to their breeding.

As mentioned earlier, the evolution of the present-day Fox Terrier began about 1860, when attention was first given to purity of breeding. There were whelped at this time four Fox Terriers—three dogs and a bitch—whose names have gone down in history: "Old Jock," "Old Trap," "Belvoir Joe," and "Grove Nettle." From these came the perfection of the Smooth that we know today, but only after careful scientific breeding to a Standard set up to achieve that perfection.

Old Jock was whelped at the kennels of the Grove Hunt and was run for two seasons with the hunt before being shown. He had several owners during his thirteen years, and, while by today's standards he may be considered "high on the leg," he passed on his type as a stamp for all Fox Terriers.

Old Trap was a more stallion-type Terrier and gameness was his outstanding virtue. He, like Old Jock, was shown, but it is

10

SMOOTH FOX TERRIER PUPPIES
Property of Col. Francis R. Appleton, Jr.

WIRE-HAIRED FOX TERRIER PUPPIES
Property of Mrs. Edmund A. Kraft

the accepted fact that he was not so good, all round, as was Jock.

Belvoir Joe was never shown. He was said to have been a coarse dog and on the large side, but the fact that he was mated with an all white bitch, Vick (of Belvoir blood), and produced Belgrave Joe, whose Terrier expression and head were representative of those of our best Smooths today, made him important in the foundation stock of the breed.

The famous bitch Grove Nettle (bred by Mr. W. Merry, Huntsman for the Grove Hounds) is always identified with the above-named trio, forming the famous quartet. And it was progeny of those four that were used by the breeders who were seriously interested in improving the breed at that time.

It was about 1860 that England's first dog show was held at Newcastle. With the coming of dog shows, it became apparent that a certain course would have to be followed among the breeds shown in order to evaluate them properly. Scales of points were formulated, relating to the different sections of the anatomy of the breeds being shown, and thereby were developed the "Standards" for the various breeds.

It is to such men as Messrs. Turner, Cox, Clarke, Vicary, Murchison, Redmond, and Burbidge, among many others, that we owe a token of thanks. For it was through their foresight, by their efforts in breeding, and by the additional efforts of Mr. Harding Cox, that the English Kennel Club was founded in 1875, and that three years later the official Standard for the breed was drawn up.

In the early days, one of the most important figures in the breeding of Wire Fox Terriers was Her Grace, the Duchess of Newcastle. Both Mr. Redmond and Mr. Vicary had bred Wires, but I believe that the most credit for this variety should go to the Duchess, who showed her first Wire in 1893. She took up Fox Terriers seriously about 1898, and her "of Notts" breeding can be traced back in all of the pedigrees of the old "greats."

The Duchess concentrated on breeding what she considered the best of Wire quality of each different strain to get the best points each possessed. She said she got her best small "V"-shaped ear and dark fiery eye from the Vicary strain, and for legs and feet she gave credit to the Redmond strain. Through careful, planned breeding, such as that carried on by the Duchess, was developed what we call scientific breeding in dogs today. And we, who love the breed, are indebted to the early lovers of Fox Terriers who recognized outstanding characteristics and endeavored to perfect the breed.

One can realize now how important the crossing of the Smooth and the Wire was, in those early days, for the purpose of producing a "good Wire Fox Terrier," and then how important it was to breed one good Wire to another in order to reproduce the desired type. In a nutshell, those first interested in the breed fortunately had the ability, the foresight, and the knowledge of what they considered a good Fox Terrier to be, to draw up a Standard and then breed the best specimens among their Smooths toward that Standard. At the same time, they had to pick those specimens that had been crossed with the rough-coated Black and Tan Terriers in order to produce the wire jacket, and in turn to breed the best of the Wires with the best Smooths, then *only* with other Wires until each variety was purebred.

I think it would be wise to mention here a few of the famous early English champions, both Smooths and Wires. If we trace our modern Fox Terriers back far enough, we will find these names appearing in their pedigrees:

Early Smooth Champions

Ch. Oxonian	Ch. Donna Fortuna
Ch. Result	Ch. The Sylph
Ch. Doncaster Dominie	Ch. Bloom
Ch. The Rattler	Ch. Cymro Queen

Early Wire Champions

Ch. Dusty Crackler	Ch. Dusty Tweak
Ch. Cocktail of Notts	Ch. Common Scamp of Notts
Ch. Dusky Siren	Ch. Cackler of Notts
Ch. Meersbrook Bristles	Ch. Cockeye of Notts

It is worthwhile to mention here a few of the reasons that these famous Smooth and Wire champions were outstanding in their

13

CH. GAINES GREAT SURPRISE OF WILDOAKS
(One of this country's greatest producing bitches)
Sire: Ch. Talavera Simon   Dam: New Town Bella Donah

day, and why their success in both the show ring and in breeding ventures lay the groundwork for the betterment of the breed.

CH. THE SYLPH was a bitch bred and owned by Mr. J. C. Tinne, the Honorable Secretary of The Fox Terrier Club, of Bashley Lodge, New Milton, England. The Sylph weighed seventeen pounds and had a white body and black head, with a slight tan on the cheeks and a white line down the center of the skull. She was sired by Verderer out of Kirry Cregeen and was a cross of Ch. Donna Fortuna in the third generation.

Whelped on July 3, 1903, The Sylph made her first appearance in the ring at Windsor under the late Walter S. Glynn in March of 1904. She won more than sixty first prizes and six championships in that year alone, a triumph for a puppy! Then in 1905 she won eight more championships. Her greatest wins were her victory over 131 champions at the Jubilee Show of The Kennel Club at the Crystal Palace, and the winning of the Grand Challenge Cup at The Fox Terrier Club shows of 1904 and 1905.

It was Mr. Tinne's success in blending the two strains of Old Foiler and Belgrave Joe which enabled him to breed a host of beautiful Terriers whose names are to be found in present-day pedigrees.

CH. DONCASTER DOMINIE was a dog bred and owned by Mrs. Bennett Edwards of Hayden Hall, Middlesex, England. He was all white except for black ears, and weighed eighteen pounds. Sired by Duke of Doncaster out of Battles of Merryweather, he began his show career in 1902. Between the years 1902 and 1905, he won thirty-five first prizes—all at the largest shows. In 1903, under Harding Cox at the Crystal Palace, he won the F.T.C. Grand Challenge Cup, the L.F.T.C. Grand Challenge Cup, the Champion of Champions Cup, and Special for best in show. His breeder, Mrs. Edwards, was one of the pioneer Fox Terrier breeders of her sex and enjoyed phenomenal success. Among her other outstanding champions were Doncaster Dodger and Doncaster Dauphine.

CH. DONNA FORTUNA was a bitch bred and owned by Mr. Francis Redmond of Totteridge, England, sired by the famous

15

Ch. Dominie out of Ch. Dame Fortuna. She was all white with the exception of her ears, which were black, and she weighed about eighteen pounds. She was aptly named for she started her show career in February 1897 as a puppy and continued to be shown until she was seven years old—and was never beaten! She won at all of England's principal shows, beginning with Cruft's in 1897, where, although yet a puppy, she defeated her illustrious dam. She captured every honor open to a Fox Terrier and her record has never yet been equaled.

At the age of seven, Ch. Donna Fortuna terminated her show career by winning both the championship and first place in the veteran class at The Fox Terrier Club show at Cheltenham. She was perhaps the best of Mr. Redmond's bitches and great credit is due this breeder for his development of the Belgrave Joe line and the many ensuing champions.

CH. OXONIAN was a dog bred by Mr. Desmond O'Connell of Sarratt, Rickmanworth, England, and later sold to Mr. Frank Reeks of Bransgore, Christchurch, England. Oxonian was a big dog, weighing nineteen and one-half pounds, with black and tan head and ears, and black body markings. He was sired by Dark Blue out of Overture. While he won in the show ring between the years 1904 and 1905, his greatest contribution to the breed was the great improvement he made in legs and feet. His owner, Mr. Reeks, used him very successfully with Mr. Redmond's bitches, and a great line of bitches descended from this cross of two dominant strains.

On the "Wire" side of the picture, it was Mr. Redmond who was responsible for the Smooth-Wire ones and the Wire-Smooth. By these terms we mean that he crossed his Smooth dogs with Wire bitches, and his Wire dogs with Smooth bitches, experimenting to see which gave the most desirable results. Mr. Redmond purchased the Wire bitch Welcome (by Meersbrook Bristles), one of the best Wires of her day, and mated her to the Smooth Ch. Donington to produce a daughter, Don't Go, founder of an outstanding line of brood bitches and winners. However, Mr. Redmond did not have as good results from his other cross, the Wire-Smooth.

16

CH. CRACKLER OF NOTTS, whelped in 1898 and shown through 1905, was bred and owned by Her Grace, the Duchess of Newcastle, Clumber, Worksop, England. Crackler was sired by Ch. Barkby Ben out of Lady Tipton of Notts and was the most outstanding stud force of his day. He sired eight champions. A white dog with tan head markings, he won fifty firsts, and won the fifty-guinea cup three times.

It was the Duchess of Newcastle who was most interested in producing Wires, and it was her "of Notts" strain that was responsible for the production of practically every bench winner in those days. Crackler was probably her most famous dog.

CH. DUSKY SIREN, whelped in 1903, was bred by Mr. Redmond but was later sold to and shown principally by Miss Hatfield of Morden Hall, Surrey, England. Dusky Siren was all white except for one tan ear and many writers of the time credit her with being the best Wire bitch that Mr. Redmond ever bred. She was sired by Ch. Commodore of Notts (a son of Crackler of Notts) out of Dusky Ruth. Her show wins were numerous and included the top awards for the breed during the years 1904 and 1905. She was six times best in show before she became the property of Miss Hatfield and won nine more times after Miss Hatfield owned her.

It is interesting to note that the weight given on both the Smooths and the Wires in those early days was approximately eighteen pounds, just what our present-day Standard calls for, although in tracing through to copies of the earliest Standards, I find that in the beginning, weight was not mentioned. And of course it is true that some of those early dogs did go to twenty pounds or better and were very high on the leg. One must remember, however, that the English were interested in a working Terrier! Also of interest is the fact that the earliest Standard did not designate a definite length of head, merely stating that "it should be long, lean, and of a modified wedge-shape, but sufficiently modelled to escape the coarseness and severe lines as exhibited by other breeds of terriers, notably the bull-terrier." When the American Fox Terrier Club was founded in 1886, the adopted Standard mentioned size, weight, and length of head.

17

INT. CH. CRACKLEY SUPREME OF WILDOAKS
(Dominant stud force in the early days of the breed)
Sire: Ch. Crackley Sensational
Dam: Eden Bridesmaid

Another note of interest to the student of these early Fox Terriers and their show records is that most all were started in the ring at a tender age—when they were between seven and eleven months old. While we start dogs in the puppy classes today, we do not find our winners coming from these classes as they apparently did then. Because the breed was in its infancy and breeders were striving so hard to perfect a winner was no doubt the answer, but in today's shows, the American-bred or open classes usually account for the winners.

Development of the Breed in America

AMONG the early breeders in this country whose Smooth Fox Terriers made history was Mr. F. H. Farwell of Texas, whose "Sabine" prefix is a byword in American Smooth Fox Terrier annals. Others whose interest lay in Smooths in the early days of the breed in America were Messrs. Belmont, Hoey, Thayer, Gooderham, Rutherford, and Kelly. Perhaps the most famous among these men was Winthrop Rutherford, whose "Warren" prefix is as indelible as that of Mr. Farwell.

Mr. Rutherford also earned the Fox Terrier fancy's undying gratitude for his many years of unselfish effort in connection with the Fox Terrier Club's activities. He was elected president of the American Fox Terrier Club in 1896 and held that office for thirty-six years. Mr. Rutherford is spoken of fondly as "that grand old sportsman of Fox Terriers," and in 1942 the Club dedicated its sixty-ninth specialty show as a tribute to him, evidence of the high esteem in which he was held by his fellow members.

The first Wire Fox Terrier to arrive in this country was Tyke, owned by Mr. Jack Grainger and shown in New York in 1883. It was not until 1892 that the first importation of an English champion occurred, with Ch. Brittle being brought over. In 1899 Mr. Charles Keyes of Boston imported Meersbrook Bristles, who has been mentioned earlier. Meersbrook Bristles stamped his quality on his get and was an important addition to the foundation stock in this country. An interesting fact about Bristles, who was whelped in 1892, was that his sire was a *Wire* dog, Knavesmire, who was nine times inbred to Old Tip, and his dam was a *Smooth* bitch, Meersbrook Cristy, who was nine times inbred to Belgrave Joe.

The American Fox Terrier Club, which was the first specialty club to become a member club of The American Kennel Club, held its first show in Newport, Rhode Island, on June 14, 1886, and the judge was the eminent Fox Terrier authority, Mr. Francis Redmond of London. There was an entry of seventy-five Smooth Fox Terriers, dogs and bitches, none of which was entered in any two classes—a departure from the custom in England. It is interesting to note that at the same show there were four Wire Fox Terriers entered. The entry that paraded before Mr. Redmond consisted mainly of imports, for breeding in this country was not yet carried on to any extent.

In his critique, which appeared in the *Fox Terrier Chronicle*, September 1886, Mr. Redmond said: "The first exhibition of The American Fox Terrier Club was held at Newport, R.I. on September 1st and 2nd, and attracted not a little interest among lovers of the dog that has become so deservedly popular in the Mother Country, and judging from the enthusiasm that exists on this side of the Atlantic, we may safely predict will have an equal share of favour here. This, I believe, is the first specialty show that has been held in America, and both numerically and in point of quality must, I submit, be considered a decided success.

"Commencing with the champion class for dogs, two old friends came before me in Splanger and Belgrave Primrose, the former had an easy win, as Belgrave Primrose, beyond his good bone and exceptional legs and feet, has little to recommend him, being much too cloddy and altogether lacking liberty; his coat, although superfluous, is too soft and piley in texture. Splanger has developed into quite a fair dog; he is the right size, has an almost perfect coat, and he is also very good behind the saddle; in head he is not what might be expected from his breeding, especially on his dam's side, being too thick in skull, and somewhat bull terrier-like, but his ears are small and well carried; he might be finer and cleaner in shoulders and front, and his legs and feet, although good, are not first-class; he would be improved with more bone, and the peculiarity of many of Picle II's descendants, to stand back at the knees, and which Splanger showed as a puppy, is still evident in a slight degree; taken all around he is a nice dog, and from his breeding, coat, and other good points, should prove useful at stud in this country."

I have quoted this part of Mr. Redmond's critique to show the great amount of improvement that was necessary in those first dogs which were imported to this country. Mr. Redmond's critique went on to say, "Wirehairs need not be mentioned, as this breed of dogs does not appear to receive much favour here."

That was in 1886. But after Mr. Keyes imported Meersbrook Bristles in 1899, Wires began to look up! Fox Terriers were "launched" in America at the turn of the twentieth century, and by 1929 had reached such heights that Westminster saw an entry of 306—an entry never achieved since!

We can conclude, then, that the Smooth and Wire Fox Terriers really became established in this country with the founding of the kennels of Messrs. August Belmont, Fred Hoey, John Thayer, Harry W. Smith, L. and W. Rutherford, G. H. Gooderham, G. M. Carnochan, R. F. Mayhew, Charles W. Keyes, F. H. Farwell, Winthrop Rutherford, George W. Quintard, and Thomas Rice Varick, and the Vickery Kennels and the kennels of Mrs. Ray A. Raincy.

The foregoing breeders were active during the years from 1887 to 1920, and it was dogs from their kennels that won the Grand Challenge Cup of The American Fox Terrier Club. Those breeders whose dogs won three times or more in competition for the cup were: August Belmont with Ch. Rachel, first in 1888, with six wins; Harry W. Smith with Ch. Cribbage, first in 1894, with three wins; August Belmont again in 1892–1895, with Ch. Blenton Victor II, for eight wins; L. and W. Rutherford won it first in 1896 with Ch. Warren Sentence, for six wins; G. M. Carnochan won it three times, the first in 1899, with Ch. Go Bang;

CH. KRIS VALE LIBERATOR
Owners, Mr. and Mrs. T. H. Veling, North Colebrook, Conn.

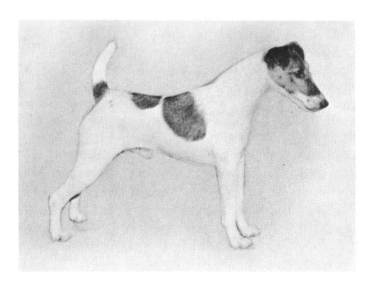

CH. STONEY MEADOWS BUOY
Owner, W. Potter Wear, Cecilton, Md.

in 1902–1903, G. H. Gooderham won it five times with his Ch. Norfolk True Blue; Winthrop Rutherford came into the picture in 1907–1910, winning the cup with his famous Ch. Warren Remedy; and H. F. Farwell won it three times in 1911, with his Ch. Sabine Rarebit. All of the foregoing dogs were Smooths, but in 1916–1920 Mrs. Roy A. Rainey won four times with her Wire, Ch. Conejo Wycollar Boy.

From this date on, more and more Wires won the Grand Challenge Cup, proving the popularity and excellence of this variety. The next fifteen years (up to 1935) found the following owners and dogs winning two times or more: Homer Gage, Jr., with Ch. Welwire Miss Springtime, in 1922; Mr. and Mrs. M. W. Newton with Ch. Chappaque Wrangler's Peggy, three times in 1923; again in 1924–1925, Homer Gage, with his great dog, Ch. Welwire Barrington Bridegroom, won five times; in 1926 Mr. and Mrs. Stanley Halle, with Ch. Signal Circuit of Halleston, won three times; Reginald Lewis won twice with Ch. Bubbling Over in 1927, and again in 1928 with his Ch. Talavera Margaret winning twice; Mr. and Mrs. R. C. Bondy won twice in 1929 with their Ch. Eden Aristocrat of Wildoaks; John G. Bates, in 1930 and 1931, won with his Ch. Pendley Calling of Blarney three times; Ch. Weltona Frizzette of Wildoaks won three times in 1930 and 1931 for Mrs. Bondy; Reginald M. Lewis again in 1932 made two wins with his Ch. Fyldelands Margaret; and Dr. and Mrs. Samuel Milbank made two wins in 1932 and 1933 with their Ch. Lone Eagle of Earlsmoor.

The span of fifteen years from 1920 to 1935 represented the heyday of the Wires, and it was not until the founding of the Wissaboo Kennels of the late James M. Austin in 1938 that the Smooths regained their former supremacy. Then for a period of ten years Mr. Austin's Ch. Nornay Saddler held the spotlight. This great dog gave much to the breed, and so today the Smooth and the Wire Fox Terriers are once more on an even keel. Interest in both coats of a breed make for a healthy situation, and both varieties of the Fox Terrier are once again claiming the popularity which they so well deserve.

It is indeed noteworthy that at the most important dog show

in this country, the Westminster Kennel Club Show at Madison Square Garden, a Smooth or Wire Fox Terrier has accounted for the coveted best-in-show award at fifteen of the shows held from 1907 to 1958. No other breed has come close to that record!

It is interesting to note, too, that for three consecutive years— 1907, 1908, and 1909—it was the late Mr. Winthrop Rutherford's fine Smooth Ch. Warren Remedy who won the top honor! This is the only instance where a dog of any breed has made three consecutive best-in-show wins at the Garden.

In 1910, Mr. Farwell's Sabine Kennels had the winner in Ch. Sabine Rarebit, another great Smooth. Then in 1915 and 1916, a Wire came to the fore—Mr. George W. Quintard's Ch. Matford Vic. The following year, 1917, and again in 1920, Mrs. Roy Rainey's Ch. Conejo Wycollar Boy, another Wire, captured that award. Others to gain the honor are as follows:

1926, Mr. and Mrs. Stanley Halle's Halleston Kennels with the Wire, Ch. Signal Circuit.

1928, Ch. Talavera Margaret, from the Wire Kennels of Mr. Reginald M. Lewis.

1930 and 1931, Mr. John G. Bates' Wire, Ch. Pendley Calling.

1934 and 1937, Halleston Kennels' Ch. Flornell Spicy Bit and Ch. Flornell Spicy Piece.

1946, the home-bred Wire, Ch. Hetherington Model Rhythm, owned by Mr. and Mrs. Thomas H. Carruthers, III.

Two Smooths and eight Wires, with a total of fifteen top awards at Westminster, is indeed a record of which any breed could well be proud!

It is regrettable that another great Fox Terrier, the Smooth Ch. Nornay Saddler, never won the top award at Westminster. I felt that, as an almost perfect specimen of the breed, he could have won and well deserved to do so—along with that great Wire, Ch. Gallant Fox of Wildoaks. It would have been a fitting triumph to add to their many other wins. However, the selection of the best-in-show dog is a matter of opinion as well as the competition on the particular day.

The Fox Terrier of today is vastly improved over the specimens entered in the shows a century ago. At the first dog show,

CH. NORNAY SADDLER, BEST IN SHOW, MORRIS & ESSEX, 1941
Mrs. M. Hartley Dodge, President of the Club, and Saddler with Mr. Austin
handling him to his triumph.

FOUR FAMOUS WILDOAKS CHAMPIONS
True Charm, Hunter, Superb, and Top Row

which was held at Newcastle-on-Tyne, England, in 1859, only Pointers and Setters were shown. But in the fall of that same year, Birmingham held its first show, and there, for the first time, Smooth Fox Terriers were shown. Three years later, Wire Fox Terriers appeared at the shows. In 1862 the Smooths had enough entries to warrant a classification of their own, but it was not until 1869, at the Darlington Show, that Wires rated their own classes.

At the first shows in those early days, judges disagreed as to just what was expected from the breed. Some gave the prizes for even markings, others on the workmanlike qualities of the dogs, and fads and fancies reigned supreme! To the serious-minded individuals in the sport, it became apparent that a governing body was needed, and in 1875 the English Kennel Club was founded. Official Standards were drawn up for the breeds, and breeders for the first time had something to guide them in their breeding programs. The Fox Terrier Standard was drawn up in 1878 and, with the exception of a change in weight, is still in use today. The American Standard was developed from the one adopted by English fanciers.

The American Fox Terrier Club, which was founded in 1885, is the parent club for both coats in this country. The author has the honor of being vice-president and on the Board of Governors of the parent club, and was one of the founders and on the Board of The Wire Fox Terrier Club of the Central States, which was organized in 1946, the author also having served as president and secretary of the latter club.

Following is a list of clubs holding specialty shows:

The American Fox Terrier Club (parent club—member club of the A.K.C.)

Western Fox Terrier Breeders Association (member club of the A.K.C.)

The Wire Fox Terrier Club of the Central States

The Lone Star Fox Terrier Club

Northern Fox Terrier Club of California

Fox Terrier Club of Chicago

Fox Terrier Club of Maryland

Fox Terrier Club of Michigan

The Fox Terrier Club of St. Louis

The fact that so many specialty clubs of this breed have been formed in this country proves how popular the breed has become.

For a breed not to show improvement during its years of development is to admit of stagnation. But no such admission need be made so far as the Fox Terrier is concerned, for improvements have been many.

The most important improvement has been the refinement in both the Smooth and the Wire. There has been a consistent tendency to bring down the size, and to breed out light eyes, bad feet, bad mouths, poor quarters, and poor coats—all to the good.

In judging the breed, I find that the dog with the light eye is an exception today; feet are greatly improved; bad mouths are seldom found any more; and soft coats are gradually disappearing.

Some of the improvements are still lacking in individual kennels, but breeders in general have become acutely aware of faults and are working to eliminate them. In those rare instances where faulty dogs do appear in the show ring, they are usually in the hands of a novice. It is safe to conclude that few breeds can boast of more improvements than have taken place in the Fox Terrier breed during the last half century. And placing the credit where it is due, it must be attributed to the sincerity and interest of the breeders as well as to the popularity of the breed.

There yet remains plenty of room for improvement of shoulders, and it would be well worth the breeders' time to study what constitutes a good shoulder. More road work, such as the English give their dogs, would improve the quarters of the Fox Terriers in America today. And two other points which breeders should strive for are the correct type and placement of ears.

Everyone who undertakes to breed a litter of Fox Terriers should study the Standard of the breed. Unfortunately, too many breeders do not know what to look for when evaluating a Fox Terrier, because they do not understand the Standard. So study of the chapter in this book entitled "Blueprint of the Breed" will also prove helpful to owners evaluating their own dogs.

Valuable information and experience can also be gained by entering the "sanction matches," which not only play a large part in our dog activities but also contribute toward the education of the novice breeder and dog lover. (See "The Exhibition of Dogs" —Part II of this book.) Every breeder and owner should take advantage of sanction matches long before he tries his hand in the bench show ring.

While some breeds of dog have run a cycle of popularity for one or two decades and then faded, that has not happened to the Fox Terrier. It is true that there has been a decline in the number of Fox Terriers entered at the shows, but I am sure that the Fox Terrier breed has steadily gained more breeders in this country than has any other breed. Today, we have fewer large kennels and more so-called "back-yard" breeders than, say, in 1935. And it was the large kennels, with entries of one to a dozen, that made for the larger show entries.

Perhaps the major reason for the drop in show entries is the

FAMOUS MOTHER AND DAUGHTER BRACE WINNING BEST IN
SHOW, WESTMINSTER KENNEL CLUB, 1946
Owner, T. H. Carruthers, handling Hetherington Navy Nurse
Handler, Jake Terhune, with Hetherington Model Rhythm

fact that the coat of the Wire variety is difficult for the novices to present properly in the show ring. Therefore, novices have been showing other breeds with less difficulty and with fewer odds against them in competition with the professional handler. The chapter entitled "Grooming the Fox Terrier" will prove helpful to the novice, for it includes illustrations as well as instructions as to the proper way to prepare a dog for the show ring.

CH. DOWNSBRAGH TWO O'CLOCK FOX
Downsbragh Kennels, Marshall, Virginia

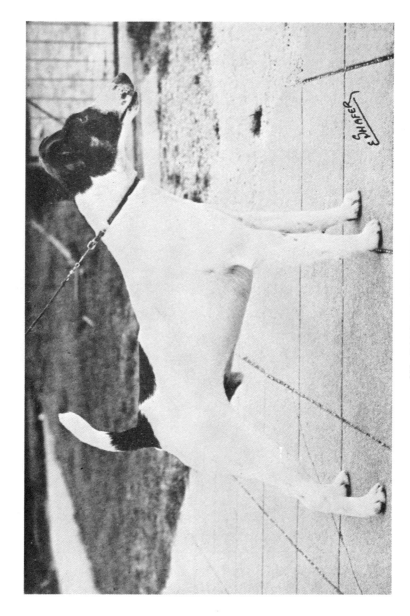

CH. FOXDEN ANTHONY
Foxden Kennels, Darien, Connecticut

Résumés of Prominent Kennels

IN America, the greater proportion of the prominent Fox Terrier owners and breeders first became interested in the dog game as a hobby. And what leads one to pursue hobbies? Usually the personal need of the individual to seek relaxation in some activity unrelated to his daily work. To one person, such relaxation may be found in an active sport of some kind; to another, just losing himself in a book for several hours may be enough; and to others, the exhibiting of dogs offers an excellent opportunity for relaxation from the stress of every-day life.

One of the leading kennels in the East today is "Downsbragh," situated in the rolling country of Marshall, Virginia, and owned by that witty, dashing country gentleman, Mr. William W. Brainard, Jr., and his gracious wife. Started as a hobby, the outstanding success of Downsbragh Kennels is confirmed by the number of Smooth Fox Terriers they have bred and shown to championship. To put it neatly in their own words, "We breed what we show and we show what we breed."

Among the leading breeders of outstanding Smooths are Mr. James A. Farrell, Jr., and his wife, whose kennels, Foxden, are located in Darien, Connecticut. The squire of Foxden, in his everyday life, is the busy executive of a steamship line, but to see this quiet, unassuming man at the ringside, completely re-laxed, watching the judging of his favorite breed, it is difficult

31

to picture him as the driving force and power of the company which bears his name. His hobby offers him the relaxation needed to carry on, and Mrs. Farrell, whose quiet charm is immediately apparent, shares his enthusiasm. While Smooth Fox Terriers are the dogs which have made Foxden Kennels famous, Mr. Farrell has also owned some well-known Wire Fox Terriers, and Mrs. Farrell is interested in Greyhounds.

Many Foxden dogs have been piloted to their wins by the well-known handlers Percy Roberts and Leonard Brumby, Jr., but it is not uncommon to see Mr. Farrell himself in the ring, showing his home-breds. The Farrells have bred more than a dozen champions, and the pleasures that they have derived from their hobby are apparent in the fact that they have been pursuing it for the past twenty years.

A gentleman who did a great deal for the Smooth Fox Terrier, helping to bring the breed definitely to the fore in recent years, was the late James M. Austin of Wissaboo Kennels in Old Westbury, Long Island, owner of the famous Nornay Saddler. During the years 1938–1948, his Wissaboo Kennels' entries were the largest in number at the shows, and his importation of Nornay Saddler made the public conscious of the Smooth Fox Terrier again. The Grand Challenge Cup of the American Fox Terrier Club had been won by Wires sixty-two out of the sixty-nine times it had been offered up to 1937. Then Nornay Saddler won the cup six times, to again bring the Smooths to the fore. Nornay Saddler is remembered, too, as the sire of more than thirty champions.

Another breeder of Smooths is that charming lady of Andley Kennels, Mrs. Barbara Lowe Fallass. Mrs. Fallass has been interested in dogs for many years and had maintained kennels in France prior to establishing her kennel in Cross River, New York. Her Smooths include the famous Ch. Buckland of Andley, Ch. Lovely Lady of Andley, and many, many others. To my mind Mrs. Fallass has an outstanding claim to fame in that her kennel has produced more home-bred champions to date than has any other kennel in the United States.

Rochester, N. Y. was the home of the Ronnoco Kennels of the late Judge James P. O'Connor, former President of The American Fox Terrier Club. Between 1946 and 1955, he had produced twenty-three homebred champions, most stemming from Saddler blood.

The late Charles Thomae, former Treasurer of the A.F.T.C. for many years, had his kennel in Attleboro, Mass., and showed under the Cotter prefix for 56 years. He handled most of the dogs himself, a feat many of us would like to think we could do!

The Wirehart Kennels of the late George H. Hartman in Lampeter, Pa., housed both Smooths and Wires. In his later years, Mr. Hartman devoted most of his time to judging. However, his Ch. Stepping Stone of Wirehart and his Ch. Promoter of Wirehart are well-known to the breeders of each respective coat, for their contribution to the breed. And none of us will forget the important part played in the breed by such fanciers as the late Robert Sedgwick, J. P. S. Harrison, E. Coe Kerr and Robert B. Neff.

Since 1936 Col. Francis R. Appleton Jr., of Ipswich, Mass. has maintained his Barberry Kennels. Most of his stock carried the famous Saddler bloodlines. Today, his dogs do not appear as often in the show ring, but when they do, they are a credit to his knowledge of breeding.

Other active breeders are Robert Brumby of the Havahome Kennels on Long Island. He will be remembered for his handling of the well-known winner, Ch. Lucky Fella, which he bred. This dog will go down as an outstanding stud of the last decade. Two active Smooth breeders are the Sandgate Kennels of the John Aitkens of Vestal, N.Y., from which a long line of champions have come, and the Arthur Gays of Dallas, Texas. From Woodcliffe and Silver-Ho Kennels in Short Creek, Va., have emerged one of the "perfect show teams" seldom seen in the ring. Dr. Nancy Lenfesty of Silver-Ho handled the outstanding Smooth, Ch. Woodcliffe Hiya Boy, owned by Mr. Albert Welty. This dog finished his championship when seven months old and piled up a record of over 90 Best of Variety wins.

Mrs. Abigail G. Jones of St. Louis, Mo., in her Welcome Kennels, established about 12 years ago, has bred 15 champions. Many buy that number in 12 years, but few breed them. To Mr. and Mrs. Henry Schley of Riverside, Calif., go the honor of breeding four champions in one litter. Also in California, the dogs from the Bronwyn Kennels of Mr. and Mrs. Ivan Gilbert are winning big. Other California breeders are the Valentines, who finished four champions recently, and the Crag Crest Kennels of the Kuskas. The Henry Speights and the Davil Halls, are on the road to success. In Ohio, we find the Shebrook Kennels of Mrs. Mary P. Trehune.

The Battle Cry Kennels of Mrs. Stewart Simmons of Bryn Mawr, Pa., have enjoyed big wins with their homebreds. And many times it is a "family affair" when brother-in-law, W. Potter Wear, faces her in the show ring with dogs from the Stoney Meadows Kennels of Cecilton, Md. Other dedicated breeders from Pennsylvania are Mrs. Judith Wolff, a newcomer who is going places, and the Pool Forge Kennels of Mr. and Mrs. W. William Wimer III, of Churchtown, the home of Ch. Thermfare and her son, Ch. Pool Forge Gold Brick.

Connecticut has three prominent breeders. One of many years' standing and again active is William Browning of Ridgefield. Mr. and Mrs. C. H. Christman's Twinbark kennel in Danbury has bred 16 champions in the same number of years, and Mr. and Mrs. T. H. Veling of North Colebrook have bred seven champions in the last four years. This last kennel, not yet ten years old and housing more of the Andley bloodlines of Mrs. Fallass than any other, is destined for success.

Although I have touched on only a few of those active in the breed today, it gives one an insight into the lives of those who have made a name for Smooth Fox Terriers in recent years. In compiling a long list of dogs and their owners, it is next to impossible to be all inclusive. It is genuinely regrettable that this is a fact, but it is. It means, unfortunately, that more than one serious breeder and dog may go unmentioned.

Statistics always play a part in any history, and the number of

Smooth champions bred by the leading kennels during the years 1946 to 1964 should prove interesting:

SMOOTH FOX TERRIER CHAMPIONS BRED IN THE U.S. DURING 1946–1964

Owner	Kennel Name	Number
Mrs. Barbara L. Fallass	Andley	30
Mr. & Mrs. W. W. Brainard, Jr.	Downsbragh	25
Judge James B. O'Connor	Ronnoco	23
Mr. Albert P. Welty	Woodcliffe	20
Mr. & Mrs. C. H. Christman	Twinbark	16
Mrs. Abigail G. Jones	Welcome	15
Mr. & Mrs. James A. Farrell	Foxden	14
Mr. & Mrs. Potter Wear	Stoney Meadows	14
Dr. Nancy Lenfesty	Silver Ho	12
Mr. John N. Simm		10
Mr. & Mrs. Arthur Gay	Gaycliff	9
Mr. Robert Sedgwick	Heathside	9
Mr. Chester Kurrash		8
Col. Francis Appleton, Jr.	Barberry	8
Mrs. Stewart Simmons	Battle Cry	7
Mr. & Mrs. T. H. Veling	Kris-Vale	7
Mr. Robert B. Neff	Fenbor	6
Mr. J. F. Delany	Mountmellick	6
Mr. William C. Browning	Ridgebury	4
Mr. & Mrs. Henry Schley	Schley Fox	4
Mr. Dan Carter		4
Mr. & Mrs. Val Valentine		4
Mr. George H. Hartman	Wirehart	4
Mr. J. P. S. Harrison	Etona	4

Each ensuing year brings to the fore new breeders as well as new dogs.

It seems only fitting while discussing the dogs I remember, that I should give you here a few side lights on perhaps one of the greatest Smooths this country will ever see. I am thankful that his career was at its height while I was still actively showing dogs. It was nice to have known "Saddler" first hand!

Brought here at the age of eleven months, four months after he had started his show career in England (where he had caused a sensation), Nornay Saddler was an exciting entry in the 1937 American Fox Terrier Club Show. This show was held only twenty-one days after his arrival in the United States and he was handled by his owner, Mr. James M. Austin.

The first judge ever to pass on Saddler was Mrs. M. V. Hughes, in England, whose comment will never be forgotten. Said Mrs. Hughes, "Nornay Saddler is a beautiful youngster, a great credit to his papa, Champion Travelling Fox. Should all go well with this child, he will have a starry future."

She was so correct.

Saddler came into his own in the United States when he won

CH. NORNAY SADDLER
From a painting by B. Vogg, 1938

36

Best of Breed at the Morris & Essex show in 1939, and he and his handler, the late Leonard Brumby, went on to victory after victory and won fame as a team. Mr. Brumby showed him fifty-five times to best in show, an enviable record indeed!

In 1941, Saddler scored his fifty-sixth best in show, again at Morris & Essex, but this time with his owner, Mr. Austin, handling. Saddler's brilliant career still had three more best-in-show awards before "finish" was written at the age of twelve years. A truly great Terrier, he sired some thirty litters and perhaps the best known combination was that of Ch. Braw Lass and Saddler, which produced the following champions: Desert Dynamic, Desert Demon, Desert Director, and Desert Deputy.

There are many interesting side lights on Saddler, some disclosed for the first time, perhaps, in that book about him entitled, *Champion of Champions*, by Don Reynolds.*

Nornay Saddler's sire was Ch. Travelling Fox, by Ch. Avon Peddler, and owned by Mr. Q. Tansey of England. In his book, Mr. Reynolds tells a fascinating story of how when Mr. Austin met Mr. Tansey at the boat which brought the noted Englishman to this country, one of the first questions he asked was:

"How long are you planning to stay in this country, Mr. Tansey?"

"One day," was the surprising reply.

"Well," asked Mr. Austin, "what brought you over for one day?"

"To see Saddler," answered Mr. Tansey, which was indeed quite a tribute to such a good little dog.

Mr. Tansey spent that afternoon and evening admiring Saddler at Mr. Austin's residence. The next day, as he approached Mr. Austin to bid farewell, he asked: "Would you do me a great favor?"

"Yes, I would be glad to if possible," was the reply.

"Then," said Mr. Tansey, "I would like to give you Peddler. I am so impressed with your love for Saddler and the home he

* By permission of the publisher and copywriter—Random House, Inc., New York.

has here, that it is my desire that his grandfather finish his days in his company."

A very pleased Mr. Austin accepted Mr. Tansey's offer, of course.

There's another interesting note about Saddler that should be told. It concerns itself with Mr. Winthrop Rutherford, who, until Mr. Austin purchased Saddler, had enjoyed the honor of owning one of the greatest Smooths in this country.

Mr. Austin was a great admirer of Mr. Rutherford, and when he became the owner of Saddler, he, along with others, more or less expected some comment from Mr. Rutherford. But, if Mr. Rutherford had anything to say, he kept it to himself.

Finally, there came a day—Mr. Rutherford was in his late seventies at the time, when Mr. Austin, along with some other gentlemen interested in dogs, found himself visiting Mr. Rutherford. It wasn't long before Mr. Rutherford volunteered what I think is one of the nicest tributes that could be paid to Saddler and his owner, and I quote Mr. Rutherford:

"Gentlemen, when I was a young man, I knew many of those men in England who wrote the Smooth Fox Terrier Standard, when it was drawn up in 1876, and I can tell you now, that when they drew up that Standard, they closed their eyes and dreamed of Saddler."

*   *   *

Turning to the Wire side of the picture, the leading kennel is unquestionably the famous Wildoaks Kennels of Mrs. Richard C. Bondy, Sr., at Goldens Bridge, New York. Mrs. Bondy and the late Mr. Bondy founded their kennel about 1924 and their success is legendary. This kennel was the foundation of the bloodlines that can be found in nearly every Wire Fox Terrier breeders' stock today. Much credit must be accorded the Bondys, who, by their importation of the best Wire blood in the world, provided the opportunity for other breeders to acquire the

CH. GALLANT FOX OF WILDOAKS
Owned by Mrs. R. C. Boudy, Goldens Bridge, N.Y.

CH. GLYNHIR GOLDEN
Owned by the late W. Luther Lewis, Briarcliff Manor, N.Y.

foundation stock to which they might not have had access otherwise.

Always, in any sport where competition is lively, jealousy is bound to rear its ugly head to some extent, and the Bondys have at times been its targets. I feel, however, that if all Wire Fox Terrier breeders were to face the truth honestly, they would have to admit that although the Wildoaks' dogs beat many of us in the show ring, we do owe our success, large or small, to use of the Bondys' stock—it has helped us to gain our own end.

And I am sure that Mrs. Bondy, one of the most charming and gracious ladies in the dog world today, must feel a personal satisfaction when she sees other kennels producing, from her stock, dogs that reflect the quality that Wildoaks has always represented.

It is thanks to Wildoaks that we have such a large number of breeders of Wires today. And, although stars rise and shine and pass on, and others take their places, Wildoaks has carved a permanent niche in Wire history. I say this because I believe that the American breeder definitely has come into his own and no longer has to depend solely on imported stock to make his success. He can breed it if he wants to do so—thanks to stock made available through Wildoaks!

For years the ringside has associated Wildoaks' dogs with their handler, Mac Silver, who put the dogs down virtually to the point of perfection. The success of Wildoaks' dogs at shows greatly popularized the Wire variety in the best way possible, and much credit is due their handler.

Mrs. Bondy takes life easier today. Although she may still be seen at almost all of the shows where her dogs are shown, she no longer enters the large numbers she once did.

From the years 1926 to 1951, the kennel running a close second to Mrs. Bondy's in the East was Glynhir, owned by the late W. L. Lewis of Briarcliff Manor, New York. Mr. Lewis, famous for the fact that he handled all of his dogs in the ring by himself, was the executive vice-president of a large manufacturing concern—another example of the well-known fact that dogs give their owners needed recreation and relaxation.

40

Mr. Lewis imported and bred many champions, but, to me, his best was the lovely Ch. Glynhir Golden. I believe that Ch. Glynhir Golden was the only Wire bitch, and Ch. Top Row of Wildoaks (who was, incidentally, bred by the Author) was the only Wire dog ever to defeat Ch. Nornay Saddler. At the time Golden and Top Row defeated Saddler, the Smooths and Wires competed against each other for best of breed.

A former New Jerseyite, where she founded her Trucote Kennels, Mrs. Joseph W. Urmston now of California, has made a name for herself with her many importations. Her Ch. Wyretex Wyns Traveller, Ch. Nugrade Nuclea and Ch. Caradochouse Spruce of Trucote are all well-known. Mrs. Urmston is a competent business woman and a top Fox Terrier judge. Another California breeder is Mrs. Barbara Worcester Sayres who, for many years, used her knowledge of breeding in producing winning West Highland Whites as well as Fox Terriers. In recent years she has bred seven Wire champions. From the same state come such successful breeders as John Lasch of Casa Blanca Kennels, Nick Calicura of Martinez, and George Law of the Lyvewyre prefix. A kennel in Iowa winning a great deal is that of Joe and Wayne Bousek. In Santa Fe, New Mexico, are the Koshare Kennels of Dr. Charlotte Jones and Evelyn Stark. Their Ch. Koshare's Striking Star has nine Bests-in-Show to her credit.

I think without a doubt that the most important breeder to come into Wires in the last ten years is Mrs. Eve Ballich of Stevenson, Md. Her Evewire Kennels have produced fifteen champions in that time, and her stud dog, Ch. Evewire Little Man has sired seven champions between the years 1960 and 1964.

Moving west to Glendale, Ohio, we have the famous Hetherington Kennels of Mr. and Mrs. Thomas H. Carruthers III. Their foundation stock started with the purchase of Gallant Knight of Wildoaks in 1930. A litter brother of Ch. Gallant Fox, and too big for the show ring, he could produce—and Hetherington was on its way! They have produced over 50 champions and today are still interested, although they do not show as often. Their bitches have brought them fame and much credit goes to Hetherington Surprise, a daughter of

41

Gallant Knight, who was bred to Ch. Newbold Teetotaler to produce that famous dog, Ch. Hetherington Surprise Model.

Model's daughters, bred to Ch. Fox Hunter of Wildoaks, Ch. Derbyshire Peter, and Midshipman of Wildoaks (who was by Invader out of Sunray), knit Hetherington's pattern closely together. Perhaps the most potent combination was that of Model and Flash, which produced the well-known Champions H. Model Bid, H. Model Manners, H. Model Minx, and H. Model Rhythm. In turn, one of these daughters—Model Minx—bred to Midshipman of W. produced the famous Ch. Hetherington Flirt, who was the dam of five champions: H. G. I. Girl, H. Pilot's Dream, H. Vindication, H. Picturesque, and H. Repetitious.

Truly, this sort of breeding proves beyond a doubt the success of the kennel, and the knowledge and ability of its owners to put into practice what they have learned.

To my mind, the Carruthers' most famous dog was Ch. Hetherington Model Rhythm, who was best of variety, best Terrier, and best in show at Westminster in 1946, and who also enjoyed the honor of winning, along with her daughter Ch. Hetherington Navy Nurse, the best brace in show at Westminster in 1944 and 1946.

In the Southwest is Hallwyre, the well-known kennel of Forest N. Hall of Dallas, Texas. Mr. Hall started his kennels in the early 1920's with the importation of Ch. Westborne Teetotaler, and then followed a succession of many champions, all stemming from this line. Among his best-known dogs were Champions Newbold Teetotaler, Hallwyre Hepatica, and Davishill Little Man.

In the Midwest there are several active breeders, including, of course, Mrs. E. A. Kraft of Pontiac, Michigan, and her Wynwyre Kennels. Mrs. Kraft, who began her kennel activities in 1937, has enjoyed remarkable success in breeding a great many champions. Perhaps the most outstanding were the dogs, Champions Wynwyre Saddle and Wynwyre Saddleson, and the bitch, Ch. Wynwyre Pamela.

In Chicago are the Harham Kennels of Mr. and Mrs. Harold Florsheim of shoe fame. While Mr. Florsheim has been identified

FAMOUS MOTHER AND DAUGHTER

CH. HETHERINGTON MODEL RHYTHM
Owned by Hetherington Kennels, Glendale, Ohio

CH. HETHERINGTON NAVY NURSE
Owned by Hetherington Kennels, Glendale, Ohio

with both Airedale and Welsh Terriers for a great many years, it is Mrs. Florsheim who is more interested in Wires. Their kennels have been known for many importations, the most outstanding being Ch. Arley Adorable and the famous Ch. Superman of Harham (whose show career we touch on elsewhere in this book). At the present time Mr. and Mrs. Florsheim have several promising litters in their kennels, and stock by Superman is beginning to reach the show ring.

Mention should be made, too, of the Derbyshire Kennels of Mr. Thomas Keator of Buffalo, New York. Mr. Keator, a banker, has been interested in Fox Terriers for the past twenty-five years. He has enjoyed great success in this line, having bred many champions, and his most outstanding stud dog was Ch. Derbyshire Peter.

Derbyshire's dogs are piloted in the show ring by that capable handler Bob Kendrick, and Mr. Keator at present devotes more time to judging than showing. He usually can be found, however, at any ringside where Wire Fox Terriers are being shown.

A kennel that enjoyed a short but exceptional period of success was that of the late Jerry Cummings and his lovely wife, who started Shiremont Kennels in upper New York State. Among their best-known champions were Shiremont Chevron and Shiremont Allure.

In Indiana are that pleasant, energetic couple, Doc Booth and his wife. Their St. Joe Kennels (so named because they live on the banks of the St. Joe River) have turned out five champions to date. The more important are, perhaps, St. Joe Julianna and Quests End Border Patrol. They purchased the latter and have used him successfully with their home-bred stock. Dr. Booth, a veterinarian, has the "know-how" for producing a "good one."

Moving on to the Pacific Coast, we have such prominent breeders as Mrs. W. B. Reis, Mr. and Mrs. F. Bilger, Mrs. H. H. Swann and the late Dr. Payne McComb, all of California; Mr. Ted Ward and Miss Lena Shortt of Canada; and many others.

Breeders of Fox Terriers can without doubt be found in every State in the United States, but recently I made a very interesting survey of the prominent breeders who have made a name for their dogs and themselves throughout the country. This comprised both Smooth and Wire breeders, and I found thirty-four States to be represented. Taking those States that are the home of five or more well-known kennels, the representation is as follows: New York leads with forty-nine; Pennsylvania has eighteen; Illinois, sixteen; California, fifteen; Ohio, thirteen; Connecticut, nine; Massachusetts, nine; New Jersey, eight; Michigan, seven; Indiana, seven; Missouri, six; and Texas, six.

The Copper Beech Kennels of Mr. and Mrs. Frederick H. Dutcher have gained notable success in recent years. Located in Stamford, Connecticut, they house such well-known winners as Ch. Copper Beech Storm, a lovely bitch who has scored four best-in-show awards, four best-of-variety wins at specialties and fifty best-of-variety wins in all breed shows. The Monestella Kennels of Mrs. Munro W. Lanier of New York have such outstanding winners as Ch. Emprise Sensational, Ch. Mac's Revelation, Ch. Glynhir Great Guns, and Ch. Citation of Wildoaks.

Also of major importance, along with the famous kennels, are the professional handlers who have been closely identified with the "stars" of these kennels. Without the ability of the handlers, I am sure many a dog would never have been made a champion.

Mr. Percy Roberts, an Englishman by birth, heads my list as the best known of our American handlers, and he has made a name for himself also as an importer of top dogs, and as the owner of the Reverly Kennels, located in Noroton, Connecticut. Mr. Roberts now devotes his time to judging and has gained an enviable reputation as the most outstanding Fox Terrier authority in our country today. Mention of his name brings back memories of the many famous dogs he handled in the past.

The late Leonard Brumby, also an Englishman, was part of the famous "team" in dogdom—that of the Smooth Fox Terrier Ch. Nornay Saddler and himself. I believe no other handler before or since his time has ever enjoyed the renown of having shown a Fox Terrier to fifty-six best-in-show wins, the record Mr. Brumby achieved with Saddler. Quiet, unassuming, and well-liked by all who knew him, Mr. Brumby was the president and the moving force in the Professional Handler's Association. And following today in his famous father's footsteps is Leonard Brumby, Jr.

There is another half of the Brumby picture, which is represented by Frank Brumby (brother of Leonard, Sr.) and his son, Robert. While Bob handles other breeds of Terriers too, he is always sure to have a Fox Terrier client. Frank Brumby has given up handling and turned to judging. Truly, the Brumbys are a family whose love of dogs in general, and of the Fox Terrier in particular, cannot be questioned.

Another Fox Terrier handler, son of a famous doggy father, is Henry Sayres, who has been showing "top" dogs for Mrs. Saunders Meade, whose latest star is Ch. Weltona Dustynight's Warrior. Another handler who has shown his share of winning dogs is Seth Campbell. Mr. Campbell has put down to perfection such well-known dogs as Ch. Wyretex Wyns Traveller, Ch. Venture of Co-Hill, Ch. Travella Allure, and, more recently, the Fox Terriers of Miss Barbara Worcester.

To the Gatelys, Tom and Kay, goes the distinction of being one of the few handling teams composed of husband and wife. Also, along with their handling, they have made a success of maintaining Gayterry—a small breeding kennel of Wires. Mr. Gately enjoys the distinction of having brought fame to Ch. Superman of Harham (owned by Mr. and Mrs. Florsheim) as well as many other top dogs.

Then, of course, there is that quiet figure always found with Mr. Brainard's Smooths—Bob Braithwaith. His dogs reflect the care and love that he gives them, and he has enjoyed the pleasure of handling a great many top ones.

Robert Snodgrass, better known to his friends as "Pete," is the owner of the Macroom Kennels. He has bred many a fine champion, and his name has been identified with top winners for years.

In the Midwest we have two very capable handlers: Jake Terhune, who handles the Carruthers' dogs to their victories, and George Ward, who learned the art of putting a Wire down to near perfection from his father, Ted Ward of Canada, who is also a well-known handler.

46

The newest handler to make his presence felt is a newcomer from England, Jimmy Butler, who intends to make this country his home. He was England's top Terrier handler, and he has in the few years since he came here made some enviable wins for his clients. His dogs reflect the nice manner he has, and—there is no getting away from it—the English do know how to put a Fox Terrier down!

It is to these professional handlers that owners owe a great deal, because it is the handlers' ability and "know-how" with their charges that leads to presentation of a pleasing picture for the judges.

Stars rise and fade in any field, and so it is with dogs and their owners. I have touched but lightly on those connected with the breed for the past twenty-five years, and many of those mentioned will drop from the dog game in the years to come. But the ensuing years will, I am sure, find other, equally interested lovers of the breed to carry on.

Returning to statistics once more, below are the number of Wire champions bred by the leading kennels during the years 1946 to 1964.

WIRE FOX TERRIER CHAMPIONS BRED IN THE U.S. DURING 1946 1964

Owner	Kennel Name	Number
Mr. Forest N. Hall	Hallwyre	69
Mr. & Mrs. T. H Carruthers	Hetherington	43
Mrs. Richard C. Bondy	Wildoaks	26
Mrs. Edward Kraft	Wynwyre	19
Mrs. Eve Ballich	Evewire	15
Mr. W. Luther Lewis	Clynhir	13
Mr. & Mrs. Thomas Gately	Gayterry	11
Mr. Thomas Keator	Derbyshire	8
Mr. George H. Hartman	Wirehart	8
Mrs. Barbara W. Sayres	Wishing Well	7
Dr. Frank R. Booth	St. Joe	7
Mrs. Paul M. Silvernail	Crack-Dale	6
Mrs. Gene Scaggs Bigelow	Raylu	6
Mrs. Franklin Koehler	Merrybrook	5
Mrs. Frederick Dutcher	Copper Beech	5
Mrs. Joseph W. Urmston	Trucote	5

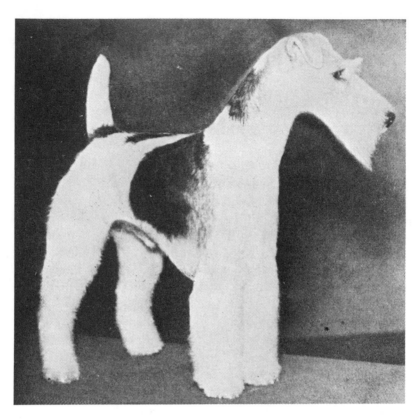

CH. TOP ROW OF WILDOAKS

Top Row, bred by the Author and sold to Mrs. Bondy at six months of age, was an outstanding dog. His wins included fourteen best-in-show awards, all breeds, and best of breed at The American Fox Terrier Club Specialty Show in 1936, at the age of eleven months. His most outstanding win was made in 1937 under the late George H. Thomas at Wissahocken, where he defeated both Ch. Glynhir Golden and Ch. Nornay Saddler, two of this country's foremost Fox Terrier champions. He was sold to the late Dr. R. Payne McComb of Santa Barbara, California, at whose kennel he passed away at twelve years of age. Top Row was the sire of five champions.

Discussions on Breeding

TO compile an all-inclusive list of dogs and their owners would be impossible. Unfortunately, many serious breeders and outstanding dogs would have to go unmentioned. However, to write a book about dogs and not include pedigrees, would be like making a cake without an icing, so we will include here the pedigrees of some of the Fox Terriers that have played an important part in the development of the breed in comparatively recent years.

We know that Webster defines *breeding* as "producing animals, especially to get improved stock," and defines *pedigree* as "ancestry and line of descent." Both *breeding* and *pedigree* are words used frequently, so their meaning and their application are highly important to the student of any breed.

A breeder is a student, for he is one who seeks knowledge of that in which he is interested, and strives to use that knowledge in his operations. To be an owner or lover of dogs, one has only to be able to keep them. To be an owner of show dogs, one has only to be able to afford them. But to be a breeder of dogs, one has to be a serious student of pedigrees and of *genetics*, a term referring to the origin of similarities and diversities between parents and offspring. The successful breeder must also have untold patience—a willingness to await the results of his labors.

Many of today's owners of show dogs are not, in the true sense of the word, *breeders*. But out of every group of people having general interest in a subject, there will be several who are interested seriously enough to get to the bottom of things to see how results are achieved. It is to such serious students that this chapter will be particularly interesting.

In the early days of the Fox Terrier, it was such breeders as Messrs. Burbidge, Clarke, Vicary, Turner, Cox, Murchison and Redmond, and the Duchess of Newcastle, who were interested enough in genetics to try to prove their theories, and when necessary, to spend years in achieving a particular goal in their breeding program. These people are mentioned repeatedly in the various volumes on dogs, and any study of Fox Terriers brings up the names of both Mr. Redmond and Mr. Vicary, and later the Duchess of Newcastle. Through their intensive research and their experimenting with various crosses and bloodlines, were laid the foundation for the two strains which made for the success of the breed.

Mr. Francis Redmond developed the Belgrave Joe strain into two channels, one of which ran through his stud Ch. Dominie, and the other through Ch. Result. Both joined issue through Brockenhurst Jim and Brockenhurst Joe, respectively, who were sired by Belgrave Joe.

Mr. Robert Vicary experimented with another strain, which was known as the Old Foiler strain, and had equal success with it in the production of his good Terrier, Ch. Oxonian. This strain is sometimes referred to as the Vicary strain. Both Mr. Redmond and Mr. Vicary were breeders who gave much thought and devoted much time to research on their own dogs, but apparently the two were somewhat bigoted as far as their own dogs and strain were concerned, for there is no record of either breeder having sent a bitch to the other's stud dog! However, there were breeders who wisely combined the best of these two celebrated kennels, with much success and improvement of the breed. Those who were most successful with these crosses were the Messrs. Doyle, Tinne, O'Connell, Burbidge, Reeks, Clarke, Glynn, and Castle, Captain Crosthwaite, and the Duchess of Newcastle in England, and F. H. Farwell of the Sabine Kennels in the United States.

50

The studies these breeders carried out so many years ago have proved the fact that to mate two winning purebred dogs will produce another purebred, but not necessarily another winner. It is the male's power of favorable reproduction and the quality of offspring that he can sire, combined with the favorable supplement of a good bitch with positive points that produce high-class stock and possible winners. This is where the study of pedigrees comes in and where the newcomer can learn from other breeders' experiences just what each line consistently produces and the dominant points of each.

Through the following examples of pedigrees, the student of the breed will see how the combining of certain bloodlines resulted in the production of champions. But he must not lose sight of the fact that the ancestors of these dogs, besides having "royal pedigrees," also were outstanding specimens of their sex.

The serious student would do well to look into and really understand the methods of breeding and what they can mean to him in his success as a breeder. As a breeder, he has it in his power to create something beautiful and near perfect, provided he uses the knowledge that is available!

The chapter on "Breeding of Dogs," in Part II of this book, covers the subject of breeding quite thoroughly, but following is a brief explanation of the three types of breeding possible.

Line breeding: following the same line on both sides. As you will see in the following pages of pedigrees, crosses in the third generation have produced the best results.

Inbreeding: breeding close relatives together, such as brother to sister, half-brother to half-sister, uncle to niece, nephew to aunt, father to daughter, or son to mother, etc.

Outcrossing: using a distinctly different line in an attempt to bring in new positive characteristics, or to intensify or strengthen attributes already present.

Line breeding and inbreeding are more or less closely related at times, and I will show you examples of this, but in pure line breeding, the same family lines are followed, although no close relatives are mated. Line breeding is slower in producing results but is generally the safest method for the novice to employ.

51

Inbreeding can only be employed with restraint, for degeneracy and weakness will usually make an appearance. It is not the method to be used by a novice, for one must be sure of the results of the strains behind it, and one must be prepared to cull ruthlessly when necessary. The breeder who uses inbreeding must possess a thorough knowledge of the virtues and faults of the individuals mated, as inbreeding tends to magnify both. For these reasons, inbreeding is not recommended for the beginner.

It is often advantageous to go outside the strain for new heredity, particularly to strengthen points. This is outbreeding, and in the next generation the breeder should revert to the original strain.

The main objective in breeding is to correct faults and improve the breed. The breeder must view his stock with an open mind and admit whatever weakness might be present. To become "kennel blind" is to become lost.

Smooths

I am going to give an example first of *outbreeding*, where the superiority of the individuals warranted the experiment. The Bowden line found in Nornay Saddler's pedigree had been proven to be a dominant line, and Saddler's sire, Travelling Fox, was a *dominant sire;* but Travelling Fox and Wyrksop Surprise, Saddler's dam, had no close common ancestors. However, the results were worth the try, for through this mating Nornay Saddler was whelped. He proved to be a very dominant sire, for almost every litter he sired had at least one champion in it. His most famous litter was one of four pups, from a mating with Ch. Braw Lass, in which all four pups became champions. Saddler's pedigree, which follows, warrants careful study.

A study of the pedigrees of Smooth Fox Terriers winning during the period between 1938 and 1948, will show the preponderance of Saddler blood. It cannot be denied that he stamped his type on his progeny and was the improvement that the breed needed in this country at that time.

Pedigree of CH. NORNAY SADDLER
Whelped March 12, 1936
Breeder, F. Coward (England)

	Ch. Avon Peddler	Homestead Aristocrat
		Avon Magnet
Sire: Ch. Travelling Fox		
	Yours Truly	Verily
		Taney
	Bowden Constable	Avon Sterling
		Bowden Picture
Dam: Wyrksop Surprise		
	Bowden Rakishly	Bowden Rakish
		Bowden Mantilla

Another very *dominant sire* at this time was Ch. Danesgate Debtor, who sired, among others, such good Smooths as Ch. Heathside Houri, Ch. Fresh Paint, Ch. Brass Tacks, and Ch. First Payment. When Debtor's offspring were mated to Saddler, the results were excellent. An example of this was the litter from Saddler and Ch. Braw Lass (granddaughter of Debtor) which produced four champions, namely, Desert Deputy, Desert Dynamic, Desert Demon, and Desert Dictator.

Following are the pedigrees of Ch. Brass Tacks and Ch. Braw Lass, both of which merit careful study.

Pedigree of CH. BRASS TACKS
Whelped March 2, 1935
Breeder, Jere R. Collins

	Chosen Collegian of Notts	Chosen Don of Notts
		China Girl of Notts
Sire: Ch. Danesgate Debtor		
	Danesgate Dot	Avon Rossiter
		Danesgate Peggy
	Ch. Southboro Satrap	Wood Lore
		Lady Muriel
Dam: Ch. Prides Hill Sonia		
	Ch. Lady Crossfield of Prides Hill	Levenside Lancer
		Alltakes' Donab

Pedigree of CH. BRAW LASS
Whelped Oct. 5, 1934
Breeder, Winthrop Rutherford

	Boreham Belton	Boreham Bismark
		Boreham Bellona
Sire: Boreham Bemark		
	Boreham Beige	Bowden Rakish
		Boreham Betrue
	Ch. Danesgate Debtor	Chosen Collegian of Notts
		Danesgate Dot
Dam: Warren Agile		
	Warren Amity	Ch. Ameybi
		Amapeppa

By studying the pedigrees of both Ch. Brass Tacks and Ch. Braw Lass, you will have discovered that the dominant sire Danesgate Debtor appears in both—as the sire of Ch. Brass Tacks, and as the grandsire (on the dam's side) of Ch. Braw Lass. It was found that when Braw Lass was bred to another dominant sire such as Saddler proved to be, excellent results could be attained, although Braw Lass and Saddler did not have any *close* common ancestors. However, because they were both such excellent specimens, they warranted *outbreeding*.

By breeding Braw Lass, a granddaughter of Debtor, to Saddler, *line breeding* was introduced, for she carried Saddler's Bowden line on her sire's side. This is not as strong line breeding as can be accomplished, as I will later point out, but, rather, the *beginning stage of line breeding*—the combining of two outstanding specimens with a view to continuing matings within the line.

To illustrate further, let us look at two more pedigrees. The first is of Ch. Stepping Stone of Wirehart, and the second is of Ch. Heathside Hurricane. Careful study of the pedigrees of both Stepping Stone and Hurricane will lead to a clearer understanding of the *line breeding* that was followed.

CH. RONNOCO RESOLUTE

Grandson of Saddler on his sire's side, and a great-grandson on his dam's side through Stepping Stone

Owned by the late Judge J. P. O'Connor, Rochester, N.Y.

CH. STEPPING STONE OF WIREHART

Daughter of Ch. Nornay Saddler

Owned by George H. Hartman, Lampeter, Penna.

Pedigree of CH. STEPPING STONE OF WIREHART
Whelped Dec. 21, 1937
Breeder, George Hartman

Sire: Ch. Nornay Saddler	Travelling Fox	Avon Peddler
		Yours Truly
	Wyrksop Surprise	Bowden Constable
		Bowden Rakishly
Dam: Ch. Golddigger of Wirehart	Ch. Clapton Goldfinder	Ch. Haven Spotlight
		Eastview Diana
	Clapton Ocean Blue	Avon Peddler
		Glenhaven Pride

Pedigree of CH. HEATHSIDE HURRICANE
Whelped April 16, 1940
Breeder, Robert Sedgwick

Sire: Ch. Desert Deputy	Ch. Nornay Saddler	Ch. Travelling Fox
		Wyrksop Surprise
	Ch. Braw Lass	Boreham Remark
		Warren Agile
Dam: Ch. Clover Club of Wissaboo	Ch. Nornay Saddler	Ch. Travelling Fox
		Wyrksop Surprise
	Ch. Krawen Cocktail of Wissaboo	Grimsbest
		Krawen Katrinka

In Stepping Stone we find the same method of introducing line breeding as was mentioned above with regard to Braw Lass. Stepping Stone is a daughter of Saddler and on her dam's side she carries some of Saddler's blood through Avon Peddler.

Now we come to what I consider the most successful line breeding. In Hurricane we find *both* grandparents sired by Saddler, which is an example of *true line breeding* in two dominant *strains*. Many similar combinations were used and most of them produced gratifying results.

Among dominant sires of the past twelve years (in addition to Nornay Saddler) is the dog called Downsbragh Mickey Finn, who was by Foxden Sundowner out of Gone to the Ground, and who has proved to be a very potent stud. He has sired some twenty or more champions, and he has a producing son in Ch. Downsbragh Night Stick, who has at least seven champions to his credit.

Other Smooths that rate high on the list of outstanding stud dogs of their time are: Landmark of Andley, Ch. Sabine Rarity, Foxden Sundowner, Ch. Lucky Fella, Ch. Downsbragh Tom Sawyer, and Ch. Downsbragh Two O'Clock Fox. I have grouped these dogs together because they either do not carry Saddler blood at all, or if it does appear, it is almost always on the dam's side in the third generation.

There is another stud who sired many champions—at least fifteen—and that is Ch. Upper Boy of Etona. It is interesting to note that his grandsire was Travelling Fox, who sired Saddler—again proving the dominance of that strain.

No mention has been made of the many sons of Saddler who went on to produce and to be a credit to their sire. The most outstanding of these, perhaps, were Ch. Lincsman and Ch. Desert Deputy.

It is important to point out that while we are all indebted to those who import "great ones," it is through the efforts of the person or persons who carry on in their own kennels and consistently *breed* "great ones" that the breed will gain. The outstanding breeder in this country in Smooths in the last twenty-five years was, without a doubt, Mrs. Barbara Lowe Fallass. May those that follow in her footsteps do as well!

There appears to be at least one kennel today that is following close in the footsteps of Mrs. Fallass, and that is the Downsbragh Kennel of Mr. and Mrs. W. W. Brainard, Jr. In the last five years this kennel has consistently walked off with the top six trophies of The American Fox Terrier Club Specialty Shows—and this speaks of success! The present star in the kennel is Downsbragh Jumpinpowder (sired by Downsbragh

Mickey Finn), and though this young champion has not proven himself a dominant stud force as yet, I predict that he will.

Wires

A great deal can be learned from the study of pedigrees, for it is the simplest way to trace producing lines, provided one does not lose sight of the quality of the individuals concerned. For a study of examples of combinations in breeding of Wires, let us begin with the pedigree of one of the "greats"—Ch. Barrington Bridegroom, a dominant stud force. Following the pedigree of Bridegroom is that of Ch. Crackley Supreme of Wildoaks, sired by Int. Ch. Crackley Sensational out of Ch. Eden Bridesmaid. Bridesmaid was Bridegroom's most famous daughter, and Int. Ch. Crackley Sensational was sired by Ch. Crackley Sensation, Bridegroom's most famous son, so the mating which produced Supreme was one of nephew to aunt. And it was Supreme and a bitch called Ch. Gaines Great Surprise (daughter of another dominant line) which really started Wildoaks on its way in this country.

Pedigree of CH. BARRINGTON BRIDEGROOM
Whelped May 19, 1919
Breeder, F. Pearse, Eng.

	Barrington Brisk	Ch. Cracker of Notts
		Barrington Crackem
Sire: Barrington Fearnought		
	Barrington Cracker	Comedian of Notts
		Gileston Prospect
	Ch. Chunkey of Notts	Comedian of Notts
		Cobnut of Notts
Dam: Sarsgrove Molly		
	Sarsgrove Pansy	Bishops Selected
		Sarsgrove Gamesters Model

Pedigree of CH. CRACKLEY SUPREME OF WILDOAKS
Whelped Jan. 2, 1926
Breeder, F. Robson, Eng.

Sire: Ch. Crackley Sensational

- Ch. Crackley Sensation
  - Ch. Barrington Bridegroom
  - Love Bird
- Kerseley Pandy
  - Pedro Toff
  - Roman Wire Girl

Dam: Ch. Eden Bridesmaid

- Ch. Barrington Bridegroom
  - Barrington Fearnought
  - Sarsgrove Molly
- Trevlac Tartlett
  - Gaffer of Gretna
  - Coffee of Notts

In the pedigree of Ch. Gallant Fox, a son of Supreme, we find the introduction of the blood of another dominant sire, Ch. Talavera Simon, through his daughter Ch. Gaines Great Surprise. We find further that when Simon blood was combined with Bridegroom stock in the right combinations, it produced outstanding results. Again, though, it was necessary for the breeder to be familiar with the individual characteristics produced by both of these lines to have success in breeding them in combination. This is an example of *outbreeding*.

Pedigree of CH. GALLANT FOX OF WILDOAKS
Whelped Dec. 23, 1929
Breeder, Mrs. R. C. Bondy

Sire: Ch. Crackley Supreme

- Ch. Crackley Sensational
  - Ch. Crackley Sensation
  - Keresley Pandy
- Ch. Eden Bridesmaid
  - Ch. Barrington Bridegroom
  - Trevlac Tartlett

Dam: Ch. Gaines Great Surprise

- Ch. Talavera Simon
  - Fountain Crusader
  - Kingsthrope Donah
- Newtown Bella Donna
  - Wycollar Trail
  - Miss Harvest Time

59

CH. FOX HUNTER OF WILDOAKS
Owned by Mrs. R. C. Bondy, Goldens Bridge, N.Y.

CH. EXTERMINATOR OF CRACK-DALE
Owned by Mrs. Paul M. Silvernail, Madison, Conn.

CH. RADAR OF WILDOAKS
Owned by Mrs. R. C. Bondy, Goldens Bridge, N.Y.

CH. DERBYSHIRE DAZZLE
Owned by Mr. Thomas Keator, Carversville, Penna.

61

Gallant Fox's two most potent sons were Ch. Gallant Invader and Ch. Fox Hunter of Wildoaks. Ch. Gallant Invader's pedigree shows the same breeding as is to be found in that of Fox, except that there is more of an intensification of Simon blood in Invader than in Fox. Invader had Simon on his sire's dam's side through Surprise, and on his dam's sire's side through Frizzette. When this combination was crossed back to bring in more Bridegroom breeding again through the dam's side, as shown in the pedigree of Ch. Top Row of Wildoaks, the results were successful. This method of *line breeding* has been used by the Author for her most successful results, and she has tried many combinations.

Pedigree of CH. TOP ROW OF WILDOAKS
Whelped June 24, 1935
Breeder, Mrs. Paul Silvernail

	Ch. Gallant Fox of Wildoaks	Ch. Crackley Supreme
		Ch. Gaines Great Surprise
Sire: Ch. Gallant Invader of Wildoaks		
	Ch. Weltona Frizzette of Wildoaks	Ch. Talavera Simon
		Oakbrook Rosebud
	Terrance of Hillcrest	Graceland Joe Simon
		Graceland Sweet Peggy
Dam: Ladysmaid of Crack-Dale		
	Lady Crack-Dale	Ch. Crackley Sensational
		Annadale Remit

Pedigree of CH. EXTERMINATOR OF CRACK-DALE
Whelped April 18, 1941
Breeder, Mrs. Paul Silvernail

	Ch. Gallant Fox of Wildoaks	Ch. Crackley Supreme
		Ch. Gaines Great Surprise
Sire: Ch. Fox Hunter of Wildoaks		
	Ch. Crackley Sunray of Wildoaks	Ch. Wyrebury Torrid Topline
		Stapenhill Barmaid
	Ch. Gallant Invader of Wildoaks	Ch. Gallant Fox of Wildoaks
		Ch. Weltona Frizzette of Wildoaks
Dam: Dangerous Lady of Crack-Dale		
	Ladysmaid of Crack-Dale	Terrance of Hillcrest
		Lady Crack-Dale

CH. HETHERINGTON FLIRT
(Dam of five champions)
Bred by Hetherington Kennels, Glen-
dale, Ohio

CH. PROMOTER OF WIREHART
Bred by George H. Hartman, Lam-
peter, Penna.
Owned by Mr. and Mrs. R. Weil, San
Francisco, Calif.

CH. HETHERINGTON PILOT   CH. HETHERINGTON CO-PILOT
(The breeding of these two dogs is interesting. Owned by Hetherington
Kennels, they are father and son and their dams are litter sisters.)

63

(The pedigree of Exterminator shows the same method used and is an interesting study of line-breeding from dominant strains of Simon and Bridegroom in sons of Invader and Fox Hunter.)

To again emphasize how dominant some lines can be, I would like to point out that Ch. Barrington Bridegroom is credited with at least ten champions; his grandson Crackley Sensational with ten; Sensational's son Ch. Crackley Supreme with nine; Supreme's son Gallant Fox with eighteen; Gallant Fox's son Gallant Invader with fourteen; and Gallant Fox's other outstanding son, Fox Hunter, with twenty-one. On the other side of the picture, Ch. Talavera Simon and his brother Ch. Talavera Jupiter produced twenty-three and sixteen, respectively.

In the early thirties, the most outstanding Wire bitch was Ch. Weltona Frizzette. Bred in England in 1928 and sired by Talavera Simon, Frizzette was brought to this country by the Bondys and won best in show for them thirty-three times! Her most outstanding litter was one with three champions in it, and was sired by Ch. Gallant Fox. These dogs were Champions Tip Topper, Irresistible, and Gallant Invader of Wildoaks.

Another outstanding Wire bitch was Ch. Hetherington Flirt, the dam of five champion daughters: Hetherington Vindication, Hetherington Picturesque, Hetherington Repetitious, Hetherington Pilot's Dream, and Hetherington G. I. Girl. It is interesting to note that Flirt was sired by Midshipman of Wildoaks (who was by Invader ex Sunray) and was out of Ch. Hetherington Model Minx.

Perhaps the most famous of the Carruthers' home-breds was that lovely bitch Ch. Hetherington Model Rhythm, whose sire was Ch. Surprise Model and whose dam was Ch. Hetherington Flash. In 1946, Model Rhythm won best in show at Westminster, and with her daughter, Ch. Hetherington Navy Nurse, won best brace in show at Westminster in 1944 and again in 1946.

Another bitch at this time was winning her share of best-in-show awards, and she was the late Luther Lewis' lovely Ch. Glynhir Golden. She was bred in England and was a daughter of Ch. Gallant Fox out of Dalewood Miss Chief (again a combination of line breeding of Simon and Supreme).

64

In Texas, the Hallwyre Kennel of Mr. Forest Hall, with the importation of Ch. Westbourne Teetotaler, was doing a great deal for the breed, turning out one champion after another. Mr. Hall had another producing stud in Florate Friar, the sire of many champions, whose daughter Hallwyre Hella Donna produced four champions.

In 1946 Mrs. Bondy imported Ch. Crackley Startrite of Wildoaks. This new stud in her kennel gave her a complete new outcross of bloodlines, and was welcomed by many breeders who felt that their stock could also use such a force. Startrite was a small dog, without the usual look of a producing stud, but, put to the right bitches, he produced satisfactory results. He sired nine champions and his son Ch. Radar of Wildoaks sired at least seven.

In 1951 a new star appeared in the field with the importation by Mr. and Mrs. Harold Florsheim of Ch. Travella Superman of Harham. He made his American debut at the Fox Terrier Club of Chicago's Specialty in 1952 and has made an enviable record for his owners. He has scored twenty-seven best-in-show wins and fifty-six Group firsts. He has been handled exclusively by Thomas M. Gately. To date he has sired five champions. Superman is a grandson of Travella Strike, a very dominant sire in England, and used with the right bitches Superman should produce. Here again is an example of how the study of pedigrees will help the breeder. The Florsheims are lucky enough to own a lovely bitch by Ch. Travella Strike—Ch. Ailey Adorable of Harham, a best-in-show winner—and it seems to me that bred to Superman she should produce something outstanding.

To bring the Carruthers' breeding up to date, they are following their usual productive line through their stud dog Ch. Hetherington Pilot and his son Ch. Hetherington Co-Pilot and the latter's son Ch. Hetherington Parapilot. The Carruthers have recently made several importations from England, and it will be interesting to students of the breed to see how these English Fox Terriers fit into their breeding program.

In the last few years the Wire has returned to winning the top spot in show awards and of course Superman of Harham heads this best-in-show list, accounting for twenty-seven. Others gaining the honor are Miss Barbara Worcester's Ch. Bluebird Ruby and Ch. Sunshower Strike; Mrs. Florsheim's Ch. Travella Staress of Harham; Mr. and Mrs. Weil's Ch. Promoter of Wirehart; Mrs. Marguerite Tyson's Ch. Nugrade Nuflame; Mrs. Frederick Dutcher's Ch. Copper Beech Storm; and Joseph W. Urmston's Ch. Mitre Miss Adorable. It appears to me that we are entering another era of renewed popularity for the Fox Terrier, both Smooth and Wire.

Pedigree of CH. RADAR OF WILDOAKS
Whelped Oct. 17, 1946
Breeder, Mrs. R. C. Bondy

	Ch. Crackley Straightaway	Ch. Crackley Supreme Again
		Crackley Sequel
Sire: Ch. Crackley Startrite of Wildoaks		
	Crackley Sportsgirl	Ch. Crackley Surething
		Crackley Sporty
	Ch. Crackley Striking of Wildoaks	Ch. Crackley Supreme Again
		Crackley Social
Dam: Ch. Radiance of Wildoaks		
	Moonbeam of Wildoaks	Ch. Fox Hunter of Wildoaks
		Ch. Glamour Girl of Wildoaks

Pedigree of CH. TRAVELLA SUPERMAN OF HARHAM
Whelped Feb. 12, 1951
Breeder, Browne-Cole, Eng.

	Ch. Travella Strike	Ch. Travella Sensation
		Travella Gloria
Sire: Travella Skyflyer		
	Travella Manequin	
	Travella Sensation	Copleydene Lucky Strike
		Copleydene Fashion Pride
Dam: Travella Carnation		
	Travella Gloria	Ch. Crackley Straightaway
		Lady Contender of Laracor

66

LIST OF SMOOTH AND WIRE
FOX TERRIERS

winning

BEST-IN-SHOW AWARDS—(All Breed Shows)—IN AMERICA
during 1955–1956–1957–1958–1959–1960–1961–1962–1963–1964

1955

Ch. Madam Moonraker	(Wire)	3 wins
Ch. Promoter of Wirehart	(Wire)	3 wins
Ch. Travella Superman of Harham	(Wire)	3 wins
Ch. Nugrade Nuclea of Trucote	(Wire)	2 wins
Ch. Travella Sunbonnet of Harham	(Wire)	2 wins
Ch. Eubray Starlet of Harham	(Wire)	1 win
Ch. Hallwyre Handy Jack	(Wire)	1 win
Ch. Oxley Diplomat	(Smooth)	1 win

1956

Ch. Travella Superman of Harham	(Wire)	6 wins
Ch. Madam Moonraker	(Wire)	4 wins
Ch. Travella Starstud of Harham	(Wire)	1 win

1957

Ch. Copper Beech Storm	(Wire)	2 wins
Ch. Mitre Miss Adorable of Trucote	(Wire)	2 wins
Ch. Bluebird Ruby of Radwyre	(Wire)	1 win
Ch. Hallwyre Hazel's Alibi	(Wire)	1 win
Ch. Promoter of Wirehart	(Wire)	1 win
Sunnybrook Special Notice	(Wire)	1 win
Ch. Travella Superman of Harham	(Wire)	1 win
Ch. Woodcliff Hiya Boy	(Smooth)	1 win
Wychway Buccaneer	(Smooth)	1 win

1958

Ch. Copper Beech Storm	(Wire)	2 wins
Ch. Hensington Society	(Wire)	2 wins
Ch. Crackerjack of Cranmore	(Wire)	1 win
Ch. Emprise Sensational	(Wire)	1 win
Ch. Mitre Miss Adorable	(Wire)	1 win
Ch. Sunshower Strike	(Wire)	1 win
Ch. Wyretex Wyns Gillian	(Wire)	1 win
Ch. Travella Special of Harham	(Wire)	1 win

1959

Ch. Sunshower Strike	(Wire)	6 wins
Ch. Cudhill Kalypso of Harham	(Wire)	5 wins
Ch. Merrbrooks Fair Reward	(Wire)	1 win
Ch. Hallwyre Halfpenny Saw Song	(Wire)	1 win
Ch. Purebeck Pride of Hehstowe	(Wire)	1 win
Ch. Travella Special of Harham	(Wire)	1 win
Ch. Woodcliffe Hiya Boy	(Smooth)	1 win
Danamic Courage	(Wire)	1 win

1960

Ch. Miss Skylight	(Wire)	11 wins
Ch. Sunshower Strike	(Wire)	2 wins
Ch. Woodcliffe Hiya Boy	(Smooth)	2 wins
Ch. Weltona Dustynight's Warrior	(Wire)	1 win

1961

Ch. Miss Skylight	(Wire)	14 wins
Ch. Falstaff Lady Fayre	(Wire)	2 wins
Ch. Star Dancer of Wildoaks	(Wire)	2 wins
Ch. Stoneygap Short Story	(Wire)	2 wins
Ch. Cairngoim Rambler	(Wire)	1 win
Ch. Merrybrooks Beautiful Belle	(Wire)	1 win
Ch. Weltona Dustynight's Warrior	(Wire)	1 win
Ch. Wildwood Cinderella	(Wire)	1 win

1962

Ch. Nugrade Nupin	(Wire)	4 wins
Ch. Merbeth Melanie	(Wire)	2 wins
Ch. Deko Druid	(Wire)	1 win
Ch. Koshare's Striking Star	(Wire)	1 win
Ch. Oxley Beau Prince	(Smooth)	1 win
Ch. Purebeck Pride of Helenstowe	(Wire)	1 win

1963

Ch. Falstaff's Lady Fayre	(Wire)	7 wins
Ch. Koshare's Striking Star	(Wire)	2 wins
Ch. Abingdon Accurate	(Smooth)	1 win

1964

Ch. Koshare's Striking Star	(Wire)	6 wins
Ch. Deko Druid	(Wire)	1 win
Ch. Koshare's Kiowa Kishi	(Wire)	1 win
Ch. Wyrecroft Briartex Trident	(Wire)	1 win
Ch. Gallant Coachman of Wildoaks	(Wire)	1 win

The Forward Look

We have been discussing what "has been." Now let us ask ourselves, "What does the breeder of today have to look forward to?"

The first and most important factor to consider in answering that question is the planning of breeding programs with an eye to the future of the breed. We must not only consider what we can win with in the show ring, but in addition, whether *what* we win with is going to further the progress of the breed. The data on previous pages have shown that concentrated effort and thought on the part of the old-time breeders produced results. In the past, there were not as many dog shows to take the attention of the breeders, and they gave more thought to their breeding operations than most do today. The trouble with today's exhibitor is that he wants to get to the top so fast that he loses his perspective of what is good for the breed.

I believe that careful planned breeding to the stud dog that suits your bitch, along her bloodlines, whoever owns the dog, is a necessity. Too often petty jealousy, because a dog has beaten his own favorite in the ring, prevents one breeder from using another's stock. What a pity! In the early days of the breed, this was also true to some extent, but it didn't take those sportsmen long to realize their mistakes and when the Duchess of Newcastle set out to "perfect" Wires, she used first one strain and then another to get the points she wanted with success. Let tomorrow's breeders take heed!

The breed is definitely staging a come-back from the slump it suffered in the early 1950's and I predict that the next ten years will find it again enjoying great popularity. Today we do have more breeders with small kennels, breeding their own champions instead of importing, and they are to be congratulated on their success. These are the people who will put Fox Terriers in their proper niche again.

Among new names in the picture of recent years is Eve Ballich (Wires) of Maryland. Her Evewire Kennels' success in the small span of seven years has been phenomenal. Mrs. Ballich's goal is to breed an American-bred champion that can stand up to his imported competition. Furthermore, all her champions have been amateur-handled with the exception of one. Her kennel houses about 30 dogs and she has been sure that each mating suited her bloodlines, rather than just breeding to top name winners. She has produced type and quality that has reproduced itself, and she should be proud of her success.

Others tasting success in Wires are Mrs. Gene Scaggs Bigelow, Raylu Kennels in Va.; Penzance Kennels of Mrs. Nell Benton Hudson, also in Va.; in Penna., Mrs. Phyllis Haage of Galliard Kennels; the Earl Greenes and Darrell Jacklins of Mich. In N. J. the Merrybrook Kennels of Mrs. Franklin Koehler continue to breed top stock. In California, we have new exhibitors in the Charles Marcks and Thomas Comans, and the leading kennels of a former Judge and long time breeder, Wm. Myers Jones, of North Hollywood, whose famous Ch. Falstaff's Lady Fayre has accounted for nine Best-in-Shows, winning in the toughest competition on both coasts. Lady Fayre is just one shining star among many in his kennel. Then the Glidewyre Kennels of Mrs. Walter Bunker of Los Angeles promises to be one to consider, with its lovely Ch. Zeloy Mooresmaid Magic piling up wins that put her at the top of the winning terriers at the present. This kennel has several outstanding imports, but I hope they will breed one that will equal "Magic!"

The *true breeder* is not so much interested in his show awards as he is in his breeding results. To support this statement, look at the record of the Smooth sire, Downsbragh Mickey Finn, of a decade ago. He produced more champions than any other stud at that time, although not a champion himself. Credit should go to the breeders who recognized his potency and put the right bitches to him.

In Wires in recent years, the top producing line proved to be that of English Ch. Travella Strike. Another English import, Ch. Kirkmoor Coachman, has proven a potent stud, and the American-bred Ch. Evewire Little Man should not be overlooked.

Approximately every decade we reach a point where we must

70

adjust our breeding programs if we are to go ahead, so take the time to study your results and honestly evaluate your progress. In my early breeding days, my dominant lines came from Bridegroom and Simon and Wildoaks lines. Then I reached a point where I felt that I should introduce new blood and I went to England and bought a bitch that was a granddaughter of Ch. Travella Strike on both her sire's and dam's sides. I returned home with her bred to Ch. Roundway Strike-a-Light, a son of Strike. This brought into my kennel the dominant producing line which I needed in a son of this breeding, Souvenir of Crack-Dale. I am very happy with my results and I guess I shall go on dreaming how to produce a better Fox Terrier as long as I live!

Breeders, besides being exhibitors, hold a responsibility for a breed. It is our hands that mold a breed and we would do well to sit back and think how we may go forward!

SOUVENIER OF CRACK-DALE
Bred by Mrs. Paul M. Silvernail, Madison, Conn.

The Blueprint of the Breed

Standard and Illustrations

A Standard for any breed is essential, for it is the outline into which the perfect picture fits. Unfortunately, in some breeds the Standards have not been as specific as they could have been. But this is not true of the Fox Terrier Standard, and I think the success of the breed over these past one hundred and fifty years has been due largely to the complete and comprehensive Standard which breeders have had as a guide.

The Standard of the breed follows. Study it carefully, and study also the illustrations which accompany it. Then I hope after reading my "Blueprint of the Breed," you will have a clear idea of what a perfect Fox Terrier should be.

Official Description and Standard of the American Fox Terrier

The following shall be the Standard of the Fox Terrier amplified in part in order that a more complete description of the Fox Terrier may be presented. The Standard itself is set forth in ordinary type, the amplification in italics.

HEAD—The skull should be flat and moderately narrow, gradually decreasing in width to the eyes. Not much "stop"

73

should be apparent, but there should be more dip in the profile between the forehead and the top jaw than is seen in the case of a Greyhound.

The cheeks must not be full.

The ears should be V-shaped and small, of moderate thickness, and drooping forward close to the cheek, not hanging by the side of the head like a Foxhound. *The top line of the folded ear should be well above the level of the skull.*

The jaws, upper and lower, should be strong and muscular and of fair punishing strength, but not so as in any way to resemble the Greyhound or modern English Terrier. There should not be much falling away below the eyes. This part of the head should, however, be moderately chiseled out, so as not to go down in a straight slope like a wedge.

The nose, toward which the muzzle must gradually taper, should be black.

It should be noticed that although the foreface should gradually taper from eye to muzzle and should tip slightly at its juncture with the forehead, it should not "dish" or fall away quickly below the eyes, where it should be full and well made up, but relieved from "wedginess" by a little delicate chiseling.

The eyes and the rims should be dark in color, *moderately* small and rather deep set, full of fire, life and intelligence and as nearly as possible circular in shape. *Anything approaching a yellow eye is most objectionable.*

The teeth should be as nearly as possible together, i.e. the *points* of the upper (*incisors*) teeth on the outside of or *slightly overlapping* the lower teeth.

There should be apparent little difference in length between the skull and foreface of a well-balanced head.

NECK—Should be clean and muscular, without throatiness, of fair length, and gradually widening to the shoulders.

SHOULDERS—Should be long and sloping, well laid back, fine at the points, and clearly cut at the withers.

CHEST—Deep and not broad.

BACK—Should be short, straight (*i.e., level*), and strong, with no appearance of slackness. *Brisket should be deep, yet not exaggerated.*

LOIN—Should be very powerful, *muscular* and very slightly arched. The foreribs should be moderately arched, the back ribs deep *and well sprung,* and the dog should be well ribbed up.

HINDQUARTERS—Should be strong and muscular, quite free from droop or crouch; the thighs long and powerful; *stifles well curved and turned neither in nor out;* hocks *well bent* and near the ground *should be perfectly upright and parallel each with the other when viewed from behind,* the dog standing well up on them like a Foxhound, and not straight in the stifle. *The worst possible form of hindquarters consists of a short second thigh and a straight stifle.*

STERN—Should be set on rather high, and carried gaily, but not over the back or curled. It should be of good strength, anything approaching a "pipe-stopper" tail being especially objectionable.

LEGS—The forelegs viewed from any direction must be straight, with bone strong right down to the feet, showing little or no appearance of ankle in front, and being short and straight in pasterns. Both forelegs and hind legs should be carried straight forward in traveling, the stifles not turning outward. The elbows should hang perpendicularly to the body, working free of the sides.

FEET—Should be round, compact and not large; the soles hard and tough; the toes moderately arched and turned neither in nor out.

COAT—Should be smooth, flat, but hard, dense and abundant. The belly and under side of the thighs should not be bare.

COLOR—White should predominate; brindle, red, or liver markings are objectionable. Otherwise this point is of little or no importance.

SYMMETRY, SIZE AND CHARACTER—The dog must present a generally gay, lively and active appearance; bone and strength in a small compass are essentials; but this must not be taken to mean that a Fox Terrier should be cloddy, or in any way coarse—speed and endurance must be looked to as well as power, and the symmetry of the Foxhound taken as a model. The Terrier, like the Hound, must on no account be leggy, nor must he be too short in the leg. He should stand like a cleverly made hunter, covering a lot of ground, yet with a short back, as before stated. He will then attain the highest degree of propelling power, together with the greatest length of stride that is compatible with the length of his body. Weight is not a certain criterion of a Terrier's fitness for his work—general shape, size and contour are the main points; and if a dog can gallop and stay, and follow his fox up a drain, it matters little what his weight is to a pound or so. *According to present-day requirements, a full-sized, well-balanced dog should not exceed 15½ inches at the withers—the bitch being proportionately lower— nor should the length of back from withers to root of tail exceed 12 inches, while, to maintain the relative proportions, the head should not exceed 7¼ inches or be less than 7 inches. A dog with these measurements should scale 18 pounds in show condition— a bitch weighing some 2 pounds less—with a margin of 1 pound either way.*

BALANCE—*This may be defined as the correct proportions of a certain point or points, when considered in relation to a certain other point or points. It is the keystone of the Terrier's anatomy. The chief points for consideration are the relative proportions of skull and foreface; head and back; height at withers and length of body from shoulder-point to buttock—the ideal of proportion being reached when the last two measurements are the same. It should be added that, although the head measurements can be taken with absolute accuracy, the height at withers and length of back and coat are approximate, and are inserted for the information of breeders and exhibitors rather than as a hard and fast rule.*

MOVEMENT—*Movement, or action, is the crucial test of conformation. The Terrier's legs should be carried straight forward while traveling, the forelegs hanging perpendicular and swinging parallel with the sides like the pendulum of a clock. The principal propulsive power is furnished by the hind legs, perfection of action being found in the Terrier possessing long thighs and muscular second thighs well bent at the stifles, which admit of a strong forward thrust or "snatch" of the hocks. When approaching, the forelegs should form a continuation of the straight line of the front, the feet being the same distance apart as the elbows. When stationary, it is often difficult to determine whether a dog is slightly out at shoulder, but directly he moves, the defect—if it exists—becomes more apparent, the forefeet having a tendency to cross, "weave," or "dish." When, on the contrary, the dog is tied at shoulder, the tendency of the feet is to move wider apart, with a sort of paddling action. When the hocks are turned in—cowhocked—the stifles and feet are turned outwards, resulting in a serious loss of propulsive power. When the hocks are turned outwards the tendency of the hind feet is to cross, resulting in an ungainly waddle.*

N.B.—*Old scars or injuries, the result of work or accident, should not be allowed to prejudice a Terrier's chance in the show ring, unless they interfere with its movement or with its utility for work or at stud.*

Wire Fox Terrier

This variety of the breed should resemble the Smooth sort in every respect except the coat, which should be broken. The harder and more wiry the texture of the coat is, the better. On no account should the dog look or feel woolly, and there should be no silky hair about the poll or elsewhere. The coat should not be too long, so as to give the dog a shaggy appearance, but, at the same time, it should show a marked and distinct difference all over from the Smooth species.

Head and ears	15
Neck	5
Shoulders and chest	10
Back and loin	10
Hindquarters	15
Stern	5
Legs and feet	15
Coat	15
Symmetry, size and character	10
Total	100 Points

DISQUALIFICATIONS

NOSE—*White, cherry, or spotted to a considerable extent with either of these colors.*
EARS—*Prick, tulip, or rose.*
MOUTH—*Much undershot, or much overshot.*

The Blueprint of the Breed

First, let me start off by asking you to sit back in your chair, close your eyes, and think about what you have just read. First, visualize the Fox Terrier as a small, rugged, compact, square-cut Terrier of about 18 pounds and 15½ inches tall at the withers, or top of the shoulder blades. He should be alert, aggressive, and elegant!

Now, let us pick him apart and see what we want in the perfect dog, and what we too often find and should avoid!

Begin with the head—remember that is important—it is what everybody sees first. Your Standard tells you it should be flat, moderately narrow, and balanced with regard to length between skull and foreface. What the judges look for in today's Fox Terriers is a long lean head. Unfortunately to my mind, sometimes too much emphasis is put on length, and the word *balance*, which is included in the Standard, is forgotten! However, what you must strive for is a *long, balanced* head in proportion with the rest of the dog—lean and narrow, not thick from the top of

EXCELLENT TYPE IN SMOOTH AND WIRE

79

FAULTS ILLUSTRATED

Wire: short in foreface; Roman nosed; cheeky; shoulders too far forward and too straight; back roached; croup falls off; tail curled; too long in body; too long in loin; straight in stifle; lacks sufficient angulation.

Smooth: dish-faced; underjaw shallow; ears semi-prick; throaty (wet); neck too thick; sway-backed; tail too short; shallow in depth; pasterns soft; over-angulated behind (hocks).

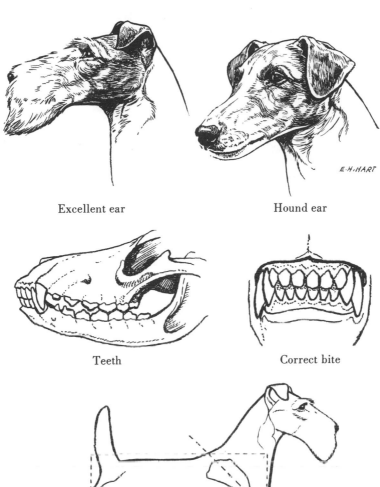

Excellent ear   Hound ear

Teeth   Correct bite

FOX TERRIER "SQUARED"
45° layback in shoulder

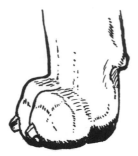 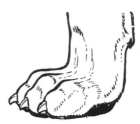

Correct cat
foot

Splay foot
(incorrect)

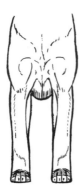  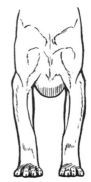

Correct

FRONTS
Toeing out
Loaded shoulder

Out at elbows
Splay-footed

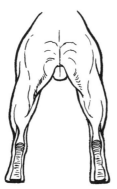 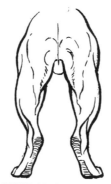 

Correct

HINDQUARTERS
Cowhocked

Barrel-legged

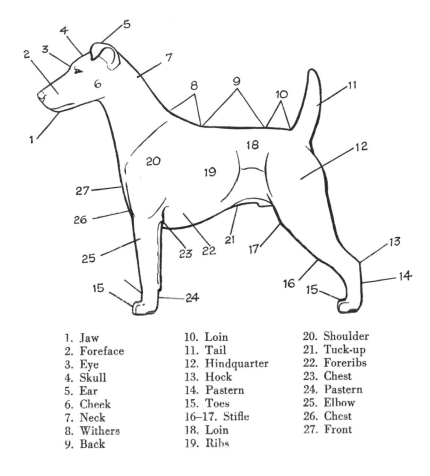

1. Jaw	10. Loin	20. Shoulder
2. Foreface	11. Tail	21. Tuck-up
3. Eye	12. Hindquarter	22. Foreribs
4. Skull	13. Hock	23. Chest
5. Ear	14. Pastern	24. Pastern
6. Cheek	15. Toes	25. Elbow
7. Neck	16–17. Stifle	26. Chest
8. Withers	18. Loin	27. Front
9. Back	19. Ribs	

the skull down to the turn of the throat. A wedgy head is to be avoided likewise. This is what the Standard means when it says, "the cheeks must not be full."

Good, well-placed ears make the "perfect" head on a Fox Terrier. They should be small, V-shaped and not too thin, and folded forward close to the cheek of the dog. The top folded line of the ear must break above the level of the skull. Nothing is more objectionable than a heavy, Hound ear on a Fox Terrier. Also, it is well to mention here that prick (one that stands up), tulip (one carried erect with a slight forward curvature), and rose ear (one that folds backwards and shows part of the inside) bring a disqualifying point. The most common ear faults found in breeding Fox Terriers are prick and Hound type ears. We breed to get small ears, but sometimes the combination of breeding produces too small ears which stand up. On the other hand, if two dogs with ears which tend to be large and heavy are bred, we will get a Hound type ear.

It is the correct eye which completes the picture of the perfect head. A light eye and a round full eye are to my mind most objectionable. The Standard calls for a small dark eye with fire and intelligence to give the "hard bitten" expression that is so desired in the breed. With the correct eye and correct eye placement, one captures the correct expression. The small V-shaped ear, properly placed, contributes toward that keen, alert expression which is so desired.

Before we leave the head, attention should be given to the mouth. The bite should be a scissors bite, the points of the upper incisors on the outside of the lower teeth, just overlapping. An undershot or overshot mouth is also a disqualifying fault. When heads are bred too long, we frequently find undershot or overshot mouths! Bad mouths are rare today, but there was a time when extreme length of head was more in vogue than proper balance of the dog, and this fault was conspicuous. The mouth was either overshot or undershot! Breeders finally learned that extreme head usually carried length of body as well as height on the leg, both of which are deplorable.

We now come to the middle portion of the body. Begin with the neck, which should be clean and muscular and of fair length, gradually widening into well-laid-back shoulders. The most common fault to be found today is a short bully neck that usually sits on a high stilted shoulder. There is nothing more beautiful in a Fox Terrier than a moderately long, well-arched neck.

To have this kind of neck, the dog must have the perfect shoulders—those that are well laid back and closely knit together. The shoulders of a good Terrier are placed at a 45 degree angle, which tends to give a freedom of movement similar to that found in the best race horses. A well-laid-back shoulder should allow the dog free movement in a straight forward action. Movement is a crucial test of the dog.

The body of a good Fox Terrier is most important. It should have a good spring of ribs with a depth of chest to take care of its stout heart and the work for which it was developed. The chest must not be *too* narrow—a fault which seems to be creeping into the breed—but do not misconstrue my meaning; it must not be broad or cloddy, but rather clean cut. If it is *too* narrow, the dog usually has a mincing gait and the shoulder is stilted. On the other hand, the chest should not be broad and giving a Bulldog appearance. Usually, a broad chest finds the dog "out at the shoulder." When viewed from the front, the shoulders and legs should sweep down in one clean-cut continuous line. With the proper shoulder placement, deep brisket and well-sprung ribs, you are bound to get the level back you desire.

Feet are of importance in the Fox Terrier. They should be small, compact and cat-like. The dog should appear "up on its toes," and the legs and feet should appear to melt into one. A long-toed, splay foot is very bad. The pads should be tough and the dog should turn neither "in" nor "out" when walking, but move with straight, free movement from the shoulders. The bone in the legs and feet should be of fair size, round and straight down to the ankle. We find too many dogs with light bone and thin feet, and usually such dogs will be down in the pastern. One must bear in mind that these dogs were hunters, and good legs and feet were essential in those early days when the dogs really went to hole after a fox. It has been my observation that when poor legs and feet get into a kennel, they take a long time to improve. This is done only by careful breeding and study of the stock on both sides. Vitamins will not provide all the bone!

We now come to the last third of the dog, the hindquarters. In our Fox Terrier this is very important because the dog gains his propelling power from his hind legs. The Fox Terrier has been likened to a cleverly made hunter, inasmuch as he covers the ground in a like manner—with speed and endurance and symmetry.

85

Understanding this, the reader knows what the Standard means when it says that the hindquarters "should be strong and muscular, free from crouch, and the thighs long and powerful." The stifles should be well turned and the hocks well bent. Viewed from behind, the hocks on the Fox Terrier should turn neither "in" nor "out" and should be "well let down," with good angulation to the quarter. The dog will then move with space between its hind legs—hocks turning neither "in" nor "out"—and the front feet, when viewed from this position, appear straight between the hind legs. Coming toward you his feet should neither "cross" nor "weave," but be put down firmly and travel forward freely in a straight line. Given a gaily carried tail, the good Fox Terrier should now be pictured in your mind.

The Fox Terrier should have a well-balanced look at all times, and this is important to remember. Your dog should "square off." In other words, the height on the leg should equal the length of the dog. To put it more clearly, if you stand a ruler alongside your dog, the height from his toes to the top of his withers should equal the length of the dog from his shoulder point to his buttocks. (See illustration.)

Up to now I have said nothing about the coat of your dog. In the chapter entitled "Grooming the Fox Terrier," I go into detail on how to groom your dog for the show ring, especially the Wire Fox Terrier, and there are step-by-step illustrations to provide emphasis. But for the record in the "Blueprint" of any breed, we must describe just what you must look for in coats, in both varieties of the breed. The coat of the Smooth should be flat, hard, dense and abundant. The coloring found on the Smooths of today is black and white or tan and white. Occasionally a dog will have a black head with tan penciling or markings. In the earliest days of the breed, there was a mixture of the three colors on a lot of the specimens. Today, most of the Smooths are just two colors.

A preponderance of the Wire specimens, however, still show all three colors. The coat of the Wire is considered a "broken" coat. It should be hard and wiry in texture and never feel woolly or silky. It should not be long enough to give the appearance of shagginess, but should be deep, and denser than that of the Smooth. The wiry texture of this coat repels water.

Exaggeration in any form is dangerous, and this is particularly true in the breeding of dogs. As I said before, there was a time when one found many poor mouths in the particular breed. This was because of exaggeration! Breeders thought an extreme length of head was what they wanted. True, it attracted attention. Perhaps it made a good first impression! But invariably with length of head came bad mouths, length of body and height on the leg. They ran hand in hand.

So for a span of a few years, the breed in this country was afflicted with these things, because that type of dog was presented to the public by the prominent kennels and we are a country made up of those who like to "follow the leader."

It took a generation or two of breeding to prove to the same kennels that things were getting out of hand. Dogs became rangy, litters inconsistent, and faults reappearing. All this only served to prove that one should not lose sight of a breed Standard that has proved over a period of a hundred years to be as near perfect as one could achieve.

"Fads" never last! Today breeders have tempered their desire for extreme points, in consideration of others, and they are breeding more closely to the original Standard than ever before.

I marvel at the foresight of those early English breeders who foresaw a perfect picture in the breed they wanted—without exaggeration—and bred toward it. That little word "balance" in the Standard is an important thing!

I think this covers pretty thoroughly what you want in a Fox Terrier and the most common pitfalls in breeding. If by now you have decided that the dog you own adds up to show caliber and that you want to show him, then there are certain things or training which you must undertake. You will find these discussed in the chapter entitled "Grooming the Fox Terrier."

87

AMERICAN FOX TERRIER CLUB SPECIALTY, 1946
Ch. Hetherington Model Rhythm, with Jake Terhune, handler, and Ch. Canadian Ambassador, with Henry Sayres, handler.

88

Establishing a Kennel

IN selecting a Fox Terrier, whether for show, for breeding, or to serve as the family pet, the best advice I can give you is to "get the best that is available, within your financial limits." The place to "get the best available" is at a kennel operated by a reliable breeder—not a breeder whose interest is aimed at making a "gold mine" by raising dogs, and whose interest will cease the minute the dogs are sold.

The reliable breeder is vitally concerned with the disposition, the health, and the appearance of the Fox Terriers he is selling, and all of those things are of importance to the purchasers, whatever their reasons may be for wanting a dog. Furthermore, the reliable breeder can serve as a model for the purchaser if he intends to breed Fox Terriers himself. Should he do so, he must realize that not every litter brings a future champion, but that every litter does consistently breed type (if bred properly), and that that is what the breeder must strive to produce.

For those dogs that do not quite come up to the high standards established for show dogs and breeding stock, a reliable breeder will find good homes where, as pets, the dogs will be recognized for the outstanding attributes they possess as far as character or personality is concerned.

The person buying a pet Fox Terrier puppy must realize that he will have to pay from $100.00 to $125.00, for each puppy costs the breeder at least that, and sometimes more! Every breeder must take into consideration the cost of his breeding stock, the dam's care, the stud fee, the cost of raising the puppy to a saleable age, veterinary costs (inoculations, etc.), and the general overhead of maintaining a kennel. A breeder is lucky if these costs do not total more than $100.00 per puppy.

Despite the comparatively high cost of the puppy, of this I am sure: by having decided on the Fox Terrier, either the Smooth or the Wire variety, you will have a dog that will repay you many times in devotion, intelligence, gameness, and gentlemanliness.

To the new breeder or kennel owner who has decided that the Fox Terrier is the breed he wants to raise, I cannot emphasize too much that the most important step is the careful consideration of foundation stock. The bitches are the mainstay of the kennel, so they must be chosen carefully. And the cost? From $150.00 and up, if it is a puppy bitch you start with, and from $250.00 and up, if it is a mature bitch.

A new kennel owner should not consider owning a stud dog for the first five years of kennel operation. By the end of that time, he will have proved to himself the ability to use the knowledge he has gained from his breeding experience, and he will also be in a position to know whether serious breeding operations are what he really wants as a hobby or a vocation. Ordinarily, the expense of maintaining a stud dog is not justified in a small breeding program. No outsider will come to a kennel to breed to a dog unless he is being shown consistently, or has made a name for himself as a champion. It is cheaper and better for the novice breeder to go out and use the best dogs to be found that are suitable for his breeding stock, than to try to support a stud dog without a proven reputation.

The success of any kennel lies in its bitches and in the breeder's knowledge of how to use them. Careful, successful breeding is the result of years of work, and of much thought on the subject. Haphazard breeding has never been successful, and it is a mistake to own a kennel just to turn out puppies.

Because the bitches are so important in making a breeding kennel a success, it is imperative that their ancestry, their pedi-

CH. HETHERINGTON MODEL RHYTHM winning the Terrier Group, Westminster Kennel Club Show. Owners, Mr. and Mrs. T. H. Carruthers III; handler, Jake Terhune; judge, George H. Hartman.

grees, be considered carefully, and that they have a history of producing ancestors and as few faults as possible. It is important, too, that the new breeder avoid purchasing any bitches or using any stud dogs with faults so pronounced that there is little or no hope of correcting them in mating.

It is a proven fact that some strains of Fox Terriers produce more typical specimens than others, as well as a greater number of winners. But another consideration is this: some dogs have won the title of champion, and while worthy of the title themselves, have been unable to reproduce their type; others have earned the title but have not reproduced for only one reason— they haven't been given a fair chance to do so.

What it all amounts to is that the breeder must know the strains represented in the pedigree of his stock, and know, too, what makes them outstanding. He must learn whether the dog he is considering as a stud can produce progeny *as good as or better than himself* (provided, of course, that the dog is mated properly). And he must not be fooled by the title of *champion!* It is important to keep in mind the record the dog has made for himself, but even more important to remember that heredity will tell. And what counts most of all is the knowledge of how to combine the chromosomes that produce the desired characteristics.

After purchasing the best matron to be found, it is advantageous to mate her with a stud dog that has similar breeding. This is called line breeding, and the idea is to combine the best in both the dam and the sire to produce the desired type of progeny.

It will be an excellent selling point for the puppies if one or both of the parents are champions, and the breeder will be able to set a higher sales price for the puppies. But a word of caution is *a propos* here: don't try to make a fortune in one litter. Give good honest value for money, and you will get more out of your breeding program in the final analysis than you will by taking a customer over the hurdles. Remember, too, that just because the bitch or the sire is a champion, it doesn't mean that the puppies are going to be champions.

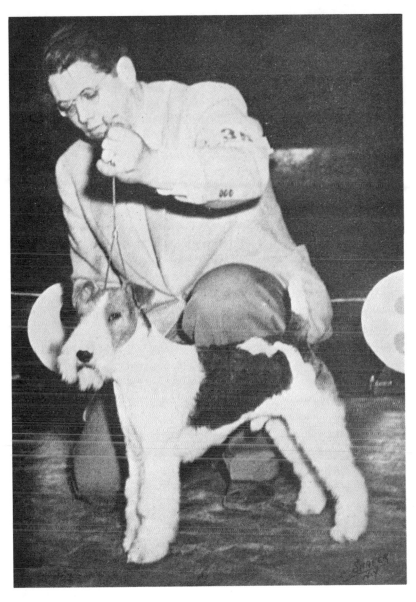

CH. RADAR OF WILDOAKS at The American Fox Terrier Club Specialty Show, February 1949. Owner, Mrs. R. C. Bondy; handler, Robert Snodgrass.

It is my belief that stud dogs produce the best progeny after they are four years old, and until they are eight years old. As for bitches, it is preferable not to breed them before their second season, and I think the quality of offspring is best when the bitch is between two and six years of age. I prefer to breed a young bitch to an older dog and vice versa, rather than to breed a young bitch to a young dog. It has been my experience that show quality pups rarely come from very young parents, and that results are more satisfactory when both the parents are at least four years old. My most successful breedings have been with the older stud dog and younger bitch.

I do not approve of breeding a bitch every time she is in season, although I have been told by some veterinarians that if the health of the female is good, it is better to keep them producing. In my opinion, this is too likely to lead to commercializing production, and the health of the bitch may suffer. If a bitch is young, I may breed her two times and then skip. If she is older, I prefer breeding every other season.

Statistics indicate that one out of every five purchasers of a female dog eventually decides to raise a litter of puppies. The temptation to have little ones around is great, especially where there are children in the home, for what better way to initiate the young into the ways of life than through their pet? But many owners seem to reach the decision to raise a litter too casually, without first taking steps to prepare for the event.

A good deal of attention must be paid to the bitch before the decision is made to breed her. First of all, a sick or thin dog should never be bred. It is important that the bitch be in good condition, and it is as bad if the bitch is too fat as it is if she is too thin. A dog is in top condition when the ribs are pleasantly covered and the tissue hard and firm from the proper exercise, not soft and flabby.

Exercise without jumping, balanced meals (not table scraps), and a bed or box in which to whelp the pups (under the eyes of the family, but not under its feet) are all that are required for the pet, although the breeder with several bitches will require more elaborate equipment and more rigid feeding and exercise schedules in order to insure the best results with a minimum of work.

It is wise to have the Wire Fox Terrier bitch plucked either just before or immediately after breeding, for then her coat will look fit rather than ragged when buyers come to look at her pups. Two weeks after breeding, the bitch should be wormed as a matter of course. And, when the pups are about three weeks old, the bitch should be wormed again. The pups must be wormed when they are eight weeks old, and it is of vital importance that the pups be inoculated as is recommended in Part II of this book.

For the pet owner, housing is not an important factor. If, however, you are thinking of starting on an extensive breeding program, it is imperative that one section of the kennel building be set aside for boxes in which to house the dogs. These are approximately two feet square and are placed on tiers. After a Fox Terrier has reached five months of age, and particularly if it is a show prospect, it is important that it be broken to these boxes or houses, for a dog kept in a pen, where it can jump up and down continually, may throw itself "out at the shoulders," thus ruining its possibilities for a career in the show ring. Large individual outside exercise runs are necessary, as are facilities for grooming the dogs (together with the proper grooming tools). The ideal kennel has proper bathing facilities, a small kitchen, and a section which can be used for isolation quarters.

It is also advantageous to have a section where matrons may whelp quietly, away from the other dogs, where the puppies may be kept for the first few months of their lives. Any "handyman" can easily make a whelping box which will be suitable either for a single pet dog or for a bitch in a large breeding kennel. For a Fox Terrier bitch, the approximate size of a whelping box should be twenty-four by thirty inches, preferably made of plywood for easy handling, on a frame of one by two inch strips, with plywood sides about six or eight inches high. Along the walls, inside the box and about four inches from the floor, a strip of wood about one inch square should be nailed. This prevents the pups from smothering if they get behind the mother, inas-

CH. CHIEF BARMAID at Newton Kennel Club, 1950
Owner, Mrs. Howard Angus; handler, Mac Silver.

much as it keeps her from lying right up against the side of the box.

To those considering embarking upon a breeding program, a final word of advice: the mainstay of your kennel will be your bitches, so choose them carefully! Quality, not quantity, counts!

Before we finish this discourse on establishing a kennel, there is one point I think should be made. That is the suitability of the individual concerned with raising dogs. One must face the fact that to do any job well, he must be suited to it, both by temperament and by ability and knowledge. I always try to discourage those people who think that by raising a litter or two of puppies they can substantially increase the family budget. Too often such people do not realize the care or cost involved, nor after the puppies arrive are they prepared to cope with them and the demands that they will make on the family life. A person must consider all this before he decides upon raising a litter just for the fun of it! I think it is a gratifying experience to have a litter of puppies, but the owner of the female must be prepared to give of their time and be able to afford such an experience, taking into full consideration that there is a possibility that remuneration may not fully cover everything, should all not go well. For this reason alone, breeders should have a genuine interest in the breed. Either they must want to improve the breed, perhaps because they have become interested in showing dogs and take this method of hoping to secure better than they own; or the desire to work with dogs may be the incentive. In any case, to love dogs is important. Breeding dogs means responsibility, some heartaches, some thrills, but for the real dog lover it does have its rewards in spite of all the work involved!

Every person seriously interested in breeding must realize the importance of evaluating his own dogs. It takes experience and knowledge and a lot of forthright honesty on the owner's part to admit his own dogs' shortcomings. I hope that by the study of the "Blueprint of the Breed," in this book, you will know what to look for and recognize in your dog.

CH. ARTLEY ADORABLE OF HARHAM
Best in show at Providence Kennel Club, 1949
Owner, Mrs. Harold Florsheim; handler, Thomas Gately; judge, Mrs.
Paul M. Silvernail.

I Remember When—

YES, I'm familiar, and so are you, with
the saying that "reminiscing is a sign of age." But, even so, I'm
willing to risk the implication if it means recalling two golden
decades of Fox Terriers that won in our largest shows—Westminster and Morris & Essex—as I remember them.

"I remember" when in 1932 there were twenty-nine Smooths
and one hundred and ten Wires entered at Westminster! At that
time the Smooths and the Wires were judged against each other
for best of breed. And in that year, such immortals as the Smooth
dogs Ch. Millhill Margin, owned by E. Coe Kerr, and Ch. Gallant
Fox, owned by Mrs. John J. Farrell, and that outstanding bitch
Ch. Daffodilly, owned by Mr. and Mrs. Wright Duryea, met the
following great Wire dogs: Champions Bobbie Burns, Gallant
Fox, and Eden Aristocrat, owned by Mrs. Bondy; Champions
Halleston Knockout and Wycollar Goldfinder, owned by Stanley
J. Halle; Ch. Westborne Teetotaler, owned by Forest Hall; and
Ch. Lone Eagle of Earlsmoor, owned by Dr. Samuel Milbank.
The bitches of the day were Ch. Delightful Lady of Wildoaks,
Ch. Earlsmoor Snowflake, Ch. Talavera Margaret and Ch. Fylde-
lands Margaret—both of the latter owned by Reginald W. Lewis.

The outcome of the judging of this marvelous array of dog
flesh found the best of winners in Wires coming from the open
class—that now famous Gallant Fox of Wildoaks, from Wildoaks
Kennels.

CH. DERBYSHIRE DUELIST
Owner, Mr. Thomas Keator; handler, Bob Kendrick.

I don't mind admitting that every time I think back to that show, I thrill again over having seen at one time such perfection in so many dogs! It makes me sad to think that these days we seldom come up with more than two or three of such caliber at the same show. Mr. Q. A. Shaw McKean (owner of the famous Wire Ch. Crackley Sensational) was the judge who did the honors.

"I remember" sitting through a drizzle, which turned into a downpour, before the judging finished at Morris & Essex in 1934. At that show, it was William Shanks of Ohio who wore the purple and sorted through twenty-seven Smooths and ninety-seven Wires.

In Smooths, I recall Moltan Fancy Man, owned by James A. Farrell, E. Coe Kerr's Flornell Special, and Jerry Collins' First Payment, all of which finished their championships. Wires saw Gallant Invader of Wildoaks, Flornell Standard of Knollton, and Ch. Leading Lady of Wildoaks fight it out for best of breed, which went to Ch. Leading Lady, a beautiful bitch owned by Mrs. Bondy.

At Westminster that same year, it was the Wire Ch. Halleston Spicy Bit, owned by Stanley J. Halle, that put the breed in top place by walking off with best-in-show honors.

"I remember" the now successful and capable "Pete" Snodgrass, white and shaken with emotion in 1935 when, at Westminster, the late George G. Thomas, the veteran judge, gave him best of breed for his home-bred Wire, Fox Trot of Macroom. At this show the entry was thirty-six Smooths and one hundred and thirty-five Wires! And had I won this—I would have been shaken too! This show found the American-bred class of Wire dogs with twenty-three entered, and the American-bred Wire bitch class with fifteen—which speaks well for the American breeders.

1935 was also the year that Brass Tacks, that lovely dog of Jerry Collins', was out along with another Smooth I admired, E. Coe Kerr's Flornell Special. They were among the entry of thirty-five Smooths and one hundred and three Wires at Morris & Essex that same year. Ch. Leading Lady of Wildoaks was best of breed in Wires, under Mr. Walter Reeves of Canada. I think

101

CH. DOWNSBRAGH TWO O'CLOCK FOX
Best in show at Montgomery County Kennel Club Show, 1951.

it interesting that the number of dogs entered at Morris & Essex in 1935 totaled 4,007.

"I remember" the year 1936 at Westminster, for that was the year that the puppy Top Row, which I had sold only two months before to Mrs. Bondy, topped a class of fifteen and went on to reserve winners. The day before he had gone best of breed at the American Fox Terrier Club's Specialty Show.

If memory serves me right, Top Row's kennel-mate, Ch. Huntsman of Wildoaks, was best of breed in Wires, and Mr. Jerry Collins' Brass Tacks was best in Smooths, out of an entry of one hundred and sixteen Wires and forty-seven Smooths. The judge for the Wires was Mr. Stanley J. Halle, and for the Smooths, Mr. William Prescott Wolcott.

Morris & Essex the same year had forty Smooths and ninety-seven Wires. The late J. W. Spring judged the Smooths and Lewis Spence of Texas, the Wires. An interesting note on the Wires is that the winners dog and the winners bitch both came through from the puppy classes. The winners dog was Top Row, bred by me and owned by Mrs. Bondy, and the winners bitch was Monopoly, bred and owned by the late William Knipe of Haverhill, Massachusetts. Monopoly went on to best Wire.

"I remember" the year 1937 as the year the famous Nornay Saddler came out in the open class at Westminster when not yet a year old. The good Smooths out at this show included Jerry Collins' Upper Crust; Frank Beer's Dancing Doll; Robert Sedgwick's Ch. Heathside Houri; and E. Coe Kerr's Solus Joy and Ch. Lad Fra Skye. There was an entry of thirty Smooths, with the late Dr. Harry Jarrett judging. And the entry was seventy-eight in Wires, with Walter Reeves judging. That ear saw, among others, such Wire dogs entered as Sea Swing Kennels' Ch. Flornell Stand Clear of Sea Swing; Mrs. Bondy's Ch. True Charm of Wildoaks; Miss Flick's (Knollton Kennels') Ch. Flornell Stand Out; W. L. Lewis' Ch. Glynhir Galahad; and George Hartman's Ch. Edgemoor Exclusive Design of Wirehart. The winner came from the open class in Stanley J. Halle's Flornell Spicypiece of Halleston, who later went on to win best in show.

"I remember" 1938, and Morris & Essex, with a total entry

103

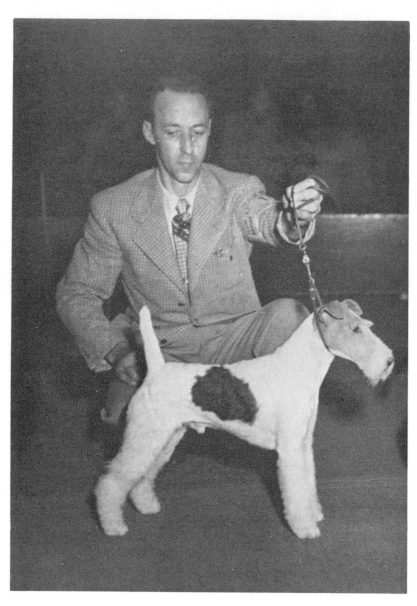

CH. WYRETEX WYNS TRAVELLER OF TRUCOTE
winning Terrier Group, Albany Kennel Club, 1951.
Owner, Mrs. Leonard Smit; handler, Seth Campbell.

104

of 4,850 dogs—including one hundred and two Wires and fifty-six Smooths. The Smooths were judged by the late Charles P. Scott and the Wires by Forest N. Hall of Hallwyre fame. Ch. Nornay Saddler walked away with the honors in Smooths, and W. L. Lewis' lovely bitch Ch. Glynhir Golden won in Wires, with Saddler winning best in show.

"I remember" the 1938 Westminster show as the one in which the late Robert Sedgwick judged an entry of thirty-three Smooths and Thomas Keator an entry of one hundred and twenty-four Wires. By that time, Mr. Austin's Wissaboo Kennels, headed by Ch. Nornay Saddler, had grown and had an entry of seven at this particular show. The Rutherfords, father and son, had an entry of ten between them. Mrs. Bondy had a new import out that year in the little bitch Crackley Sunray of Wildoaks.

The specials class saw ten champions, among them W. L. Lewis' Glynhir Golden; Pete Snodgrass' Fox Trotter of Macroom (a son of his previous winner, Fox Trot); Mrs. Bondy's Flying Fox (an Invader son); George Hartman's Edgemoor Everest; Mr. and Mrs. Carruthers' Hetherington Knight Stormer; Mrs. Florence Floren's Good News of Floranda, and Halleston Kennels' Flornell Spicypiece.

"I remember" the year 1939 because Morris & Essex hit the 5,000 mark in total entry of dogs. Smooths were sixty-three strong and Wires one hundred, but at that point, while total entries in shows were increasing, the entries in Smooths and Wires were slowly decreasing.

Westminster that year saw an entry of fifty-seven Smooths and one hundred and ten Wires, and the total entry of the show was over the 3,400 mark. Today, fire laws make it necessary to limit the entries at Westminster to 2,500.

In June that same year, at Katonah, New York, on the estate of Mrs. Sherman Hoyt, the North Westchester Kennel Club Show had a total entry of 1,880. (This show, which is no longer held, used to be an extremely popular Eastern event.) That year, Mrs. Wini Barber of England judged the Fox Terriers and had an entry of seventy, both coats. Fox Hunter of Wildoaks went best Wire, coming through from the classes. I had had the pleasure

105

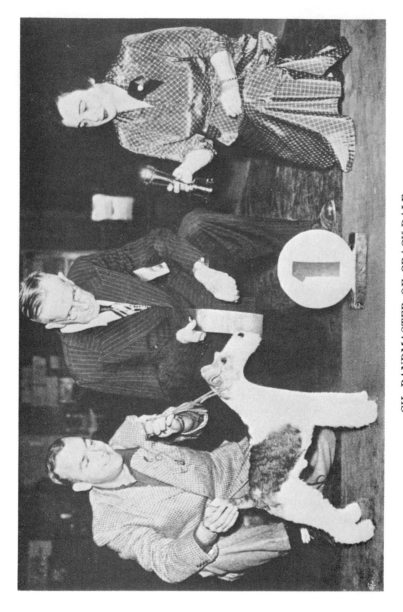

CH. BANDMASTER OF CRACK-DALE
winning Terrier Group, Tampa Bay Kennel Club.
Owner, Mrs. Edward N. Snowdon; handler, Jerry Rigdon; judge, C. J. Casselman.

of passing on this dog at his first show in Worcester, Massachusetts, six months earlier and had also taken him from the classes over very strong competition to best of breed. He went on to take the Group, and after passing on him I predicted a rosy future, remarking that I considered him the "best home-bred" of the Bondys.

"I remember" 1940 as one of those in-between years—nothing startling out in either Smooths or Wires. Westminster had an entry of sixty-six Smooths and eighty-seven Wires. The fact that the Smooth entry had grown each year after Saddler came out was interesting. This, of course, was due to the fact that Mr. Austin had established his kennels and showed so many dogs. At the 1940 Westminster Show he accounted for twenty-five entries! Saddler won in Smooths, and Fox Hunter of Wildoaks in Wires.

Morris & Essex in 1940 had Mr. Sedgwick and Mr. Austin for judges, doing the Smooths and Wires, respectively. There were forty-three Smooths and eighty-seven Wires, and without the Wissaboo dogs, that was a good entry. Such good Smooths as Ch. Buckland of Andley, Ch. Flornell Checkmate, Ch. Alwen Foxcatcher, Ch. Desert Deputy, and Andley Lovely Lady were out. In Wires, it was a new import for Mrs. Bondy—Ch. Crackley Striking of Wildoaks; and in specials, it was Ch. Crackley Sunray, Ch. Invader's Sun Beau, Ch. Glynhir Golden, and two litter sisters, imports, Wynstead Wonderful and Wynstead Wireclad of Sarhelm, fighting it out. At this show the Wire and the Smooth both appeared in the Group, the rule having been changed.

"I remember" 1941, 1942, and 1943 as the war years. Shows felt the pinch of gas rationing, and brown-outs were in order in the large cities, but between strikes, storms, and war, a few hardy souls got to the shows. All shows were held as benefits for the Red Cross, Dogs for Defense, or some other worthwhile cause, and War Bonds were prizes at the shows. Entries suffered, of course, because of the restrictions on travel, and were of necessity quite localized.

An interesting side light about the war years lies in the fact that in 1940, just after the Battle of Britain, the editor of *Our*

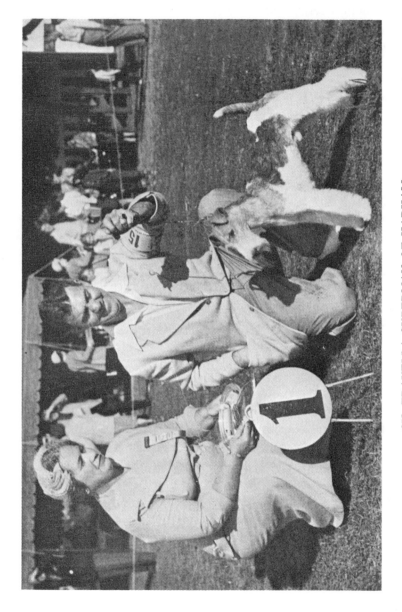

CH. TRAVELLA SUPERMAN OF HARHAM
winning Terrier Group, Ox Ridge Kennel Club, 1953.
Owner, Mrs. Harold Florsheim; handler, Thomas Gately; judge, Mrs. Paul M. Silvernail.

Dogs, an English magazine which was conducting a campaign for the Air Fighter Fund, received the following cable (accompanied by instructions to a bank to credit the fund with the amount)—"I sink my teeth into Adolf Hitler with this draft of 1,200 dollars. I earned it all myself in stud fees. Signed, Champion Nornay Saddler, New York."

"I remember" that by 1944 and 1945, things were a little better. Westminster in 1944 had an entry of forty-one Smooths, with Mr. Jerry Collins judging, and best of variety went to Mrs. Fallass' She's Bonney of Andley. There were fifty-two Wires, with Mr. Stanley Halle judging, and Mr. and Mrs. Thomas Carruthers' Ch. Hetherington Model Rhythm took the purple and gold. There was a big drop in Smooths in 1945—only twenty-eight entered—and sixty-eight Wires, both coats being judged by Walter Reeves. Par Value of Wissaboo, owned by Lt. Robert W. Craig, went to the top in Smooths. Wires found the Carruthers having another field day. Their previous year's winner's daughter, Ch. Hetherington Navy Nurse, went to the top. And in 1946, they had the supreme thrill of going best in show with that grand bitch Ch. Hetherington Model Rhythm.

"I remember" 1947 as the year that Ch. Crackley Startrite of Wildoaks was out in Wires. This newest import of the Bondys had an extreme head and was on the small side, but in his famous son, Ch. Radar of Wildoaks, he left his stamp as a sire. There were eighty-one Wires and forty-two Smooths at Westminster that year. Mrs. Cora Charters of England judged both coats and found Mr. J. P. S. Harrison's Ch. Oppidan of Etona in Smooths, and Crackley Startrite in Wires, as her best-of-variety winners. Morris & Essex that year found the entry down to forty-eight Smooths and sixty-four Wires.

In Smooths, 1947 found the Downsbragh Kennels becoming active. Also, there was a lovely Smooth out in Ch. Canadian Ambassador, bred by Frank Beer. This was the year that the Gayterry Kennels had lovely Ch. Boarzell Brightest Star out.

It seemed to me that the quality of the Wires at the time was, on the whole, somewhat on the downward path. I think it noteworthy to mention here, for comparison with today's scale of

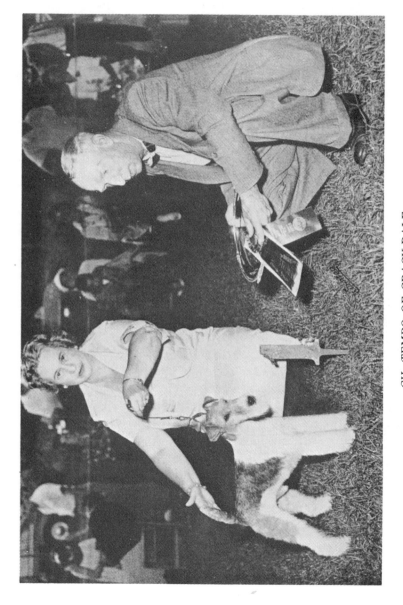

CH. TEMPO OF CRACK-DALE
winning Terrier Group, Adirondack Kennel Club, 1953.
Owner and handler, Mrs. Paul M. Silvernail; judge, Ernest Crowley.

championship points, that at that time twelve Smooths and twenty-two Wires were needed for five points, against twelve and fourteen now. Today, the scale is divided by sex, but because it wasn't then, I am using the larger figure in the present scale.

"I remember" James J. Farrell, Jr., judging forty-seven Smooths at Westminster in 1948, and having such fine specials as the Brainard's Ch. Downsbragh Groundwork; Aliber Kennels' Ch. Canadian Ambassador; Wissaboo Kennels' Valuable of Wissaboo; Derek Rayne's Ch. The Young Pretender of Andley; Ch. Oppidam of Etona; Ch. Mountmellick March Wind; Ch. Heathside Heads Up II; and Colonel Appleton's Barberry Vivian.

The classes at that show were filled with many that finished their championships, among them Downsbragh Night Stick (a beautiful dog), Downsbragh Speak Easy, Barberry Verity, and Barberry Vanity.

Mr. Jerry O'Callahan, from the Boston area, judged the Wires and, out of sixty-six, came up with J. P. Hackett's Faith of Piety Hill. Also in the Wire classes there was some outstanding stock which finished: Hetherington Minstrel Man; Marquis of Ar-For; Quests End Border Patrol; Wyretes Wyns Royalist of Glynhir; Radar of Wildoaks; Derbyshire Duelist; Wyretex Wyns Jupiter of Glynhir; Hetherington Navy Patrol; Shiremont Allure; and others.

In retrospect it truly seems that the enforced rest of the war years gave us a fine crop of young material in both Smooths and Wires.

"I remember" 1949 as the year that any judge would have been thrilled to pass on the specials class of Smooths at Westminster. They were a sight to see—eighteen, all good ones—and the job fell to Robert Sedgwick, a tribute to this man who had so long been identified with this breed, and one of his last judging assignments. Out of a total entry of forty-nine, the winner was Ch. Downsbragh Night Stick, owned by Mr. and Mrs. W. W. Brainard, Jr. The Wires were judged by Mrs. Kenneth Marlett of Canada, and she also had forty-nine to pass on. Mrs. Edward Kraft of Michigan won with her Wynwyre Warrior.

111

CH. MADAM MOONRAKER
best of breed, Westchester Kennel Club, 1953.
Owner, J. Donald Duncan; handler, Seth Campbell.

112

"I remember" with regret that the year 1950 saw a distinct drop in the breed at three of the largest Eastern shows—New York, Boston, and Morris & Essex, all ranging in total entries from 1,500 to 2,600. We managed, however, to dig up a total entry (both coats) of eighty-nine, forty-two, and seventy-five, respectively. Ch. Radar of Wildoaks was the outstanding Wire at the time, accounting for innumerable bests of breed, Groups, and bests in show. His closest contenders in Smooths were Ch. Ronnoco Resolute, owned by the late Judge O'Connor, and Ch. Lucky Fella, owned by the late Robert Sedgwick.

"I remember" 1951 and 1952 as the years that saw more good ones to the fore. In Smooths were Foxden Molly Brazen, Assault of Andley, Sandate Storm, Ch. Farham's First Flight, and Ch. Downsbragh Two O'Clock Fox. Walter Reeves judged both coats at Westminster in 1951 and Ch. Ronnoco Resolute was best of variety in Smooths. Best of variety in Wires was Mrs. Florsheim's Ch. Foxbank Entertainer of Harham. At Boston that year, Lucky Fella was best Smooth. Morris & Essex in 1952 found Ch. Two O'Clock Fox the winner in Smooths and Mrs. Leonard Smit's Ch. Wyretex Wyns Traveller in Wires. Mr. Forest Hall did the judging. Traveller was also the Garden winner that year under Mr. John Marvin, with an entry of eighty-nine in both coats.

"I remember" 1953 as the year that the quality of both the Smooth and Wire seemed to improve, even if show entries did not take a big jump. At Westminster that year, with Mr. Thomas Keator judging the Smooths, best of variety was Mrs. Fallass' Ch. Indicator of Andley. Now some new names are consistently appearing among the Smooth entries: Silver-Ho Kennels, Mr. and Mrs. C. Huntley Christman, W. Potter Wear, and Dr. Charles Thompson. Forty Wires made an appearance for Mrs. Thomas Carruthers to judge, and her best of variety was Mrs. Smit's Ch. Wyretex Wyns Traveller of Trucote.

"I remember" 1954 as the year that Mr. George Hartman judged a Smooth entry of thirty-two at the Westminster show, with such quality in the specials class as Ch. Ronnoco Romancer, Ch. Argonaut of Andley, Ch. Flicker of Kidsgrove, Ch. Foxden Anthony, and Ch. Oxley Diplomate. The Wires had an entry of

113

forty-nine for General Edward McKinley to pass on, and as I look back, it is interesting to me to note that out of the open dog class of six, only two made their championship. Further checking shows me that there were seven in the open bitch class and of those, five, possibly six, made their championship! It was a nice specials class of eleven with Ch. Travella Superman of Harham, owned by Mrs. Florsheim, winning top honors.

"I remember" 1955 as the year our visitor from England, Mrs. Cyril Pacey, passed on the breed at Westminster. A nice entry of thirty-nine Smooths and fifty Wires greeted her. In Smooths, her best of variety came from the classes and was the Brainard's Downsbragh Diana's Dream. In Wires it was the Florsheim's Ch. Travella Surelooker of Harham who won and then placed fourth in the Group.

"I remember" 1956 as the year Mr. Thomas Carruthers judged both coats, with an entry of twenty-two Smooths and thirty-one Wires. Ch. Downsbragh Red Vixen was the Smooth winner, with Ch. Dancer of Wildoaks the Wire winner at this Westminster show.

"I remember" that Mr. James Farrell judged the Smooths and Mr. Hartman the Wires at Westminster in 1957. The entry was nineteen Smooths and forty Wires. Mr. Farrell picked Ch. Downsbragh Jumpinpowder as his winner, and Mr. Hartman found his winner in the open class in Caradochouse Spruce of Trucote, the new import that year of Mrs. Urmston, and the Wire that placed third in the Group.

"I remember" that Westminster in 1958 saw a slight increase in entries: twenty-three Smooths for General McKinley to pass on, from which he found his winner in Ch. Woodcliffe Hiya Boy owned by Mr. Welty. The late Mr. Thomas Mullins passed on fifty Wires and picked Mrs. Munro W. Lanier's Emprise Sensational from the classes, and he went on to win a tough Terrier Group.

"I remember" that in 1959 Mrs. Eileen McEachren of Canada did the honors at Westminster, with an entry of nineteen Smooths and thirty-nine Wires. Mr. Welty's Ch. Woodcliffe Hiya Boy was best of variety in Smooths and Mrs. Harold Florsheim's

Cudhill Kalypso of Harham came from the open class to take best of variety in Wires, and second in the Group.

"I remember" that Mrs. Duncan Henderson judged an entry of nineteen Smooths and forty-one Wires at Westminster in 1960. She put Mr. and Mrs. T. H. Veling's Ch. Jeopardy of Andley Best of Variety in Smooths, and Mrs. Murno Lanier's Ch. Mac's Revelation Best of Variety in Wires. A lot of good ones were out this year and in looking back I find that most all of the class dogs in both coats made their championships.

"I remember" 1961 as the year that Ross Proctor officiated at Westminster with an entry of seventeen Smooths and forty-one Wires. Ch. Lucky Find owned by James McMorris was best in Smooths, and in Wires the west coast was represented by Ch. Miss Skylight owned by the Wyldwest Kennels as Best of Variety.

"I remember" the late George Hartman passing on a total of forty-four at Westminster in 1962. In a small entry of only six Smooths Mrs. Stewart Simmons's Ch. Battlecry Biff went to the top. In Wires, it was a field day for the Wyldwest Kennels of California. They accounted for Winners Dogs with Kirkmoor Coachman, Winners Bitches with Kirkmoor Cockleshell (a daughter of Coachman), and Best of Variety for a second year with Ch. Miss Skylight! The same placing was made the day before at the A.F.T.C. Specialty with Tom Carruthers judging.

"I remember" 1963 as the year that the late Gen. Edward B. McKinley had an entry of twenty Smooths and thirty Wires at Westminster. He found his Best of Variety in Smooths in the Wm. Wimers' Ch. Thermfare, and in Wires for the third consecutive year a west coast entry took Best of Variety. This time it was Wm. Myers Jones' Ch. Falstaff Lady Fayre that was Best of Variety.

"I remember" John Marvin judging Westminster in 1964 with an entry of twenty-two Smooths and twenty-eight Wires. His Best of Variety in Smooths was the Downsbragh Kennels' Ch. Downsbragh Gold Cup, and in Wires Wm. Myers Jones of California won again for a second year with his Ch. Falstaff Lady Fayre.

So we see a trend—for the first time, eastern exhibitors have to bow to their western competitors! The beautiful Morris & Essex show has written finis to its span and no longer do the eastern shows hold the spotlight. Indeed, six out of the top ten shows with the largest entries in the country are western shows! The International Kennel Club show in Chicago, the Heart of America show in Kansas City, and in California the Santa Barbara Kennel Club, Golden Gate Kennel Club and the Harbor Cities Kennel Club, have each passed the 2000 mark in entries! While Fox Terriers are not the largest terrier entries, a slow gradual increase is to be noted, with emphasis on the increase of breeders and the popularity the breed is experiencing again.

It is interesting to note that at the three 1964 Specialty Shows of the Parent Club, The American Fox Terrier Club, the entries ran: eighty-nine both coats at New York in February, twenty-seven both coats in April at International in Chicago, and in the fall specialty at Montgomery County in October found both coats boasting of an entry of one hundred and five. In 1965 they had a total entry of one hundred for Club President, Tom Keator, to pass on in New York, and at International in Chicago in April a entry of thirty-eight. I believe the Chicago entry may suffer because it follows the N. Y. shows so closely.

And so over a period of three decades, I hope your memory was refreshed on the "dogs of the years." It is indeed a good idea to take a look backward at the winnings of the dogs to see what each has accomplished through the years.

Comparison of English and American Kennels, Dogs, and Judging

RECENTLY I visited England, and while there I had the pleasure of judging at two of their championship shows, the Southern Counties Canine Association at Brighton, and the City of Birmingham Show at Birmingham. I also had the opportunity of visiting several leading kennels and meeting many people interested in dogs. As a result of my visit, I have come to the conclusion that while both England and the United States have the same Standard for the Fox Terrier, the interpretation of the Standard is different, for the interpretation depends on the interpreter. Also, it is only natural that each country thinks it produces the best! Let it suffice to report that we have produced England's equals and may well be proud of our home-breds.

Around every "import" there is that certain glamour of the newcomer—the foreigner to these shores—and sometimes glamour dazzles. For this reason, one should always keep in mind the Standard of the breed and judge the specimen according to the Standard, not by its history of past performances. Too often one forgets that circumstances alter results, and that competition and quality must be reckoned with. This applies in evaluating all specimens, whether imported or home-bred, and that is where the Standard *should* fit in—the Standard should be the criterion for evaluating the individual dog!

On the whole, there are more dogs per person in England than

117

there are in this country. The English are truly a dog-loving people. Kennels are large and there are a great many of them—it would seem that almost every person owns a dog or two. Also, it is interesting to note that many owners of dogs in England establish a kennel name and then have "out to walk" or "farm out" a number of bitches, but actually do not maintain a kennel.

In Fox Terriers, the number entered at the shows has declined in recent years, just as it has in America. The most obvious reason lies in the increase of professional handlers, and their ability to condition and show the dogs to advantage over amateur owners. In England, handlers seem to be employed only for the Terrier breeds, whereas in this country they are seen in almost every ring and with various breeds. It is interesting to note, too, that the majority of dogs shown in England, all breeds, are handled by women. I think perhaps one reason for this might be that the shows are held during the week, not just on week-ends, as in this country, and shows are never held in England on Sunday. Since many of the men are not able to attend because they are employed, more of the dogs are shown by women.

I would say that on the whole, and probably because of the climate of the country, English Fox Terriers possess better coats than do ours. I also think that at the present time the heads are longer and more impressive than those found on the American specimens. However, with longer heads are usually found longer bodies and more daylight underneath, and this I found particularly true of the English Fox Terriers. Because English dogs are walked more than their American cousins, they possess better legs and feet, and I found that the Smooths, especially, excelled in these parts. It is my opinion that when it comes to size, the American breeder at the present time has the Standard of the breed more clearly in mind than does his English cousin, especially among the Wire breeders, for bone, substance, and size can be controlled by breeding and by the extent one inbreeds along certain family lines.

Differences in living habits of countries influence the lives of the dogs as well as the people. In England, where central heating is the exception rather than the rule, kennels do not employ the one-house units that are so common in kennels in America. Instead, most kennels house their dogs in a series of small buildings, each with its individual run attached. These buildings range from a small six-foot by nine-foot affair to perhaps a twelve- by twelve-foot, or larger, building. Much depends, of course, on the type of dog housed.

For Fox Terriers, most kennels use the smaller type buildings, with three or more dogs quartered in one house. The arrangement consists of three pens, three feet by four feet, with an aisle across the front, from which opens a large run for the use of the dogs quartered within. The size of the pens depends on the size of the building. This common practice of keeping a few dogs in one kennel has its logical reason for being: with no heat, the compactness of the kennel tends to reduce the cold, which would be a problem in a larger space, although in England the temperature seldom goes below thirty degrees in the winter.

All sizeable kennels employ kennel maids to do the work, and, depending on the size and the number of dogs kept in the kennels, the help varies from one to four or six girls, with a kennel manager or head kennel maid in charge of the larger kennels. With individual units such as are used, each girl is responsible for a certain number of houses and dogs. She is also responsible for the feeding, cleaning, and walking of those dogs in her houses.

Wages are lower in England, but the kennel help is compensated in part by being provided room and board, with many of the larger kennels maintaining separate living quarters or cottages for the kennel help. While in the employ of kennels, the girls learn the art of caring for, trimming, and showing dogs. There are also schools that train kennel help and then place them. It seems to be the ambition of every kennel maid to some day open her own shop or beauty parlor for dogs, and in the London area, many such establishments may be found. The girls take their work with the dogs very seriously and I believe a good deal of the success the English kennels have with their dogs should be credited to the kennel maids. It is a problem to get competent kennel help in the United States, as almost everyone who has run a large kennel has found out. And rarely is the

119

kennel help that we get in this country really interested in the dogs. Rather, the employment is just a source of income.

In England, the judging method at shows is entirely different from ours. In America, we have the same classes at each show—a rule set up by The American Kennel Club. But in England, the classes included are left to the discretion of the show secretaries, and hence vary from show to show. There is a wide variety of possible classes, and the secretaries include those which they think will draw the most entries from a particular locality.

The classes are listed in "Schedules," or "Premium Lists," as we know them. A few of the usual classes are listed below so that you may see how different they are from ours.

First, there is the usual PUPPY class, similar to ours.

JUNIOR class, for dogs over six and not exceeding eighteen months of age.

SPECIAL YEARLING class, for dogs six and not over twenty-four months of age.

MAIDEN class, for dogs not having won a first prize of over one pound.

NOVICE class, which compares pretty much to ours, for dogs which have not won more than two first prizes, the value of which is not over one pound.

TYRO class, for dogs which have not won more than four first prizes of more than one pound.

DEBUTANT class, for dogs which have not won a first prize of over two pounds.

UNDERGRADUATE class, for dogs which have not won more than two first prizes, each of the value of two pounds or more.

POST GRADUATE class, for dogs which have not won more than four first prizes of two pounds or more. This is one of the most used classes.

LIMIT class, for dogs which have not won three challenge certificates under three different judges or more than six first prizes in all, each of the value of two pounds.

OPEN class, for all dogs. If confined to a breed or variety, for all dogs of that breed or variety.

SPECIAL BEGINNERS class, for dogs shown by an exhibitor who has never won a challenge certificate in the breed. (Note—here it is the exhibitor who has to qualify, not the dog.)

I think that the first thing about English classes (besides the variety and number) that impresses Americans, is the fact of the importance laid to the prize money won—especially in this country where we are lucky if we ever win any prize money!

Second, I was impressed by the fact that in some of their classes the dogs and bitches were judged together! Again, this is left to the discretion of the show secretary when making up the classes for the shows.

Third, I was amazed at the number of entries made at a show in the different classes, against the number of dogs entered. For example, at Birmingham I judged Smooth Fox Terriers and I had eighty-seven entries with forty-seven dogs. I attribute this entry of dogs in so many different classes to the fact that the entry fees at the shows are very low in comparison to ours— about $1.75 to $2.10, depending on the shows—and the fact that all the shows offered prize money in each class of two pounds, one pound, and twelve shillings, for first, second, and third places. That would be approximately $5.70, $2.85, and $1.68 in our money. I am referring only to English championship shows, which were what I attended.

Two types of shows are held in England—open and championship shows, at the latter of which the championship certificates are given (these compare with our points). It takes three championship certificates (challenge certificates, as they are called) to make a dog a champion. Certificates are not offered at the open shows.

Of all the shows held during the year, the percentage of championship shows is very small indeed. The number to be held during the year in any breed is governed by the number of entries in that breed during the year—so that the rating is changed each year. To show you what I mean, I quote statistics I have for the

121

year 1954. There were twenty-two championship shows held for Smooths and twenty-six for Wires. This would mean that there were forty-four challenge certificates awarded in Smooths (an equal division between the sexes) and fifty-two challenge certificates in Wires. It so happens that of the winners in 1954, two Wires have reached these shores: Ch. Travella Suredo, a best-in-show winner, and Ch. Madam Moonraker, a five times best-in-show winner considered the best bitch England had to offer that year.

The fact that the entry fee is so much lower than ours, and that there is a chance to win more in prize money, may account for the repeat entry of the same dogs in several classes at a show, particularly at the championship shows. The arrangement has its advantages, for when a dog is entered in many classes, the competition in each is bound to be different, and with the large classes, an exhibitor is offered the opportunity of meeting many different entries on the same day. It is not unusual to find anywhere from eight to fifteen dogs entered in one class, and in some of the very popular breeds, such as Poodles, these will run to twenty or more entries per class!

Cards are given out at the shows in lieu of the ribbons which we give at our shows. The challenge certificate is called a "ticket," and there is also a reserve "ticket" given. The dog and bitch which win the certificates do not compete for best of winners and then against the champions in the "specials" class as they do here. Instead, in the open class in England, the champions are entered along with the other entries, so the certificate winner, when he gets his "ticket," has already met the champions in his or her sex. Therefore, each certificate winner of a breed goes into the Group (if they have them—it is optional with the show-giving club), to compete for best in show. In other words, the English place the stress on BREED wins, rather than on GROUP or BEST-IN-SHOW wins. Frankly, I think this is the best method as far as the breed is concerned.

Another unique feature about English dog shows is the judges' critique. This is a "must" and looked forward to by breeders and exhibitors alike. It is published within the week following the show in the two leading English dog papers, *Dog World* and *Dog News*. The practice requires that the judge prepare his notes in duplicate and send each paper his report. There is much to be said for constructive criticism—properly presented and accepted, it can do a great deal of good. To me the most important person in the picture is the dog owner, and in England the owners seem to look forward to these reports, something which I can't make myself believe the American exhibitors would ever do.

I cannot speak too highly of the really sporting enthusiasm of the English people. They love their dogs, they take them seriously, and they do not commercialize them to the extent the American show-public does. They can lose in the show ring, walk out of it and talk to their winning opponent without a chip on the shoulder—a lesson we can well afford to learn! A show the next week is immediately looked forward to and it is amazing to realize how they can and will discuss the good points and the faults of each other's dogs—something almost never done here, where for an owner to admit his own dog's faults is almost a *faux pas!*

Exhibitors do not travel long distances to and from shows as we do, and with the exception of a few of the larger shows, what traveling is done is via the railroads, on which special cars are made up to carry exhibitors and dogs together to the shows at special rates. There are also, for some shows, a number of "coach parties" made up, stopping at various places en route to pick up exhibitors. Some of these even start at midnight the day prior to the show.

Another thing which impressed me was the fact that there is no organization which supervises the shows, such as we have. The American show-public is very apt to enjoy and take for granted the conveniences of a well-run show and its organization by the show superintendent. Granted, we pay well for it, but in comparison with shows having no organization, it's well worth it. In England, where small shows draw entries of from 1,000 to 4,000 dogs, on to the larger fixtures like Crufts with over 11,000

123

entered, a superintendent's organization would be a wonderful thing.

The love of the sport of showing dogs is fundamentally the same the world over. The American show dog lives a more "plush" life than his overseas brother when it comes to housing, traveling, eating, and being shown, but the goal is the same: to win that first prize and go on to championship!

In England, as well as in this country, kennel names become synonymous with owners and the breed. For this reason, it was especially interesting to have had the pleasure of meeting the owners of many of the famous Fox Terrier kennels there.

I visited in Coventry with Mr. Jack Barlow of the famous Crackley Kennels, who has sent many famous dogs to the Wildoaks Kennels of Mrs. Bondy. Mr. Bob Barlow, his father, will be remembered by many in this country who met him on the several occasions that he was over here showing the Wildoaks imports. He has since retired from the dog game, but his son is carrying on. The leading stud dog in that kennel when I was there was Crackley Standard, by Crackley Splendid, who is the sire of Ch. Crackley Security. Security won more challenge certificates than any other of his sex during the year 1954. It was a visit to which I had looked forward, inasmuch as my first Wire carried the Crackley prefix, being a daughter of Ch. Crackley Sensational.

The old-timers in Fox Terriers in the United States will remember Mr. Joe Cartledge, who handled Wires for Mr. and Mrs. Warrick of the Warwell Kennels. I visited at the kennels of his nephew, young Joe Cartledge, who has the Ryslip Kennels and handles such famous dogs as Ch. Crackley Security, who is the property of Mr. Stanley Thorne.

The most interesting and by far the largest kennel of Wires I visited was the famous Roundway Kennels of Mrs. Josephine Creasy. Without a doubt, these kennels housed more dogs of a consistent type than did any other I saw. Mrs. Creasy has earned an enviable reputation as a judge in England and many other countries. The stock in her kennel proves that as a judge and breeder she keeps the Standard of the breed constantly in mind.

124

When I was there, her outstanding stud dog was Ch. Roundway Strike-A-Light, the sire of five English and two American champions. His sire is the famous Ch. Travella Strike, an outstanding dog. Another stud which I saw there and thought equal to Strike-A-Light, was Roundway Surprise Model, also by Travella Strike. This kennel is strong in its bitches, a very important feature for correct breeding, and the young stock I saw there promises the owner much fun in the show ring in the forthcoming years.

I also met Miss Emery of the Hermon Kennels of Smooths. Her dogs have been imported by Mrs. Fallass, Mr. H. Sansom (owner of the Quakertown Kennels and president of the English Fox Terrier Club), Mr. J. Hamilton (another Smooth and Wire breeder), Miss Linda Beak of the well-known Newmaidly Kennels of Wires, Mr. W. G. Nelmes of Arley fame (he will be remembered as the breeder of Ch. Arley Adorable of Harham), Mrs. F. L. Williams of the Penda Kennels (some of whose dogs have found their way over here), Mr. J. Lowe (a Smooth breeder), and Miss B. Cliff of the Wyrecliff prefix in Wires.

Unfortunately for me, there were two owners of very well-known kennels that I did not have the opportunity to meet: Mr. Brown-Cole of the Travella Kennels and Mr. A. Churchill of Weltona fame. The latter's great bitch Ch. Weltona Frizzette of Wildoaks was a great favorite of mine and his Ch. Weltona Dustynight was the sire of Ch. Madam Moonraker. Of course, the import from Mr. Brown-Cole's kennels that has kept him before the American dog public is the famous Wire Ch. Travella Superman of Harham, belonging to Mr. and Mrs. Harold Florsheim.

After having visited the land in which the Fox Terrier originated and its leading kennels, and having seen the dogs of the day, I returned home happy in the knowledge that our breeders can be justly proud of our home-breds. It is unfortunate that it is not as easy for us to export (because of quarantine restrictions) as it is to import—for it would be fun to have as many of our home-breds find their way into the English show ring, as do English imports into ours, and then to compare the results.

AMERICAN FOX TERRIER CLUB SPECIALTY, 1955
"Daughter Tops Sire"
Best of variety, Ch. Downsbragh Red Vixen
Best of opposite sex, Ch. Downsbragh Top Sawyer

Grooming the Fox Terrier

GROOMING plays a large part in the care of the Wire Fox Terrier, but not so much in the care of his brother—the Smooth. For the owner of the Wire, it becomes a matter of necessity and personal pride: necessity because the Wire is a double-coated dog, and nature provides that he shed his coat and grow a complete new one about every six months, and personal pride because every owner wants his dog to appear at his best.

The Wire Fox Terrier's coat must be removed when it is dead, and the term applied to this removal is called "plucking," a process whereby the old coat is pulled out and a new jacket grows. The owner of the Smooth escapes most of this, for actually there is little to do to him other than brushing him daily to remove what few loose hairs there might be. The Smooth's coat is tight and smooth and short, but it does require brushing to keep it healthy, and a bit of fine trimming of the "frills" for the show ring.

In contrast, the grooming of the Wire for the show ring is quite another thing; as a matter of fact, it is an "art." Very few amateurs acquire the knowledge needed to put a dog down in show shape and to compete successfully against the professional handler who makes this his business. Owners, after enough experience, can acquire this knack if they have the patience, but it has been my observation that too few have the patience or want to spend the time required to do it.

127

Your Fox Terrier should be properly groomed and presented in a right manner in the show ring. Trimming is not faking! It is the art of making the coat fit the dog in such a way that he shows every point to advantage, in much the same manner that a tailor shapes a coat or suit to show off a woman's figure. In condition, and perfectly groomed, the Fox Terrier looks the part of the aristocrat that he truly is.

To get your Wire ready for the show ring is an art, and when you read that "your Wire was in superb condition," it proves a mastery of the art! I shall attempt a step by step description of how to trim, and hope that the text and pictures will give you the incentive to try to do it yourself.

The work of conditioning a Fox Terrier for the show ring begins about eight weeks before the show. It means the dogs must be stripped or plucked at this time and worked on each day continually until the show.

Your tools are important. You must provide yourself with a strong steady table on which to stand your dog. Attached to this table should be a post to hold a collar, to enable you to have both hands free, and to keep your dog standing quietly while you are stripping him.

There are three sizes of so-called "stripping knives" that are used: course, medium, and fine. The coarse is used for the body. The medium knife is used for the neck and shoulders. And the fine knife is used for the head and ears. Start at the neck and take a few hairs, lifting them with the thumb and turning them over the blade of the knife, and with the thumb against the blade give a sharp pull. When the coat is what we commonly term as "ripe," stripping is a painless task and the dog does not mind it. Continue the process and go all the way down the neck and shoulders. I might mention here that in England, most Englishmen trim their Fox Terriers by the "finger and thumb" method. They do not use stripping knives as freely as we do, and their method takes longer, but I must admit they do a good job!

In trimming the body of the animal you should change to the coarse knife, and do the back and both sides of the animal exactly the same way you did the neck and shoulders. Then the tail should be trimmed very close, especially in the back of the tail, right up to the top. Next, do one hindquarter and then the other, down to the hocks. Bear in mind that a Fox Terrier is supposed to be short coupled, and therefore trimming the hindquarters close is a "must," for it tends to emphasize the shortness of the dog. The same holds true when you strip your dog's throat and front.

Next do the head, and here use the fine knife. Starting at a point between the eyes, clean the skull very close and clean right back to the starting point of the neck. You can leave quite a bit of eyebrow at this time—say, probably about a half inch back from the eye. Proceed to trim the side of the head, commonly known as the cheek, from the side of the eye right straight back to the ear. Do the other side in the same manner.

After this is done, grasp the dog by the muzzle, lifting his head so you can get at his throat (this action tends to pull the skin taut). Starting at the opening of the mouth, work back and clean the throat just as close as you can possibly get it. Now you can do the ears, doing the outside first, but remember the ears are very tender. The inside of the ear might prove to be a bit of a problem and sometimes it is necessary to use scissors to cut away some of the hair. Be very careful that no hair falls into the ear opening, as it may cause an ear canker.

At this point, you may find yourself confronted with considerable eyebrows and whiskers. Take a steel comb, comb the eyebrows and whiskers forward, and with the stripping knife thin these down to get the appearance of a straight line from the cheek forward to the muzzle. Some hair can be taken from under the eye, but avoid taking too much for it might give a "hollowed out" appearance.

Next comes the underside of the dog. This can be accomplished with the dog standing on the table, but it is considerably easier if you have someone to help and you lay the dog on its side. Start from between the front legs and work back. The hair at the brisket need not be taken too close, but the "tuck-up" should be taken off clean. Then trim the inside of the hind legs. Now

129

stand your dog up again. Comb out his front legs and trim these as round as possible. The hair on the toes and between the pads should be trimmed close, so that the finished foot has a very round effect. Next, do the same for the hind legs, trimming them from the hock down to the toes, so the hair is round and even. The hind feet should be trimmed in the same manner as the front ones.

The last step in the preparation of your dog is trimming its nails. Lift the foot and be careful not to cut through the quick of the nail. This is the point where the red line of blood shows. With nail clippers, cut to within a fraction of an inch of this red line, on all the toes. Some nails are black, which makes it difficult to tell where the line is, so with your nail clippers clip off a little at a time, until the nail appears tender. After the clipping is completed, the sharp edges are filed off with a heavy nail file.

The dog, to be kept in show shape, requires a complete, full plucking from the rough, and then must be continually worked on during the eight weeks preceding the show at which it is to be shown. A coat may be held over a long period of shows, with the continual daily grooming and trimming that is required. Of course, in due time, the coat will get to a stage where it needs complete removal again. A term we use for this stage is that the coat is "blown." One thing to remember is that the more work one does on a dog's coat, the more the texture improves.

The pictures* that appear in this chapter should help you in your attempt to "pluck" your Wire Fox Terrier. It takes a lot of practice and your first job will not be a professional one, but you may enjoy it. If you find, however, that you are not able after several attempts to master this "art," then I advise you to seek the services of a professional, especially if you plan to continue exhibiting your dog.

I have taken you through the steps of stripping your dog to get him ready for a show, but there is more hard work ahead. This will begin after he is stripped and about eight weeks before you plan to show him.

* Photographs appearing in this chapter are the work of Mr. Hodio.

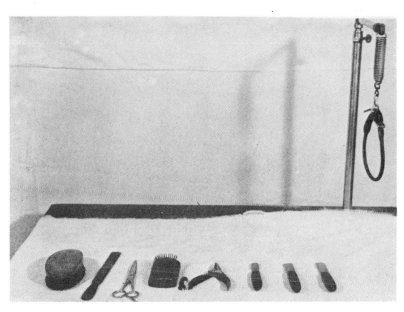

TOOLS NECESSARY FOR GROOMING

Left to right: brush, nail file, scissors, wire brush, comb, nail clippers, three sizes of stripping knives, and post to hold dog.

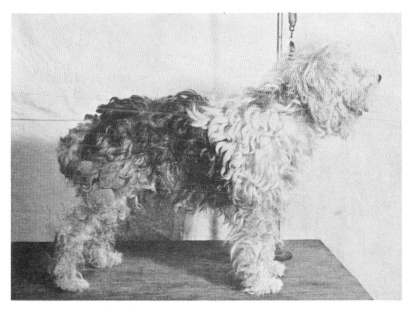

THE SUBJECT: a dog "in the rough."

131

STEP 1: the proper method of holding the stripping knife and the hair.

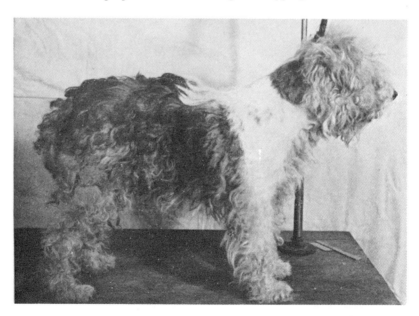

STEP 2: the dog with neck and shoulders stripped.

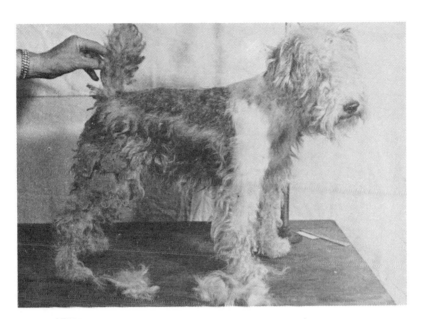

STEP 3: the dog with the neck, shoulder, and back finished.

STEP 4: the dog with the "tuck-up" done; next step is to go down quarter.

133

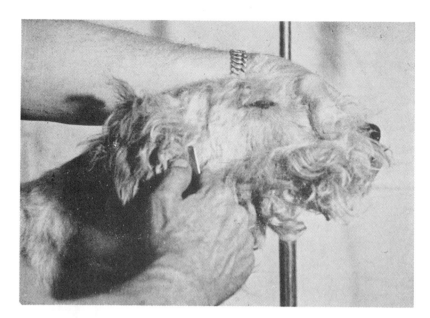

STEP 5: manner of holding head and starting work on cheek.

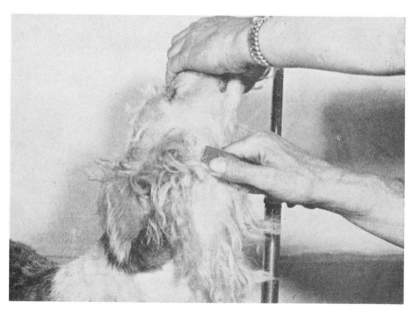

STEP 6: trimming the neck and throat.

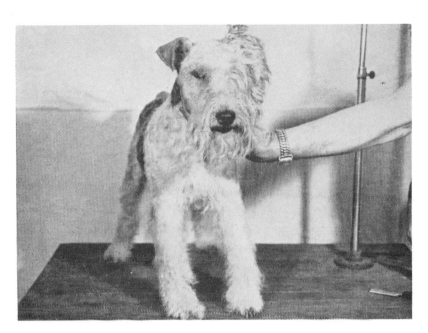

STEP 7: the dog after one half has been completed.

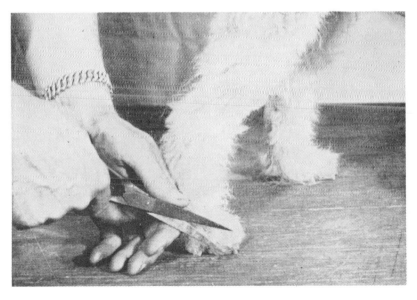

STEP 8: trimming the feet.

135

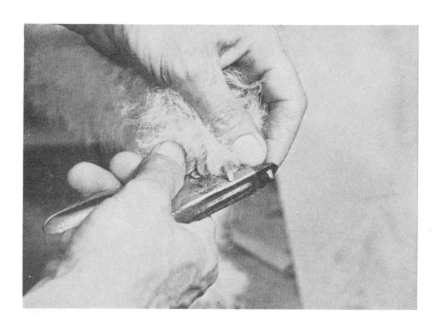

STEP 9: cutting the nails.

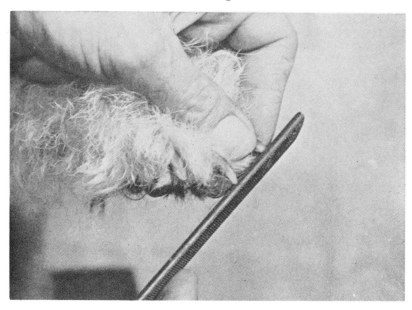

STEP 10: filing the nails.

136

RESULTS OF WORK.

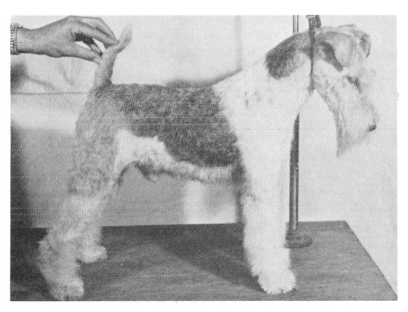

THE FINISHED ARTICLE—Ch. Tempo of Crack-Dale.

137

To begin with, the dog's body must be clean. Give him a bath, using warm water and a good quality liquid shampoo. After he is thoroughly dry, put him back on the grooming table and, using a brush that has bristles about an inch long, brush thoroughly. To remove any snarls in the whiskers and legs, brush the hair up and down quite vigorously, but not hard enough to break off the brittle leg coat. Then take a steel comb and straighten out the hair. Your dog should be brushed and combed several times a day. As the coat grows, the hair on the head and neck will have to be trimmed several times, as you do not want the coat on those parts the same length as the body coat. It is going to take a bit of practice for the novice to be able to trim his dog in such a manner that the coat fits the body as it should. The coat on the shoulders must be blended at the withers into the body coat.

It would be wise, two or three weeks after the dog has been trimmed, to "rug" him. This means simply putting a folded, medium-sized Turkish towel over the dog's body. This is sometimes called a blanket. Pin the towel around the dog's neck with a safety pin and use another pin to secure it at his "tuck-up." The object of the towel or blanket is to keep the coat in place and lying flat. It is very important that the dog be sponged off with warm water, dried, and then brushed and combed each day. Make sure that his coat is lying flat before you put the blanket on him. A word of caution here—in combing the whiskers and the leg coat of your Wire, be careful not to pull any out. Those hairs are precious! If they are removed, it takes a long time to grow them again.

Along with the daily care of your dog's coat, you must also tend his manners! To take an untrained Fox Terrier into a show ring is to defeat all your other hard work. If the owner has attended a few dog shows himself, he probably knows the general procedure of showing a dog: which hand to hold the lead in, and how to pose or stand the dog. This is the part that takes the training. Probably here-to-fore you have let your dog jump all over you or anyone else who might stop and pet him. Also, you have no doubt let him have his own way about running around on the lead. For the show dog, those days are over! He must be taught to stand quietly and allow himself to be examined, and to walk sedately on the lead. With Fox Terriers this is easily accomplished once they understand what you want, for they are very bright and will respond to your training readily.

I am assuming that anyone who is thinking of showing a dog has attended a dog show or at least a sanction match. This would make him familiar with the fundamentals of handling the dog in the ring. It is not too early to start when the puppy is three or four months old.

First, get your dog accustomed to a collar and lead, walking— not pulling! Put a light-weight collar on the dog, and use a light-weight lead. It is natural for the dog immediately to see how far he can go on that lead! Always do your training in your own back yard and not on the street. When the puppy goes to the end of the lead, gently pull him back, at the same time speaking to him in a low, friendly voice. Never use too many commands in training any dog, for this will only tend to confuse him. When I am lead-breaking a dog, I always use the words "steady," "come," and the dog's name. A great many people also use the term "heel," which is used in obedience training. I have found that a slight jerk on the lead about every third step tends to keep the dog at my side and reminds him of my presence, before he gets a chance to go to the end of the lead. Always keep the lead well up under his chin, keeping his nose off the ground. Walk up and down with him until he will walk at your side without pulling, and then the lesson for the day should end. I might add here that the first time you put a puppy on the lead, before you start to make him walk with you, it is wise to give him a few minutes for sniffing and running around—on the lead, of course. This relieves the strangeness of the collar and lead, and he will work better for you. Remember always to hold the lead in your left hand and walk the dog on your left side. So much for lesson one and lead work.

The next step is to get your dog accustomed to a table and to stand him on it each day to comb and brush him. After doing this, pose your puppy in the same manner that dogs are posed in the show ring: head erect, tail up, and front legs straight. Then gently stroke your dog, getting him used to holding this position for a long time. Practice this for many days until he gets to understand what is required of him and will hold the pose; then the next time you have him out on the lead, you can try standing him in the same manner with the lead on him. You will find that he is more easily distracted out-of-doors, so posing him will take more time. A third step is to get your dog used to walking around in a circle, not pulling—and keeping his head up. For some reason it is harder to make dogs walk in a circle than up and down. Remember to keep the dog at your left side. The reason for this is that the judge usually stands in the middle of the ring and the dogs are always on the side facing him. I might mention here that in walking any dog, the owner must adjust his stride to fit the gait of the dog.

Perfection of the above three steps comes when your dog gaits perfectly, poses indefinitely without moving, and will allow you or anyone else to examine him or walk around him—without his moving himself and thereby throwing himself out of position. This is not all accomplished in a few lessons, but rather in many *regular* lessons. Take it in easy stages each day, gradually lengthening the time you work with the dog, both on the lead and on the table. When he is on the table being groomed, it is just as important that he hold the correct position as it is when he is on the lead. In training, patience is the greatest virtue!

So now the ground work is laid, it's up to you from here on in. If you have a good dog and you have been to a few shows, no doubt you have already been bitten by the "show bug." It's a lot of hard work, but lots of fun. And now, just a few parting thoughts: the most important and hardest lesson to learn is to fight against becoming "kennel blind." The novice, after several years of breeding, would be wise to try his hand at showing; it will be a solid method for him to evaluate his success.

I think the ambition of every serious novice and breeder is to see his or her dog in the show ring. It is a matter of personal pride and satisfaction to have the knowledge and ability to produce a specimen superior enough to defeat the competition of others with the same ambition, and take home the blue ribbon. It is far more difficult than it might appear, but if you have absorbed the information supplied in the preceding chapters, you have learned how to select the correct structure, how to best breed a good specimen, how to correct points in your breeding, and how to prepare your dog for the show ring. Showing is the final test of your ability to succeed in your efforts!

It is human nature for everyone to think that his or her dog is best. It takes an open mind, a lot of courage and determination, and a sense of fair play to participate in the sport of showing dogs, and it *is* a sporting event. I like to think of it in this manner, rather than as a place where one takes the fruits of his efforts to try to down another, to his own satisfaction and delight. If commercialism could be avoided, it would be a much nicer thing. However, it is almost impossible to keep this factor out of the dog game. In the world today, commercialism is something which seems impossible to separate from our lives. Those who show just to satisfy their own desire for publicity or to satisfy their ego, are superficial. But, to the person who is wholeheartedly interested in breeding, showing is a part of the structure of producing. It is the final criterion of your efforts. And these people, these exhibitors, who have this in mind, are usually the ones who have been in the game at least ten years. Unlike those who have just purchased specimens to show and exhibit and win with, these veteran exhibitors have taken the time to gain the knowledge, and through their own efforts have produced that final specimen as near perfect to their interpretation of the Standard as is possible. It is one thing which is always held out in front for the serious breeder to grasp, and therefore, exhibiting is, to him, a necessity. It is a place and a way in which he can measure his own success. A dog lover who has not yet taken in a dog show has missed a most exciting and thrilling event! (See page 11, Part II, for details of dog shows and judging procedures.)

To the judges fall the decisions, and by their decisions the ringsiders are also governed with their reactions toward a dog show. These ringsiders are made up largely of our potential

141

novice exhibitors, and their reactions are important to the dog fancy. It is with this in mind that I say: "All judges, breeders, exhibitors and professional handlers have an obligation to other dog lovers. It is up to these people to educate the public about one of the grandest sports there is—the art of showing your dog and winning with him, and the ability of understanding both sides of the art, before it is undertaken."

Too often from the ringside I have heard the remark, "That man is a professional handler, he shows Mr. X's dogs, and you can't beat him!" That is not fair. Perhaps it is true that he wins often, but are not his dogs in better condition and showing to advantage over the others? Let people realize that showing dogs is an art and business that must be mastered. I say that the amateur has just as good a chance as the professional, when he *understands* the dog show game. Showing dogs is a wonderful sport, and we should all work together, understand each other, and help one another along to continue it. We all want to win. But, since all of us can't win, let's be sure that the one who does come through does it with the intelligent cooperation of all dog lovers. In that way the best dog must win!

One thing about judging is certain: within limits, there is ample room for difference of opinion. Therefore, any criticism of the judges' decisions should be made with good temper and due toleration, which is not always the case. "Judge not that ye shall not be judged."

The Fox Terrier's size, adaptability, disposition and heartiness make him an ideal, all-round companion, especially suited for those who live in apartments or small homes. He is also aristocratic enough to grace the most imposing estates. He is as game as they come, loyal to the end, intelligent, alert, even-tempered, dressy, and an excellent pet and companion, particularly for children. I've never been more positive in my life than I am about the future of the Fox Terrier. He is here to stay. Every serious breeder and handler has a responsibility. The welfare of the breed should be their constant care. Its future is in their hands!

And so, in closing, let me leave you with this thought about our friend—an anonymous and semi-humorous description of the Fox Terrier:

"The Fox Terrier is a small black and white disturbance which afflicts and delights many families. The Fox Terrier has straight legs, an active expressive face, a lean well-shaped head, talkative eyes, and a nose which leads him from one misdemeanor to another. Originally he had a liberal tail, but it has been edited and revised by man. This was done because when a Fox Terrier's tail was as active as his head, it took two people to watch him.

"The Fox Terrier is a house pet, and is clean and dainty in his habits. He lives on meat, milk, potatoes, mice, old shoes, curtains, books, hats and tableclothes. In return for this diet he guards the house with unremitting ferocity. No burglar can come near without dislodging an eruption of barks from the faithful brute. He also guards the house against all cats, dogs, taxicabs, late pedestrians, dead leaves and moonbeams which may chance to pass at night.

"After a family has got used to a Fox Terrier and has lost him temporarily, it can sleep through a boiler explosion and a fire next door. The Fox Terrier is vivacious, audacious, ingenious, merciful, hysterical, wheedlesome, companionable, affectionate, optimistic, fickle, restless, and irrepressible. He is, in fact, the Chorus Girl of the dog family."

CH. WELCOME HERE AND THERE
American Fox Terrier Club Specialty, 1959
Owner, Mrs. Abigail Goss Jones; judge, William Kendrick

Showing and Sportsmanship

A PROFESSIONAL handler is a person who earns a living by showing and conditioning dogs. He or she usually spends several years of apprenticeship before really becoming a success. Handling professionally takes a lot of hard work and a thorough knowledge of dogs in general—their care, the study of the Standards of the different breeds and the traits of each breed, and knowledge of how to train and groom each different breed. Then there is the training for the show ring, which takes hours upon hours of work. Showing is a highly competitive sport and to win, one must really work at it.

This brings me down to a point which I believe very few people have taken into consideration. The difference between a novice exhibitor, an amateur exhibitor, and a professional handler exhibiting. I think that anyone considering showing a dog should give this some thought.

Almost always, we hear of only two distinctions—a novice and a professional—and there has been much said about both. I'm sure that if the dog-conscious public could be educated to the fact that there are really three distinctions in the art of showing, it would tend to make for better relations between the seasoned exhibitor and breeder, and the beginner. In every other sport today, we have the novice, the amateur, and the professional. A novice skater is a beginner. An amateur is an experienced skater who skates for the love and thrill of it—it is his hobby. The professional is one who makes his living by his mastering of the art.

145

So is all this true of the dog lover. To the person who asks me, while he gazes over the head of his two-months-old pup, "Can I win with him?" my answer is, "If your dog has and properly develops its show possibilities, you can show, but your chances of winning are somewhat limited!"

This is our novice—and to him I say, "You must remember that the art or sport of showing dogs is also a business. Like any other business, it is run along certain lines and I believe that experience and only experience, regardless of how tough it may be, is still the best teacher!

Because the dog game needs this novice with his unbounded enthusiasm, it is up to the veteran breeder to educate him. Do not paint a rosy picture of his pet's future in the show ring and then have him leave the ring dejected because he did not win— and lost to us! Instead, help him to see both sides of the picture. Fundamentally, he may have the best dog in the ring, *but* the dog's show manners or condition, or the owner's handling, could not let the dog win over a properly presented specimen.

This must all be explained to the novice in order to give him the incentive to continue showing and improving, or to place his dog with a professional. It takes hours upon hours of grooming any dog, especially a Terrier, to get it ready for the show ring. It also takes hours of training to get it ready. Furthermore, it takes many experiences of the owner, before he himself presents the proper picture of coordination in the show ring with his dog—to make the perfect team! This is something that too few novices realize, or have ever thought about.

If the novice has the time (and it can't be accomplished in a few hours, but rather over a period of years), I'm certain the novice *can* win, but by doing so consistently, he then becomes an amateur! There are in our show rings today, amateurs who possess more years of experience than some of the younger professional handlers! But, here again, we come to a fine point. The professional makes his living by his dogs and he normally puts in his eight-hour day (and more often it is a ten-hour day) with his dogs. The amateur spends only his leisure hours with his dogs. So while I believe that an amateur can develop and

146

possess the same degree of technique as the professional, it takes him twice as long to do so. In all breeds, we have some very fine amateur exhibitors. These amateurs can and do hold their own with the professionals. If they have the specimens, they can and do win! It is just a little harder struggle for them, because the human element enters into their winning more than it does in a professional's winning. The amateurs have spent many of their leisure hours on their pet subject—their dogs—and when they go into the ring, and everything is equal, their win (or loss) has greater emotional significance for them than it does for their professional opponent! For, win or lose, the professional is getting paid for his work. Nevertheless, I believe that everybody who owns a good dog should have a "go" at the show ring.

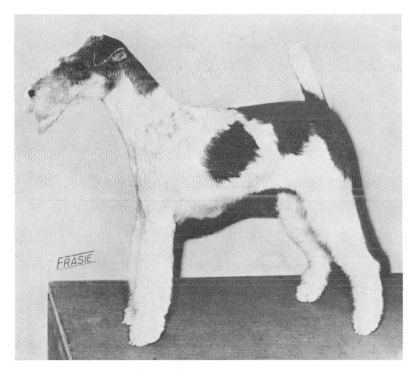

CH. SAINT JOE JULIANA
Owned by Dr. Frank Booth, Elkhart, Ind.

147

Gallery of Stars

THIS chapter is a presentation of pictures of leading Fox Terriers of their day and should prove of great interest to students of the breed. A comparison of the old and the new should be a lesson in progress. It is my hope that the fanciers of tomorrow will heed the wisdom of the founders of the breed of over a century ago, and remember that "blood will tell" and that the study of pedigrees and specimens is all-important in the success of production.

It seems only fitting to me that I close Part I of this book with these "Fox Terrier Stars" and the hope that those who carry on for the breed in the next generation will enjoy the success that is deserving of such a fine breed!

CH. SIGNAL WARILY OF WILDOAKS
Owner, Mrs. R. C. Bondy, Goldens Bridge, N.Y.

CH. EDEN ARISTOCRAT OF WILDOAKS
Owner, Mrs. R. C. Bondy, Goldens Bridge, N.Y.

149

CH. TRUE CHARM OF WILDOAKS
Owner, Mrs. R. C. Bondy, Goldens Bridge, N.Y.

CH. CRACKLEY STARTLER OF WILDOAKS
Owner, Mrs. R. C. Bondy, Goldens Bridge, N.Y.

CH. DOWNSBRAGH TOP SAWYER
Owned by Downsbragh Kennels, Marshall, Va.

CH. DOWNSBRAGH NIGHT STICK
Owned by Downsbragh Kennels, Marshall, Va.

151

CH. HETHERINGTON PARAPILOT
Owned by Mr. and Mrs. T. H. Carruthers III, Glendale, Ohio.

CH. HETHERINGTON FORGET-ME-NOT
Owned by Mr. and Mrs. T. H. Carruthers III, Glendale, Ohio.

152

CH. CITATION OF WILDOAKS
Owned by Mrs. Munro Lanier, New York, N.Y.

CH. GALLANT COACHMAN OF WILDOAKS
Owner, Revlis Kennels of Mac Silver, Swansea, Mass.

153

CH. DERBYSHIRE DELPHINE
Owner, Thomas Keator, Carversville, Penna.

CH. GOOD DEAL OF CRACK-DALE
Owners, Mr. and Mrs. R. E. Greuter, Weston, Conn.

CH. DANYCRAIG LIBERTY BELLE OF WIREHART
Owner, George H. Hartman, Lampeter, Penna.

CH. DEKO DRUID
Owner, T. H. Carruthers III, Glendale, Ohio

155

CH. TRAVELLA ALLURE
Owner, Mrs. Frederick H. Dutcher, Stamford, Conn.

CH. EVEWIRE LITTLE MAN
Owner, Mrs. Eve Ballich, Stevenson, Md.

CH. CRACKLEY STRIKING OF WILDOAKS
Owner, Mrs. R. C. Bondy, Goldens Bridge, N.Y.

CH. CHORUS GIRL OF CRACK-DALE
Owner, Mrs. Paul M. Silvernail, Madison, Conn.

157

CH. CRACKLEY STARTRITE OF WILDOAKS
Owner, Mrs. R. C. Bondy, Goldens Bridge, N.Y.

CH. RADAR OF WILDOAKS
Breeder, Mrs. R. C. Bondy, Goldens Bridge, N.Y.
(This is an interesting father and son comparison. Startrite is the sire of Radar.)

CH. FALSTAFF'S LADY FAYRE
Owner, Wm. Meyers Jones, North Hollywood, Calif.

(Lady Fayre won her championship easily in England, being the top winning Wire in that country in 1959 and acquiring two Best-in-Show awards. Imported to America, she became the ninth top winning Terrier in 1961 and when retired from competition in 1964, she had eleven American Best-in-Shows to her credit.)

CH. ZELOY MOOREMAIDES MAGIC
Owner, Mrs. Walter Bunker, Los Angeles, Calif.

(Magic came to America in 1963 and the author had the pleasure of being the first judge to pass on her at the New York Specialty where she went from the Open Class to Best of Opposite Sex over a strong field. Since then Magic's career has been outstanding with no defeats in her breed up to press time and five Best-in-Show wins.)

160

Part II

GENERAL CARE AND TRAINING
OF YOUR DOG

by

Elsworth S. Howell

Milo G. Denlinger

A. C. Merrick, D.V.M.

Introduction

THE normal care and training of dogs involve no great mysteries. The application of common sense and good judgment is required, however. The pages that follow distill the combined experience and knowledge of three authorities who have devoted most of their lives to dogs.

Milo Denlinger wrote many books out of his rich and varied experience as a breeder, exhibitor and owner of a commercial kennel. Elsworth Howell has been a fancier since young boyhood and claims intimate knowledge of 25 different breeds; he is an American Kennel Club delegate and judge of the sporting breeds. Dr. A. C. Merrick is a leading veterinarian with a wide practice.

The chapter on "Training and Simple Obedience" covers the basic behavior and performance every dog should have to be accepted by your friends, relatives, neighbors and strangers. The good manners and exercises described will avoid costly bills for damage to the owner's or neighbor's property and will prevent heartbreaking accidents to the dog and to the people he meets. The instructions are given in simple, clear language so that a child may easily follow them.

"The Exhibition of Dogs" describes the kinds of dog shows, their classes and how an owner may enter his dog and show it. If one practices good sportsmanship, shows can be enjoyable.

The chapter on feeding offers sound advice on feeding puppies,

3

adult dogs, the stud dog and the brood bitch. The values of proteins, carbohydrates, fats, minerals and vitamins in the dog's diet are thoroughly covered. Specific diets and quantities are not given because of the many variations among dogs, even of the same breed or size, in their individual needs, likes, dislikes, allergies, etc.

"The Breeding of Dogs" contains the fundamental precepts everyone who wishes to raise puppies should know. Suggestions for choosing a stud dog are given. The differences among outcrossing, inbreeding and line breeding are clearly explained. Care tips for the pregnant and whelping bitch will be found most helpful.

The material on "External Vermin and Parasites" gives specific treatments for removing and preventing fleas, lice, ticks and flies. With today's wonder insecticides and with proper management there is no excuse for a dog to be infested with any of these pests which often cause secondary problems.

"Intestinal Parasites and Their Control" supplies the knowledge dog owners must have of the kinds of worms that invade dogs and the symptoms they cause. While drugs used for the removal of these debilitating dog enemies are discussed, dosages are not given because it is the authors' and publisher's belief that such treatment is best left in the hands of the veterinarian. These drugs are powerful and dangerous in inexperienced hands.

The chapter on "Skin Troubles" supplies the information and treatments needed to recognize and cure these diseases. The hints appearing on coat care will do much to prevent skin problems.

One of the most valuable sections in this book is the "instant" advice on "FIRST AID" appearing on pages 95-98. The publisher strongly urges the reader to commit this section to memory. It may save a pet's life.

The information on diseases will help the dog owner to diagnose symptoms. Some dog owners rush their dogs to the veterinarian for the slightest, transitory upsets.

Finally, the chapters on "Housing for Dogs" and "Care of the Old Dog" round out this highly useful guide for all dog lovers.

4

Training and
Simple Obedience

E VERY DOG that is mentally and physically sound
can be taught good manners and simple obedience by any normal
man, woman, or child over eight years old.

Certain requirements must be met by the dog, trainer and the
environment if the training is to be enjoyable and effective. The
dog must be rested and calm. The trainer must be rested, calm,
gentle, firm, patient and persistent. The training site should be
dry, comfortable and, except for certain exercises, devoid of distrac-
tions.

Proper techniques can achieve quick and sure results. Always
use short, strong words for commands and always use the *same* word
or words for the same command. Speak with authority; never
scream or yell. Teach one command or exercise at a time and make
sure the dog understands it and performs it perfectly before you
proceed to the next step. Demand the dog's undivided attention;
if he wavers or wanders, speak his name or pat him smartly or
jerk his leash. Use pats and praise plentifully; avoid tidbit training
if at all possible because tidbits may not always be available in
an emergency and the dog will learn better without them. Keep
lessons short; when the dog begins to show boredom, stop and
do not resume in less than two hours. One or two ten-minute
lessons a day should be ample, especially for a young puppy. Dogs
have their good and bad days; if your well dog seems unduly lazy,

5

tired, bored or off-color, put off the lesson until tomorrow. Try to make lessons a joy, a happy time both for you and the dog, but do demand and get the desired action. Whenever correction or punishment is needed, use ways and devices that the dog does not connect with you; some of these means are given in the following instructions. Use painful punishment only as a last resort.

"NO!"

The most useful and easily understood command is "NO!" spoken in a sharp, disapproving tone and accompanied with a shaking finger. At first, speak the dog's name following with "NO!" until the meaning of the word—your displeasure—is clear.

"COME!"

Indoors or out, let the dog go ten or more feet away from you. Speak his name following at once with "COME!" Crouch, clap your hands, pick up a stick, throw a ball up and catch it, or create any other diversion which will lure the dog to you. When he comes, praise and pat effusively. As with all commands and exercises repeat the lesson, until the dog *always* comes to you.

THE FIRST NIGHTS

Puppies left alone will bark, moan and whine. If your dog is not to have the run of the house, put him in a room where he can do the least damage. Give him a Nylabone and a strip of beef hide (both available in supermarkets or pet shops and excellent as teething pacifiers). A very young puppy may appreciate a loud-ticking clock which, some dog trainers say, simulates the heart-beat of his former litter mates. Beyond providing these diversions, grit your teeth and steel your heart. If in pity you go to the howling puppy, he will howl every time you leave him. Suffer one night, two nights or possibly three, and you'll have it made.

The greatest boon to dog training and management is the wooden or wire crate. Any two-handed man can make a $\frac{3}{8}''$ plywood crate. It needs only four sides, a top, a bottom, a door on hinges and

6

with a strong hasp, and a fitting burlap bag stuffed with shredded newspaper, cedar shavings or 2″ foam rubber. Feed dealers or seed stores should give you burlap bags; be sure to wash them thoroughly to remove any chemical or allergy-causing material. The crate should be as long, as high and three times as wide as the dog will be full grown. The crate will become as much a sanctuary to your dog as a cave was to his prehistoric ancestor; it will also help immeasurably in housebreaking.

HOUSEBREAKING

The secret to housebreaking a healthy normal dog is simple: take him out every hour if he is from two to six months old when you get him; or the first thing in the morning, immediately after every meal, and the last thing at night if he is over six months.

For very young puppies, the paper break is indicated. Lay eight or ten layers of newspapers in a room corner most remote from the puppy's bed. By four months of age or after two weeks in a new home if older, a healthy puppy should not need the paper *IF* it is exercised outdoors often and *IF* no liquid (including milk) is given after 5 P.M. and *IF* it is taken out not earlier than 10 P.M. at night and not later than 7 A.M. the next morning.

When the dog does what it should when and where it should, praise, praise and praise some more. Be patient outdoors: keep the dog out until action occurs. Take the dog to the same general area always; its own traces and those of other dogs thus drawn to the spot will help to inspire the desired action.

In extreme cases where frequent exercising outdoors fails, try to catch the dog in the act and throw a chain or a closed tin can with pebbles in it near the dog but not on him; say "NO!" loudly as the chain or can lands. In the most extreme case, a full 30-second spanking with a light strap may be indicated but be sure you catch the miscreant *in the act*. Dog memories are short.

Remember the crate discussed under "THE FIRST NIGHTS." If you give the dog a fair chance, he will NOT soil his crate.

Do not rub his nose in "it." Dogs have dignity and pride. It is permissible to lead him to his error as soon as he commits it and to remonstrate forcefully with "NO!"

7

COLLAR AND LEASH TRAINING

Put on a collar tight enough not to slip over the head. Leave it on for lengthening periods from a few minutes to a few hours over several days. A flat collar for shorthaired breeds; a round or rolled collar for longhairs. For collar breaking, do NOT use a choke collar; it may catch on a branch or other jutting object and strangle the dog.

After a few days' lessons with the collar, attach a heavy cord or rope to it without a loop or knot at the end (to avoid snagging or catching on a stump or other object). Allow the dog to run free with collar and cord attached a few moments at a time for several days. Do not allow dog to chew cord!

When the dog appears to be accustomed to the free-riding cord, pick up end of the cord, loop it around your hand and take your dog for a walk (not the other way around!). DON'T STOP WALKING if the dog pulls, balks or screams bloody murder. Keep going and make encouraging noises. If dog leaps ahead of you, turn sharply left or right whichever is *away* from dog's direction—AND KEEP MOVING! The biggest mistake in leash training is stopping when the dog stops, or going the way the dog goes when the dog goes wrong. You're the leader; make the dog aware of it. This is one lesson you should continue until the dog realizes who is boss. If the dog gets the upper leg now, you will find it difficult to resume your rightful position as master. Brutality, no; firmness, yes!

If the dog pulls ahead, jerk the cord—or by now, the leash—backward. Do not pull. Jerk or snap the leash only!

JUMPING ON PEOPLE

Nip this annoying habit at once by bumping the dog with your knee on his chest or stepping with authority on his rear feet. A sharp "NO!" at the same time helps. Don't permit this action when you're in your work clothes and ban it only when dressed in glad rags. The dog is not Beau Brummel, and it is cruel to expect him to distinguish between denim and silk.

8

THE "PROBLEM" DOG

The following corrections are indicated when softer methods fail. Remember that it's better to rehabilitate than to destroy.

Biting. For the puppy habit of mouthing or teething on the owner's hand, a sharp rap with a folded newspaper on the nose, or snapping the middle finger off the thumb against the dog's nose, will usually discourage nibbling tactics. For the biter that means it, truly drastic corrections may be preferable to destroying the dog. If your dog is approaching one year of age and is biting in earnest, take him to a professional dog trainer and don't quibble with his methods unless you would rather see the dog dead.

Chewing. For teething puppies, provide a Nylabone (trade mark) and beef hide strips (see "THE FIRST NIGHTS" above). Every time the puppy attacks a chair, a rug, your hand, or any other chewable object, snap your finger or rap a newspaper on his nose, or throw the chain or a covered pebble-laden tin can near him, say "NO!" and hand him the bone or beef hide. If he persists, put him in his crate with the bone and hide. For incorrigible chewers, check diet for deficiencies first. William Koehler, trainer of many movie dogs including *The Thin Man's* Asta, recommends in his book, *The Koehler Method of Dog Training*, that the chewed object or part of it be taped crosswise in the dog's mouth until he develops a hearty distaste for it.

Digging. While he is in the act, throw the chain or noisy tin can and call out "NO!" For the real delinquent Koehler recommends filling the dug hole with water, forcing the dog's nose into it until the dog thinks he's drowning and he'll never dig again. Drastic perhaps, but better than the bullet from an angry neighbor's gun, or a surreptitious poisoning.

The Runaway. If your dog wanders while walking with you, throw the chain or tin can and call "COME!" to him. If he persists, have a friend or neighbor cooperate in chasing him home. A very long line, perhaps 25 feet or more, can be effective if you permit the dog to run its length and then snap it sharply to remind him not to get too far from you.

9

Car Chasing. Your dog will certainly live longer if you make him car-wise; in fact, deathly afraid of anything on wheels. Ask a friend or neighbor to drive you in *his* car. Lie below the windows and as your dog chases the car throw the chain or tin can while your neighbor or friend says "GO HOME!" sharply. Another method is to shoot a water pistol filled with highly diluted ammonia at the dog. If your dog runs after children on bicycles, the latter device is especially effective but may turn the dog against children.

The Possessive Dog. If a dog displays overly protective habits, berate him in no uncertain terms. The chain, the noisy can, the rolled newspaper, or light strap sharply applied, may convince him that, while he loves you, there's no percentage in overdoing it.

The Cat Chaser. Again, the chain, the can, the newspaper, the strap—or the cat's claws if all else fails, but only as the last resort.

The Defiant, or Revengeful, Wetter. Some dogs seem to resent being left alone. Some are jealous when their owners play with another dog or animal. Get a friend or neighbor in this case to heave the chain or noisy tin can when the dog relieves himself in sheer spite.

For other canine delinquencies, you will find *The Koehler Method of Dog Training* effective. William Koehler's techniques have been certified as extremely successful by directors of motion pictures featuring dogs and by officers of dog obedience clubs.

10

OBEDIENCE EXERCISES

A well-mannered dog saves its owner money, embarrassment and possible heartbreak. The destruction of property by canine delinquents, avoidable accidents to dogs and children, and other unnecessary disadvantages to dog ownership can be eliminated by simple obedience training. The elementary exercises of heeling, sitting, staying and lying down can keep the dog out of trouble in most situations.

The only tools needed for basic obedience training are a slip collar made of chain link, leather or nylon and a strong six-foot leather leash with a good spring snap. Reviewing the requirements and basic techniques given earlier, let's proceed with the dog's schooling.

Heeling. Keep your dog on your left side, with the leash in your left hand. Start straight ahead in a brisk walk. If your dog pulls ahead, jerk (do not pull) the leash and say "Heel" firmly. If the dog persists in pulling ahead, stop, turn right or left and go on for several yards, saying "Heel" each time you change direction.

If your dog balks, fix leash *under* his throat and coax him forward by repeating his name and tapping your hip.

Whatever you do, don't stop walking! If the dog jumps up or "fights" the leash, just keep moving briskly. Sooner than later he will catch on and with the repetition of "Heel" on every correction, you will have him trotting by your side with style and respect.

Sit. Keeping your dog on leash, hold his neck up and push his rump down while repeating "Sit." If he resists, "spank" him lightly several times on his rump. Be firm, but not cruel. Repeat this lesson often until it is learned perfectly. When the dog knows the command, test him at a distance without the leash. Return to him every time he fails to sit and repeat the exercise.

Stay. If you have properly trained your dog to "Sit," the "Stay" is simple. Take his leash off and repeat "Stay" holding your hand up, palm toward dog, and move away. If dog moves toward you, you must repeat the "sit" lesson until properly learned. After your

11

dog "stays" while you are in sight, move out of his sight and keep repeating "Stay." Once he has learned to "stay" even while you are out of his sight, you can test him under various conditions, such as when another dog is near, a child is playing close to him, or a car appears on the road. (Warning: do not tax your dog's patience on the "stay" until he has learned the performance perfectly.)

Down. For this lesson, keep your dog on leash. First tell him to "sit." When he has sat for a minute, place your shoe over his leash between the heel and sole. Slowly pull on the leash and repeat "Down" while you push his head down with your other hand. Do this exercise very quietly so that dog does not become excited and uncontrollable. In fact, this performance is best trained when the dog is rather quiet. Later, after the dog has learned the voice signal perfectly, you can command the "Down" with a hand signal, sweeping your hand from an upright position to a downward motion with your palm toward the dog. Be sure to say "Down" with the hand signal.

For more advanced obedience the following guides by Blanche Saunders are recommended:

The Complete Novice Obedience Course
The Complete Open Obedience Course
The Complete Utility Obedience Course (with Tracking)
Dog Training for Boys and Girls (includes simple tricks.)
All are published by Howell Book House at $3.00 each.

OBEDIENCE TRIALS

Booklets covering the rules and regulations of Obedience Trials may be obtained from The American Kennel Club, 51 Madison Avenue, New York, N.Y. 10010. In Canada, write The Canadian Kennel Club, 667 Yonge Street, Toronto, Ontario.

Both these national clubs can give you the names and locations of local and regional dog clubs that conduct training classes in obedience and run Obedience Trials in which trained dogs compete for degrees as follow: CD (Companion Dog), CDX (Companion Dog Excellent), UD (Utility Dog), TD (Tracking Dog) and UDT (Utility Dog, Tracking.)

The Exhibition
of Dogs

NOBODY should exhibit a dog in the shows unless he can win without gloating and can lose without rancor. The showing of dogs is first of all a sport, and it is to be approached in a sportsmanlike spirit. It is not always so approached. That there are so many wretched losers and so many supercilious winners among the exhibitors in dog shows is the reason for this warning.

The confidence that one's dog is of exhibition excellence is all that prompts one to enter him in the show, but, if he fails in comparison with his competitors, nobody is harmed. It is no personal disgrace to have a dog beaten. It may be due to the dog's fundamental faults, to its condition, or to inexpert handling. One way to avoid such hazards is to turn the dog over to a good professional handler. Such a man with a flourishing established business will not accept an inferior dog, one that is not worth exhibiting. He will put the dog in the best possible condition before he goes into the ring with him, and he knows all the tricks of getting out of a dog all he has to give. Good handlers come high, however. Fees for taking a dog into the ring will range from ten to twenty-five dollars, plus any cash prizes the dog may win, and plus a bonus for wins made in the group.

Handlers do not win all the prizes, despite the gossip that they do, but good handlers choose only good dogs and they usually

13

finish at or near the top of their classes. It is a mistake to assume that this is due to any favoritism or any connivance with the judges; the handlers have simply chosen the best dogs, conditioned them well, and so maneuvered them in the ring as to bring out their best points.

The services of a professional handler are not essential, however. Many an amateur shows his dogs as well, but the exhibitor without previous experience is ordinarily at something of a disadvantage. If the dog is good enough, he may be expected to win.

The premium list of the show, setting forth the prizes to be offered, giving the names of the judges, containing the entry form, and describing the conditions under which the show is to be held, are usually mailed out to prospective exhibitors about a month before the show is scheduled to be held. Any show superintendent is glad to add names of interested persons to the mailing list.

Entries for a Licensed show close at a stated date, usually about two weeks before the show opens, and under the rules no entry may be accepted after the advertised date of closing. It behooves the exhibitor to make his entries promptly. The exhibitor is responsible for all errors he may make on the entry form of his dog; such errors cannot be rectified and may result in the disqualification of the exhibit. It therefore is wise for the owner to double check all data submitted with an entry. The cost of making an entry, which is stated in the premium list, is usually from six to eight dollars. An unregistered dog may be shown at three shows, after which he must be registered or a statement must be made to the American Kennel Club that he is ineligible for registry and why, with a request for permission to continue to exhibit the dog. Such permission is seldom denied. The listing fee for an unregistered dog is twenty-five cents, which must be added to the entry fee.

Match or Sanctioned shows are excellent training and experience for regular bench shows. Entry fees are low, usually ranging from fifty cents to a dollar, and are made at the show instead of in advance. Sanctioned shows are unbenched, informal affairs where the puppy may follow his owner about on the leash and become accustomed to strange dogs, to behaving himself in the ring, and to being handled by a judge. For the novice exhibitor, too, Sanctioned shows will provide valuable experience, for ring procedure is similar to that at regular bench shows.

14

The classes open at most shows and usually divided by sex are as follows: Puppy Class (often Junior Puppy for dogs 6 to 9 months old, and Senior Puppy for dogs 9 to 12 months); Novice Class, for dogs that have never won first in any except the Puppy Class; Bred-by-Exhibitor Class, for dogs of which the breeder and owner are the same person or persons; the American-bred Class, for dogs whose parents were mated in America; and the Open Class, which is open to all comers. The respective first prize winners of these various classes compete in what is known as the Winners Class for points toward championship. No entry can be made in the Winners Class, which is open without additional charge to the winners of the earlier classes, all of which are obligated to compete.

A dog eligible to more than one class can be entered in each of them, but it is usually wiser to enter him in only one. A puppy should, unless unusually precocious and mature, be placed in the Puppy Class, and it is unfair to so young a dog to expect him to defeat older dogs, although an exceptional puppy may receive an award in the Winners Class. The exhibitor who is satisfied merely that his dog may win the class in which he is entered is advised to place him in the lowest class to which he is eligible, but the exhibitor with confidence in his dog and shooting for high honors should enter the dog in the Open Class, where the competition is usually the toughest. The winner of the Open Class usually (but by no means always) is also the top of the Winners Class; the runner-up to this dog is named Reserve Winners.

The winner of the Winners Class for dogs competes with the Winners Bitch for Best of Winners, after competing for Best of Breed or Best of Variety with any Champions of Record which may be entered for Specials Only. In the closing hours of the show, the Best of Breed or Best of Variety is eligible to compete in the respective Variety Group to which his breed belongs. And if, perchance, he should win his Variety Group, he is obligated to compete for Best Dog in Show. This is a major honor which few inexperienced exhibitors attain and to which they seldom aspire.

Duly entered, the dog should be brought into the best possible condition for his exhibition in the show and taught to move and to pose at his best. He should be equipped with a neat, strong collar without ornaments or spikes, a show lead of the proper length, width and material for his size and coat, and a nickel bench chain

15

of strong links with which to fasten him to his bench. Food such as the dog is used to, a bottle of the water he is accustomed to drink, and all grooming equipment should be assembled in a bag the night before departure for the show. The exhibitor's pass, on which the dog is assigned a stall number, is sent by mail by the show superintendent and should not be left behind, since it is difficult to have the pass duplicated and it enables the dog's caretaker to leave and return to the show at will.

The time of the opening of the show is stated in the premium list, and it is wise to have one's dog at the show promptly. Late arrivals are subject to disqualification if they are protested.

Sometimes examination is made by the veterinarian at the entrance of the show, and healthy dogs are quickly passed along. Once admitted to the show, if it is a "benched" show, it is wise to find one's bench, the number of which is on the exhibitor's ticket, to affix one's dog to the bench, and not to remove him from it except for exercising or until he is to be taken into the ring to be judged. A familiar blanket or cushion for the bench makes a dog feel at home there. It is contrary to the rules to remove dogs from their benches and to keep them in crates during show hours, and these rules are strictly enforced. Many outdoor shows are not "benched," and you provide your own crate or place for your dog.

At bench shows some exhibitors choose to sit by their dog's bench, but if he is securely chained he is likely to be safe in his owner's absence. Dogs have been stolen from their benches and others allegedly poisoned in the shows, but such incidents are rare indeed. The greater danger is that the dog may grow nervous and insecure, and it is best that the owner return now and again to the bench to reassure the dog of his security.

The advertised program of the show permits exhibitors to know the approximate hour of the judging of their respective breeds. Although that time may be somewhat delayed, it may be depended upon that judging will not begin before the stated hour. The dog should have been groomed and made ready for his appearance in the show ring. When his class is called the dog should be taken unhurriedly to the entrance of the ring, where the handler will receive an arm band with the dog's number.

When the class is assembled and the judge asks that the dogs be paraded before him, the handler should fall into the counter-clock-

16

wise line and walk his dog until the signal to stop is given. In moving in a circle, the dog should be kept on the inside so that he may be readily seen by the judge, who stands in the center of the ring. In stopping the line, there is no advantage to be gained in maneuvering one's dog to the premier position, since the judge will change the position of the dogs as he sees fit.

Keep the dog alert and facing toward the judge at all times. When summoned to the center of the ring for examination, go briskly but not brashly. It is unwise to enter into conversation with the judge, except briefly to reply to any questions he may ask. Do not call his attention to any excellences the dog may possess or excuse any shortcomings; the judge is presumed to evaluate the exhibit's merits as he sees them.

If asked to move the dog, he should be led directly away from the judge and again toward the judge. A brisk but not too rapid trot is the gait the judge wishes to see, unless he declares otherwise. He may ask that the movement be repeated, with which request the handler should respond with alacrity. It is best not to choke a dog in moving him, but rather to move him on a loose lead. The judge will assign or signal a dog to his position, which should be assumed without quibble.

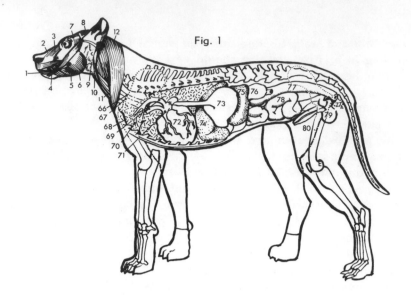

Fig. 1

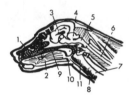

Fig. 2

Fig. 1

1 Orbicularis oris.
2 Levator nasolabialis.
3 Levator labii superioris proprius (levator of upper lip).
4 Dilator naris lateralis.
5 Zygomaticus.
6 Masseter (large and well developed in the dog).
7 Scutularis.
8 Parotid Gland.
9 Submaxillary Gland.
10 Parotido-auricularis.
11 Sterno-hyoideus.
12 Brachio-cephalicus.

(Between figures 8 and 12 on top the Elevator and Depressor muscles of the ear are to be seen.)

66 Œsophagus (gullet).
67 Trachea (wind pipe).
68 Left Carotid Artery.
69 Anterior Aorta.
70 Lungs.
71 Posterior Aorta.
72 Heart.
73 Stomach.

74 Liver. (The line in front of Liver shows the Diaphragm separating Thoracic from Abdominal cavity.)
75 Spleen.
76 Kidney (left).
77 Rectum.
77A Anal Glands (position) just inside rectum.
78 Intestine.
79 Testicle.
80 Penis.
(Midway between 76 and 79 is the seat of the Bladder and behind this the seat of the Prostate gland in males, uterus in females.)

Fig. 2

Section of Head and Neck.
1 Nasal septum.
2 Tongue.
3 Cerebrum.
4 Cerebellum.
5 Medulla oblongata.
6 Spinal Cord.
7 Œsophagus (gullet).
8 Trachea (wind pipe).
9 Hard palate.
10 Soft palate.
11 Larynx, containing vocal cords.

18

The Feeding of Dogs,
Constitutional Vigor

IN selecting a new dog, it is quite as essential that he shall be of sound constitution as that he shall be of the correct type of his own particular breed. The animal that is thoroughly typical of his breed is likely to be vigorous, with a will and a body to surmount diseases and ill treatment, but the converse of this statement is not always true. A dog may have constitutional vigor without breed type. We want both.

Half of the care and effort of rearing a dog is saved by choosing at the outset a puppy of sound constitution, one with a will and an ability to survive and flourish in spite of such adversity and neglect as he may encounter in life. This does not mean that the reader has any intention of obtaining a healthy dog and ill treating it, trusting its good constitution to bring it through whatever crises may beset it. It only means that he will save himself work, expense, and disappointment if only he will exercise care in the first place to obtain a healthy dog, one bred from sound and vigorous parents and one which has received adequate care and good food.

The first warning is not to economize too much in buying a dog. Never accept a cull of the litter at any price. The difference in first cost between a fragile, ill nourished, weedy, and unhealthy puppy and a sound, vigorous one, with adequate substance and the will to survive, may be ten dollars or it may be fifty dollars. But whatever it may be, it is worthwhile. A dog is an investment and it

19

is not the cost but the upkeep that makes the difference. We may save fifty dollars on the first price of a dog, only to lay out twice or five times that sum for veterinary fees over and above what it would cost to rear a dog of sound fundamental constitution and structure.

The vital, desirable dog, the one that is easy to rear and worth the care bestowed upon him, is active, inquisitive, and happy. He is sleek, his eyes free from pus or tears, his coat shining and alive, his flesh adequate and firm. He is not necessarily fat, but a small amount of surplus flesh, especially in puppyhood, is not undesirable. He is free from rachitic knobs on his joints or from crooked bones resultant from rickets. His teeth are firm and white and even. His breath is sweet to the smell. Above all, he is playful and responsive. Puppies, like babies, are much given to sleep, but when they are awake the sturdy ones do not mope lethargically around.

An adult dog that is too thin may often be fattened; if he is too fat he may be reduced. But it is essential that he shall be sound and healthy with a good normal appetite and that he be active and full of the joy of being alive. He must have had the benefit of a good heredity and a good start in life.

A dog without a fundamental inheritance of good vitality, or one that has been neglected throughout his growing period is seldom worth his feed. We must face these facts at the very beginning. Buy only from an owner who is willing to guarantee the soundness of his stock, and before consummating the purchase, have the dog, whether puppy or adult, examined by a veterinarian in order to determine the state of the dog's health.

If the dog to be cared for has been already acquired, there is nothing to do but to make the best of whatever weaknesses or frailties he may possess. But, when it is decided to replace him with another, let us make sure that he has constitutional vigor.

20

THE FEEDING AND NUTRITION OF
THE ADULT DOG

The dog is a carnivore, an eater of meat. This is a truism that cannot be repeated too often. Dog keepers know it but are prone to disregard it, although they do so at their peril and the peril of their dogs. Despite all the old-wives' tales to the contrary, meat does not cause a dog to be vicious, it does not give him worms nor cause him to have fits. It is his food. This is by no means all that is needed to know about food for the dog, but it is the essential knowledge. Give a dog enough sound meat and he will not be ill fed.

The dog is believed to have been the first of the animals that was brought under domestication. In his feral state he was almost exclusively an eater of meat. In his long association with man, however, his metabolism has adjusted itself somewhat to the consumption of human diet until he now can eat, even if he cannot flourish upon, whatever his master chooses to share with him, be it caviar or corn pone. It is not to be denied that a mature dog can survive without ill effects upon an exclusive diet of rice for a considerable period, but it is not to be recommended that he should be forced to do so.

Even if we had no empirical evidence that dogs thrive best upon foods of animal origin, and we possess conclusive proof of that fact, the anatomy and physiology of the dog would convince us of it. An observation of the structure of the dog's alimentary canal, superimposed upon many trial and error methods of feeding, leads us to the conclusion that a diet with meat predominating is the best food we can give a dog.

To begin with, the dental formation of the dog is typical of the carnivores. His teeth are designed for tearing rather than for mastication. He bolts his food and swallows it with a minimum of chewing. It is harmless that he should do this. No digestion takes place in the dog's mouth.

The capacity of the dog's stomach is great in comparison with the size of his body and with the capacity of his intestines. The amounts of carbohydrates and of fats digested in the stomach are minimal. The chief function of the dog's stomach is the digestion of proteins. In the dog as in the other carnivores, carbohydrates

21

and fats are digested for the most part in the small intestine, and absorption of food materials is largely from the small intestine. The enzymes necessary for the completion of the digestion of proteins which have not been fully digested in the stomach and for the digestion of sugars, starches, and fats are present in the pancreatic and intestinal juices. The capacity of the small intestine in the dog is not great and for that reason digestion that takes place there must be rapid.

The so-called large intestine (although in the dog it is really not "large" at all) is short and of small capacity in comparison with that of animals adapted by nature to subsist wholly or largely upon plant foods. In the dog, the large gut is designed to serve chiefly for storage of a limited and compact bulk of waste materials, which are later to be discharged as feces. Some absorption of water occurs there, but there is little if any absorption there of the products of digestion.

It will be readily seen that the short digestive tract of the dog is best adapted to a concentrated diet, which can be quickly digested and which leaves a small residue. Foods of animal origin (flesh, fish, milk, and eggs) are therefore suited to the digestive physiology of the dog because of the ease and completeness with which they are digested as compared with plant foods, which contain considerable amounts of indigestible structural material. The dog is best fed with a concentrated diet with a minimum of roughage.

This means meat. Flesh, milk, and eggs are, in effect, vegetation partly predigested. The steer or horse eats grain and herbage, from which its long digestive tract enables it to extract the food value and eliminate the indigestible material. The carnivore eats the flesh of the herbivore, thus obtaining his grain and grass in a concentrated form suitable for digestion in his short alimentary tract. Thus it is seen that meat is the ideal as a chief ingredient of the dog's ration.

Like that of all other animals, the dog's diet must be made up of proteins, carbohydrates, fats, minerals, vitamins, and water. None of these substances may be excluded if the dog is to survive. If he fails to obtain any of them from one source, it must come from another. It may be argued that before minerals were artificially supplied in the dog's diet and before we were aware of the existence of the various vitamins, we had dogs and they (some of them) appeared to thrive. However, they obtained such substances in their foods, although we were not aware of it. It is very likely that few dogs obtained much more than their very minimum of requirements of the minerals and vitamins. It is known that rickets were more prevalent before we learned to supply our dogs with ample calcium, and black tongue, now almost unknown, was a common canine disease before we supplied in the dog's diet that fraction of the vitamin B complex known as nicotinic acid. There is no way for us to know how large a portion of our dogs died for want of some particular food element before we learned to supply all the necessary ones. The dogs that survived received somewhere in their diet some of all of these compounds.

PROTEIN

The various proteins are the nitrogenous part of the food. They are composed of the amino acids, singly or in combination. There are at least twenty-two of these amino acids known to the nutritional scientists, ten of which are regarded as dietary essentials, the others of which, if not supplied in the diet, can be compounded in the body, which requires an adequate supply of all twenty-two. When any one of the essential ten amino acids is withdrawn from the diet of any animal, growth ceases or is greatly retarded. Thus, a high protein content in any food is not an assurance of its food value if taken alone; it may be lacking in one or more of the essential ten amino acids. When the absent essential amino acids are added to it in sufficient quantities or included separately in the diet, the protein may be complete and fully assimilated.

Proteins, as such, are ingested and in the digestive tract are broken down into the separate amino acids of which they are composed. These amino acids have been likened to building stones, since they are taken up by the blood stream and conveyed to the various parts of the animal as they may be required, where they are deposited and re-united with other complementary amino acids again to form bone and muscles in the resumed form of protein.

To correct amino acid deficiencies in the diet, it is not necessary to add the required units in pure form. The same object may be accomplished more efficiently by employing proteins which contain the required amino acids.

Foods of animal origin—meat, fish, eggs, and milk—supply proteins of high nutritive value, both from the standpoint of digestibility and amino acid content. Gelatin is an exception to that statement, since gelatin is very incomplete.

Even foods of animal origin vary among themselves in their protein content and amino acid balance. The protein of muscle meat does not rank quite as high as that of eggs or milk. The glandular tissues—such as liver, kidneys, sweetbreads or pancreas—contain proteins of exceptionally high nutritive value, and these organs should be added to the dog's diet whenever it is possible to do so. Each pint of milk contains two-thirds of an ounce (dry weight) of particularly high class protein, in addition to minerals, vitamins, carbohydrates, and fats. (The only dietary necessity absent

24

from milk is iron.) Animal proteins have a high content of dietary-essential amino acids, which makes them very effective in supplementing many proteins of vegetable origin. The whites of eggs, while somewhat inferior to the yolks, contain excellent proteins. The lysine of milk can be destroyed by excessive heat and the growth promoting value of its protein so destroyed. Evaporated tinned milk has not been subjected to enough heat to injure its proteins.

Thus we can readily see why meat with its concentrated, balanced, and easily assimilated proteins should form the major part of dry weight of a dog's ration.

It has never been determined how much protein the dog requires in his diet. It may be assumed to vary as to the size, age, and breed of the dog under consideration; as to the individual dog, some assimilating protein better, or utilizing more of it than others; as to the activity or inactivity of the subject; and as to the amino acid content of the protein employed. When wheat protein gliadin is fed as the sole protein, three times as much of it is required as of the milk protein, lactalbumin. It has been estimated that approximately twenty to twenty-five percent of animal protein (dry weight) in a dog's diet is adequate for maintenance in good health, although no final conclusion has been reached and probably never can be.

Our purpose, however, is not to feed the dog the minimum ration with which he can survive or even the minimum ration with which he can flourish. It is rather to give him the maximum food in quantity and balance which he can digest and enjoy without developing a paunch. Who wants to live on the minimum diet necessary for adequate sustenance? We all enjoy a full belly of good food, and so do our dogs.

Roy G. Daggs found from experimentation that milk production in the dog was influenced by the different kinds of proteins fed to it. He has pointed out that relatively high protein diets stimulate lactation and that, in the bitch, animal proteins are better suited to the synthesis of milk than plant proteins. He concluded that liver was a better source of protein for lactation than eggs or round steak.

THE CARBOHYDRATES

The carbohydrates include all the starches, the sugars, and the cellulose and hemicellulose, which last two, known as fiber, are the chief constituents of wood, of the stalks and leaves of plants, and of the coverings of seeds. There remains considerable controversy as to the amount of carbohydrates required or desirable in canine nutrition. It has been shown experimentally that the dog is able to digest large quantities of cornstarch, either raw or cooked. Rice fed to mature dogs in amounts sufficient to satisfy total energy requirements has been found to be 95 percent digested. We know that the various commercial biscuits and meals which are marketed as food for dogs are well tolerated, especially if they are supplemented by the addition of fresh meat. There seems to be no reason why they should not be included in the dog's ration.

Carbohydrates are a cheap source of energy for the dog, both in their initial cost and in the work required of the organism for their metabolism. Since there exists ample evidence that the dog has no difficulty in digesting and utilizing considerable amounts of starches and sugars for the production of energy, there is no reason why they should be excluded from his diet. Some carbohydrate is necessary for the metabolism of fats. The only danger from the employment of carbohydrates is that, being cheap, they may be employed to the exclusion of proteins and other essential elements of the dog's diet. It should be noted that meat and milk contain a measure of carbohydrates as well as of proteins.

Thoroughly cooked rice or oatmeal in moderate quantities may well be used to supplement and cheapen a meat diet for a dog without harm to him, as may crushed dog biscuit or shredded wheat waste or the waste from manufacture of other cereal foods. They are not required but may be used without harm.

Sugar and candy, of which dogs are inordinately fond, used also to be *verboten*. They are an excellent source of energy—and harmless. They should be fed in only moderate quantities.

FATS

In the dog as in man, body fat is found in largest amounts under the skin, between the muscles and around the internal organs. The fat so stored serves as a reserve source of heat and energy when the caloric value of the food is insufficient, or for temporary periods when no food is eaten. The accumulation of a certain amount of fat around vital organs provides considerable protection against cold and injury.

Before fats can be carried to the body cells by means of the circulating blood, it is necessary for them to be digested in the intestines with the aid of enzymes. Fats require a longer time for digestion than carbohydrates or proteins. For this reason, they are of special importance in delaying the sensations of hunger. This property of fats is frequently referred to as "staying power."

It is easily possible for some dogs to accumulate too much fat, making them unattractive, ungainly, and vaguely uncomfortable. This should be avoided by withholding an excess of fats and carbohydrates from the diets of such dogs whenever obesity threatens them. There is greater danger, however, that dogs may through inadequacy of their diets be permitted to become too thin.

Carbohydrates can in part be transformed to fats within the animal body. The ratio between fats and carbohydrates can therefore be varied within wide limits in the dog's ration so long as the requirements for proteins, vitamins, and minerals are adequately met. Some dogs have been known to tolerate as much as forty percent of fat in their diets over prolonged periods, but so much is not to be recommended as a general practice. Perhaps fifteen to twenty percent of fat is adequate without being too much.

Fat is a heat producing food, and the amount given a dog should be stepped up in the colder parts of the year and reduced in the summer months. In a ration low in fat it is particularly important that a good source of the fat-soluble vitamins be included or that such vitamins be artificially supplied. Weight for weight, fat has more than twice the food value of the other organic food groups— carbohydrates and proteins. The use of fat tends to decrease the amount of food required to supply caloric needs. The fats offer a means of increasing or decreasing the total sum of energy in the diet with the least change in the volume of food intake.

27

It is far less important that the dog receive more than a minimum amount of fats, however, than that his ration contain an adequate amount and quality balance of proteins. Lean meat in adequate quantities will provide him with such proteins, and fats may be added to it in the form of fat meat, suet, or lard. Small quantities of dog biscuits, cooked rice, or other cereals in the diet will supply the needed carbohydrates. However, cellulose or other roughage is not required in the diet of the carnivore. It serves only to engorge the dog's colon, which is not capacious, and to increase the volume of feces, which is supererogatory.

MINERALS

At least eleven minerals are present in the normal dog, and there are probably others occurring in quantities so minute that they have not as yet been discovered. The eleven are as follows: Calcium (lime), sodium chloride (table salt), copper, iron, magnesium, manganese, phosphorus, zinc, potassium, and iodine.

Of many of these only a trace in the daily ration is required and that trace is adequately found in meat or in almost any other normal diet. There are a few that we should be at pains to add to the diet. The others we shall ignore.

Sodium chloride (salt) is present in sufficient quantities in most meats, although, more to improve the flavor of the food than to contribute to the animal's nutrition, a small amount of salt may be added to the ration. The exact amount makes no material difference, since the unutilized portions are eliminated, largely in the urine. If the brand of salt used is iodized, it will meet the iodine requirements, which are very small. Iodine deficiency in dogs is rare, but food crops and meats grown in certain areas contain little or no iodine, and it is well to be safe by using iodized salt.

Sufficient iron is usually found in meat and milk, but if the dog appears anemic or listless the trace of iron needed can be supplied with one of the iron salts—ferric sulphate, or oxide, or ferrous gluconate. Iron is utilized in the bone marrow in the synthesis of hemoglobin in the blood corpuscles. It is used over and over; when a corpuscle is worn out and is to be replaced, it surrenders its iron before being eliminated.

When more iron is ingested than can be utilized, some is stored in the liver, after which further surplus is excreted. The liver of the newborn puppy contains enough iron to supply the organism up until weaning time. No iron is present in milk, which otherwise provides a completely balanced ration.

A diet with a reasonable content of red meat, especially of liver or kidney, is likely to be adequate in respect to its iron. However, bitches in whelp require more iron than a dog on mere maintenance. It is recommended that the liver content of bitches' diets be increased for the duration of pregnancy.

Iron requires the presence of a minute trace of copper for its utilization, but there is enough copper in well nigh any diet to supply the requirements.

Calcium and phosphorous are the only minerals of which an insufficiency is a warranted source of anxiety. This statement may not be true of adult dogs not employed for breeding purposes, but it does apply to brood bitches and to growing puppies. The entire skeleton and teeth are made largely from calcium and phosphorus, and it is essential that the organism have enough of those minerals.

If additional calcium is not supplied to a bitch in her diet, her own bone structure is depleted to provide her puppies with their share of calcium. Moreover, in giving birth to her puppies or shortly afterward she is likely to go into eclampsia as a result of calcium depletion.

The situation, however, is easily avoided. The addition of a small amount of calcium phosphate diabasic to the ration precludes any possible calcium deficiency. Calcium phosphate diabasic is an inexpensive substance and quite tasteless. It may be sprinkled in or over the food, especially that given to brood bitches and puppies. It is the source of strong bones and vigorous teeth of ivory whiteness.

But it must be mentioned that calcium cannot be assimilated into the bone structure, no matter how much of it is fed or otherwise administered, except in the presence of vitamin D. That is D's function, to facilitate the absorption of calcium and phosphorus. This will be elaborated upon in the following discussion of the vitamins and their functions.

VITAMINS

Vitamins have in the past been largely described by diseases resulting from their absence. It is recognized more and more that many of the subacute symptoms of general unfitness of dogs may be attributable to an inadequate supply in the diet of one or more of these essential food factors. It is to be emphasized that vitamins are to be considered a part of the dog's food, essential to his health and well being. They are not to be considered as medication. Often the morbid conditions resultant from their absence in the diet may be remedied by the addition of the particular needed vitamin.

The requirements of vitamins, as food, not as medication, in the diet cannot be too strongly emphasized. These vitamins may be in the food itself, or they may better be added to it as a supplement to insure an adequate supply. Except for vitamin D, of which it is remotely possible (though unlikely) to supply too much, a surplus of the vitamin substances in the ration is harmless. They are somewhat expensive and we have no disposition to waste them, but if too much of them are fed they are simply eliminated with no subsequent ill effect.

It must be realized that vitamins are various substances, each of which has a separate function. It is definitely not safe to add to a dog's (or a child's) diet something out of a bottle or box indefinitely labeled "Vitamins," as is the practice of so many persons. We must know which vitamins we are giving, what purpose each is designed to serve, and the potency of the preparation of the brand of each one we are using.

Any one of the "shotgun" vitamin preparations is probably adequate if administered in large enough dosages. Such a method may be wasteful, however; to be sure of enough of one substance, the surplus of the others is wasted. It is much better to buy a product that contains an adequate amount of each of the needed vitamins and a wasteful surplus of none. Such a procedure is cheaper in the long run.

There follows a brief description of each of the various vitamins so far discovered and a statement of what purpose in the diet they are respectively intended to serve:

*Vitamin A—*This vitamin in some form is an absolute requisite for good health, even for enduring life itself. Symptoms of advanced deficiency of vitamin A in dogs are an eye disease with resulting impaired vision, inflammation of the conjunctiva or mucous membranes which line the eyelid, and injury to the mucous membranes of the body. Less easily recognized symptoms are an apparent lowered resistance to bacterial infection, especially of the upper respiratory tract, retarded growth, and loss of weight. Diseases due to vitamin A deficiency may be well established while the dog is still gaining in weight. Lack of muscular coordination and paralysis have been observed in dogs and degeneration of the nervous system. Some young dogs deprived of vitamin A become wholly or partially deaf.

The potency of vitamin A is usually calculated in International Units, of which it has been estimated that the dog requires about 35 per day for each pound of his body weight. Such parts as are not utilized are not lost, but are stored in the liver for future use in time of shortage. A dog well fortified with this particular vitamin can well go a month or more without harm with none of it in his diet. At such times he draws upon his liver for its surplus.

It is for its content of vitamins A and D that cod-liver oil (and the oils from the livers of other fish) is fed to puppies and growing children. Fish liver oils are an excellent source of vitamin A, and if a small amount of them is included in the diet no anxiety about deficiency of vitamin A need be entertained. In buying cod-liver oil, it pays to obtain the best grade. The number of International Units it contains per teaspoonful is stated on most labels. The vitamin content of cod-liver oil is impaired by exposure to heat, light, and air. It should be kept in a dark, cool place and the bottle should be firmly stopped.

Another source of vitamin A is found in carrots but it is almost impossible to get enough carrots in a dog to do him any good. It is better and easier to use a preparation known as carotene, three drops of which contains almost the vitamin A in a bushel of carrots.

Other natural sources of vitamin A are liver, kidney, heart, cheese, egg yolks, butter and milk. If these foods, or any one of them, are generously included in the adult dog's maintenance ration, all other sources of vitamin A may be dispensed with. The ration for all puppies, however, and for pregnant and lactating bitches should be copiously fortified either with fish liver oil or with tablets containing vitamin A.

32

Vitamin B. What was formerly known as a single vitamin B has now been found to be a complex of many different factors. Some of them are, in minute quantities, very important parts of the diets of any kind of animals. The various factors of this complex, each a separate vitamin, are designated by the letter B followed by an inferior number, as B_1, B_2, or B_6.

The absence or insufficiency in the diet of Vitamin B_1, otherwise known as thiamin, has been blamed for retarded growth, loss of weight, decreased fertility, loss of appetite, and impaired digestion. A prolonged shortage of B_1 may result in paralysis, the accumulation of fluid in the tissues, and finally in death, apparently from heart failure.

It is not easy to estimate just how much B_1 a dog requires per pound of body weight, since dogs as individuals vary in their needs, and the activity of an animal rapidly depletes the thiamin in his body. The feeding of 50 International Units per day per pound of body weight is probably wasteful but harmless. That is at least enough.

Thiamin is not stored in the system for any length of time and requires a daily dosage. It is destroyed in part by heat above the boiling point. It is found in yeast (especially in brewer's yeast), liver, wheat germ, milk, eggs, and in the coloring matter of vegetables. However, few dogs or persons obtain an optimum supply of B_1 from their daily diet, and it is recommended that it be supplied to the dog daily.

Brewer's yeast, either in powdered or tablet form affords a cheap and rather efficient way to supply the average daily requirements. An overdose of yeast is likely to cause gas in the dog's stomach.

Another factor of the vitamin B complex, riboflavin, affects particularly the skin and hair. Animals fed a diet in which it is deficient are prone to develop a scruffy dryness of the skin, especially about the eyes and mouth, and the hair becomes dull and dry, finally falling out, leaving the skin rough and dry. In experiments with rats deprived of riboflavin the toes have fallen off.

Riboflavin is present in minute quantities in so many foods that a serious shortage in any well balanced diet is unlikely. It is especially to be found in whey, which is the explanation of the smooth skin and lively hair of so many dogs whose ration contains cottage cheese.

33

While few dogs manifest any positive shortage of riboflavin, experiments on various animals have shown that successively more liberal amounts of it in their diets, up to about four times as much as is needed to prevent the first signs of deficiency, result in increased positive health.

Riboflavin deteriorates with exposure to heat and light. Most vitamin products contain it in ample measure.

Dogs were immediately responsible for the discovery of the existence of vitamin B_2, or nicotinic acid, formerly known as vitamin G. The canine disease of black tongue is analogous with the human disease called pellagra, both of which are prevented and cured by sufficient amounts of nicotinic acid in the diet. Black tongue is not a threat for any dog that eats a diet which contains even a reasonable quantity of lean meat, but it used to be prevalent among dogs fed exclusively upon corn bread or corn-meal mush, as many were.

No definite optimum dosage has been established. However, many cases of vaguely irritated skin, deadness of coat, and soft, spongy, or bleeding gums have been reported to be remedied by administration of nicotinic acid.

It has been demonstrated that niacin is essential if a good sound healthy appetite is to be maintained. Pantothenic acid is essential to good nerve health. Pyridoxin influences proper gastro-intestinal functions. Vitamin B_{12}, the "animal protein factor," is essential for proper growth and health in early life. And the water soluble B factor affects the production of milk.

Vitamin C, the so-called anti-scorbutic vitamin, is presumed to be synthesized by the dog in his own body. The dog is believed not to be subject to true scurvy. Vitamin C, then, can well be ignored as pertains to the dog. It is the most expensive of the vitamins, and, its presence in the vitamin mixture for the dog will probably do no good.

Vitamin D, the anti-rachitic vitamin, is necessary to promote the assimilation of calcium and phosphorus into the skeletal structure. One may feed all of those minerals one will, but without vitamin D they will pass out of the system unused. It is impossible to develop sound bones and teeth without its presence. Exposure to sunshine unimpeded by glass enables the animal to manufacture vitamin D in his system, but sunshine is not to be depended upon for an entire supply.

Vitamin D is abundant in cod-liver oil and in the liver oils of some other fish, or it may be obtained in a dry form in combination with other vitamins. One International Unit per pound of body weight per day is sufficient to protect a dog from rickets. From a teaspoonful to a tablespoonful of cod-liver oil a day will serve well instead for any dog.

This is the only one of the vitamins with which overdosage is possible and harmful. While a dog will not suffer from several times the amount stated and an excess dosage is unlikely, it is only fair to warn the reader that it is at least theoretically possible.

Vitamin E is the so-called fertility vitamin. Whether it is required for dogs has not as yet been determined. Rats fed upon a ration from which vitamin E was wholly excluded became permanently sterile, but the finding is not believed to pertain to all animals. Some dog keepers, however, declare that the feeding of wheat germ oil, the most abundant source of vitamin E, has prevented early abortions of their bitches, has resulted in larger and more vigorous litters of puppies, has increased the fertility of stud dogs, has improved the coats of their dogs and furthered the betterment of their general health. Whether vitamin E or some other factor or factors in the wheat germ oil is responsible for these alleged benefits is impossible to say.

Vitamin E is so widely found in small quantities in well nigh all foods that the hazard of its omission from any normal diet is small.

Numerous other vitamins have been discovered and isolated in recent years, and there are suspected to be still others as yet unknown. The ones here discussed are the only ones that warrant the use of care to include them in the dog's daily ration. It is well to reiterate that vitamins are not medicine, but are food, a required part of the diet. Any person interested in the complete nutrition of his dog will not neglect them.

It should go without saying that a dog should have access to clean, fresh, pure drinking water at all times, of which he should be permitted to drink as much or as little as he chooses. The demands of his system for drinking water will depend in part upon the moisture content of his food. Fed upon dry dog biscuits, he will probably drink considerable water to moisten it; with a diet which contains much milk or soup, he will need little additional water.

35

That he chooses to drink water immediately after a meal is harmless. The only times his water should be limited (but not entirely withheld from him) is after violent exercise or excitement, at which times his thirst should be satisfied only gradually.

The quantities of food required daily by dogs are influenced and determined by a number of factors: the age, size, individuality, and physical condition of the animal; the kind, quality, character, and proportions of the various foods in the ration; the climate, environment and methods of management; and the type and amount of work done, or the degree of exercise. Of these considerations, the age and size of the dog and the kind and amount of work are particularly important in determining food requirements. During early puppyhood a dog may require two or three (or even more) times as much food per pound of body weight as the same dog will require at maturity.

Any statement we should make here about the food requirements of a dog as to weight or volume would be subject to modification. Dogs vary in their metabolism. One dog might stay fat and sleek on a given amount of a given ration, whereas his litter brother in an adjoining kennel might require twice or only half as much of the same ration to maintain him in the same state of flesh.

The only sound determiners of how much to feed a dog are his appetite and his condition. As a general rule, a dog should have as much food for maintenance as he will readily clean up in five or ten minutes, unless he tends to lay on unwanted fat, in which case his intake of food should be reduced, especially its content of fats and carbohydrates. A thin dog should have his ration increased and be urged to eat it. The fats in his ration should be increased, and he may be fattened with a dessert of candy, sugar, or sweet cake following his main meal. These should never be used before a meal, lest they impair the appetite, and they should not be given to a fat dog at all. Rightly employed, they are useful and harmless, contrary to the prevalent belief.

Growing puppies require frequent meals, as will be discussed later. Pregnant and lactating bitches and frequently used stud dogs should have at least two meals, and better three, each day. For the mere maintenance of healthy adult dogs, one large meal a day appears to suffice as well as more smaller ones. Many tenderhearted dog keepers choose to divide the ration into two parts and to feed their dogs twice each day. There can be no objection offered to such a program except that it involves additional work for the keeper. Whether one meal or two, they should be given at regular hours, to which dogs soon adjust and expect their dinner at a given time.

It is better to determine upon an adequate ration, with plenty of meat in it, and feed it day after day, than to vary the diet in the assumption that a dog tires of eating the same thing. There is no evidence that he does, and it is a burden upon his carnivorous digestion to be making constant adjustments and readjustments to a new diet.

Today there are available for dogs many brands of canned foods, some good and others not so good. But it is safe to feed your dog exclusively—if you do not object to the cost—a canned dog food which has been produced by a reliable concern. Many of the producers of canned dog foods are subject to Federal inspection because they also process meat and meat products for human consumption. The Federal regulations prohibit the use of diseased or unsuitable by-products in the preparation of dog food. Some of the canned dog foods on the market are mostly cereal. A glance at the analysis chart on the label will tell you whether a particular product is a good food for your dog.

If fish is fed, it should be boned—thoroughly. The same is true of fowl and rabbit meats. Small bones may be caught in the dog's throat or may puncture the stomach or intestines. Large, raw shank bones of beef may be given to the dog with impunity, but they should be renewed at frequent intervals before they spoil. A dog obtains much amusement from gnawing a raw bone, and some nutrition. Harm does not accrue from his swallowing of bone fragments, which are dissolved by the hydrochloric acid in his stomach. If the dog is fed an excessive amount of bones, constipation may result. When this occurs, the best way to relieve the condition is by the use of the enema bag. Medicinal purges of laxatives given at this time may cause irreparable damage.

Meat for dogs may be fed raw, or may be roasted, broiled, or boiled. It is not advisable to feed fried foods to dogs. All soups, gravies and juices from cooked meat must be conserved and included in the food, since they contain some of the minerals and vitamins extracted from the meat.

37

A well-known German physician selected a medium sized, strong, healthy bitch, and after she had been mated, he fed her on chopped horse meat from which the salts were to a large extent extracted by boiling for two hours in distilled water. In addition to this she was given each day a certain quantity of fried fat. As drink she had only distilled water. She gave birth to six healthy puppies, one of which was killed immediately, and its bones found to be strong and well built and free from abnormalities. The other puppies did not thrive, but remained weak, and could scarcely walk at the end of a month, when four died from excessive feebleness. And the sixth was killed two weeks later. The mother in the meantime had become very lean but was tolerably lively and had a fair appetite. She was killed one hundred and twenty-six days after the beginning of the experiment, and it was then found that the bones of her spine and pelvis were softened—a condition known to physicians as osteomalacia.

The results of this experiment are highly interesting and instructive, showing clearly as they do that the nursing mother sends out to her young, in her milk, a part of her store of lime, which is absolutely essential to their welfare. They show also that if proper food is denied her, when in whelp and when nursing, not only her puppies but she as well must suffer greatly in consequence. And in the light of these facts is uncovered one of the most potential causes of rickets, so common among large breeds.

It may therefore be accepted that bitches in whelp must have goodly quantities of meat; moreover, that while cooking may be the rule if the broth is utilized, it is a wise plan to give the food occasionally in the raw state.

There is little choice among the varieties of meat, except that pork is seldom relished by dogs, usually contains too much fat, and should be cooked to improve its digestibility when it is used at all. Beef, mutton, lamb, goat, and horse flesh are equally valuable. The choice should be made upon the basis of their comparative cost and their availability in the particular community. A dog suddenly changed from another diet to horse flesh may develop a harmless and temporary diarrhea, which can be ignored. Horse flesh is likely to be deficient in fats, which may be added in the form of suet, lard or pure corn oil.

The particular cuts of whatever meat is used is of little consequence. Liver and kidney are especially valuable and when it is possible they should be included as part of the meat used. As the only meat in the ration, liver and kidney tend to loosen the bowels. It is better to include them as a part of each day's ration than to permit them to serve as the sole meat content one or two days a week.

It makes no difference whether meat is ground or is fed to the dog in large or medium sized pieces. He is able to digest pieces of meat as large as he can swallow. The advantage of grinding meat is that it can be better mixed with whatever else it is wished to include in the ration, the dog being unable to pick out the meat and reject the rest. There is little harm in his doing so, except for the waste, since it is the meat upon which we must depend for the most part for his nutrition.

Fresh ground meat can be kept four or five days under ordinary refrigeration without spoiling. It may be kept indefinitely if solidly frozen. Frozen ground horse meat for dogs is available in many markets, is low in price, and is entirely satisfactory for the purpose intended.

A suggested ration is made as follows: Two-thirds to three-quarters by weight of ground meat including ten to twenty percent of fat and a portion of liver or kidney, with the remainder thoroughly cooked rice or oatmeal, or shredded wheat, or dog biscuit, or wheat germ, with a sprinkling of calcium phosphate diabasic. Vitamins may be added, or given separately.

If it is desired to offer the dog a second meal, it may be of shredded wheat or other breakfast cereal with plenty of milk, with or without one or more soft boiled eggs. Evaporated canned milk or powdered milk is just as good food for the dog as fresh milk. Cottage cheese is excellent for this second meal.

These are not the only possible rations for the dog, but they will prove adequate. Leavings from the owner's table can be added to either ration, but can hardly be depended upon for the entire nourishment of the dog.

The dog's food should be at approximately body heat, tepid but never hot.

Little consideration is here given to the costs of the various foods. Economies in rations and feeding practices are admittedly desirable, but not if they are made at the expense of the dog's health.

SOME BRIEF PRECEPTS ABOUT FEEDING

Many dogs are overfed. Others do not receive adequate rations. Both extremes should be avoided, but particularly overfeeding of grown dogs. Coupled with lack of exercise, overfeeding usually produces excessive body weight and laziness, and it may result in illness and sterility. Prolonged undernourishment causes loss of weight, listlessness, dull coats, sickness, and death.

An adequate ration will keep most mature dogs at a uniform body weight and in a thrifty, moderately lean condition. Observation of condition is the best guide in determining the correct amount of food.

The axiom, "One man's meat is another man's poison," is applicable to dogs also. Foods that are not tolerated by the dog or those that cause digestive and other disturbances should be discontinued. The use of moldy, spoiled, or rotten food is never good practice. Food should be protected from fouling by rats or mice, especially because rats are vectors of leptospirosis. The excessive use of food of low energy content and low biological values will often result in poor condition and may cause loss of weight and paunchiness.

All feeding and drinking utensils must be kept scrupulously clean. They should be washed after each using.

It is usually desirable to reduce the food allotment somewhat during hot weather. Dogs should be fed at regular intervals, and the best results may be expected when regular feeding is accompanied by regular, but not exhausting, exercise.

Most dogs do not thrive on a ration containing large amounts of sloppy foods, and excessive bulk is to be avoided especially for hardworking dogs, puppies, and pregnant or lactating bitches. If the ration is known to be adequate and the dog is losing weight or is not in good condition, the presence of intestinal parasites is to be suspected. However, dogs sometimes go "off feed" for a day or two. This is cause for no immediate anxiety, but if it lasts more than two or three days, a veterinarian should be consulted.

FOOD FOR THE STUD DOG

The stud dog that is used for breeding only at infrequent intervals requires only the food needed for his maintenance in good health, as set forth in the foregoing pages. He should be well fed with ample meat in his diet, moderately exercised to keep his flesh firm and hard, and not permitted to become too thin or too fat.

More care is required for the adequate nutrition of the dog offered at public stud and frequently employed for breeding. A vigorous stud dog may very handily serve two bitches a week over a long period without a serious tax upon his health and strength if he is fully nourished and adequately but not excessively exercised. Such a dog should have at least two meals a day, and they should consist of even more meat, milk (canned is as good as fresh), eggs, cottage cheese, and other foods of animal origin than is used in most maintenance rations. Liver and some fat should be included, and the vitamins especially are not to be forgotten. In volume this will be only a little more than the basic maintenance diet, the difference being in its richness and concentration.

An interval of an hour or two should intervene between a dog's meal and his employment for breeding. He may be fed, but only lightly, immediately after he has been used for breeding.

The immediate reason that a stud dog should be adequately fed and exercised is the maintenance of his strength and virility. The secondary reason is that a popular stud dog is on exhibition at all times, between the shows as well as at the shows. Clients with bitches to be bred appear without notice to examine a dog at public stud, and the dog should be presented to them in the best possible condition—clean, hard, in exactly the most becoming state of flesh, and with a gleaming, lively coat. These all depend largely upon the highly nutritious diet the dog receives.

FOOD FOR THE BROOD BITCH

Often a well fed bitch comes through the ordeal of rearing a large litter of puppies without any impairment of her vitality and flesh. In such case she may be returned to a good maintenance ration until she is ready to be bred again. About the time she weans her puppies her coat will be dead and ready to drop out, but if she is healthy and well fed a new and vigorous coat will grow in, and she will be no worse off for her maternal ordeal. Some bitches, either from a deficient nutrition or a constitutional disposition to contribute too much of their own strength and substance to the nutrition of the puppies, are thin and exhausted at the time of weaning. Such a bitch needs the continuance of at least two good and especially nutritious meals a day for a month or more until her flesh and strength are restored before she is returned to her routine maintenance ration, upon which she may be kept until time comes to breed her again.

At breeding time a bitch's flesh should be hard, and she should be on the lean side rather than too fat. No change in her regular maintenance diet need be made until about the fourth or fifth week of her pregnancy. The growth of the fetus is small up until the middle of the pregnancy, after which it becomes rapid.

The bitch usually begins to "show in whelp" in four to six weeks after breeding, and her food consumption should be then gradually stepped up. If she has been having only one meal a day, she should be given two; if she has had two, both should be larger. Henceforth until her puppies are weaned, she must eat not merely for two, as is said of the pregnant woman, but for four or five, possibly for ten or twelve. She is not to be encouraged to grow fat. Especial emphasis should be laid upon her ration's content of meat, including liver, milk, calcium phosphate, and vitamins A and D, both of which are found in cod-liver oil.

Some breeders destroy all but a limited number of puppies in a litter in the belief that a bitch will be unable adequately to nourish all the puppies she has whelped. In some extreme cases it may be necessary to do this or to obtain a foster mother or wet nurse to share the burden of rearing the puppies. However, the healthy bitch with normal metabolism can usually generate enough milk to feed adequately all the puppies she has produced, pro-

42

vided she is well enough fed and provided the puppies are fed additionally as soon as they are able to eat.

After whelping until the puppies are weaned, throughout the lactating period, the bitch should have all the nourishing food she can be induced to eat—up to four or five meals a day. These should consist largely of meat and liver, some fat, a small amount of cereals, milk, eggs, cottage cheese, calcium phosphate, and vitamins, with especial reference to vitamins A and D. At that time it is hardly possible to feed a bitch too much or to keep her too fat. The growth of the puppies is much more rapid after they are born than was their growth in the dam's uterus, and the large amount of food needed to maintain that rapid growth must pass through the bitch and be transformed to milk, while at the same time she must maintain her own body.

THE FEEDING OF PUPPIES

If the number of puppies in a litter is small, if the mother is vigorous, healthy, and a good milker, the youngsters up until their weaning time may require no additional food over and above the milk they suck from their dam's breasts. If the puppies are numerous or if the dam's milk is deficient in quality or quantity, it is wise to begin feeding the puppies artificially as soon as they are able and willing to accept food. This is earlier than used to be realized.

It is for the sake of the puppies' vigor rather than for the sake of their ultimate size that their growth is to be promoted as rapidly as possible. Vigorous and healthy puppies attain early maturity if they are given the right amounts of the right quality of food. The ultimate size of the dog at maturity is laid down in his germ plasm, and he can be stunted or dwarfed, if at all, only at the expense of his type. If one tries to prevent the full growth of a dog by withholding from him the food he needs, one will wind up with a rachitic, cowhocked dog, one with a delicate digestive apparatus, a sterile one, one with all of these shortcomings combined, or even a dead dog.

Growth may be slowed with improper food, sometimes without serious harm, but the dog is in all ways better off if he is forced along with the best food and encouraged to attain his full size at an early age. Dogs of the smaller breeds usually reach their full maturity several months earlier than those of the larger breeds. A well grown dog reaches his sexual maturity and can be safely used for limited breeding at one year of age.

As soon as teeth can be felt with the finger in a puppy's mouth, which is usually at about seventeen or eighteen days of age, it is safe to begin to feed him. His first food (except for his mother's milk) should be of scraped raw beef at body temperature. The first day he may have $\frac{1}{4}$ to 2 teaspoonfuls, according to size. He will not need to learn to eat this meat; he will seize upon it avidly and lick his chops for more. The second day he may have $\frac{1}{3}$ to 3 teaspoonfuls, according to size, with two feedings 12 hours apart. Thereafter, the amount and frequency of this feeding may be rapidly increased. By the twenty-fifth day the meat need not be scraped, but only finely ground. This process of the early feeding of raw meat to puppies not only gives them a good start in life, but

44

it also relieves their mother of a part of her burden of providing milk for them.

At about the fourth week, some cereal (thoroughly cooked oatmeal, shredded wheat, or dried bread) may be either moistened and mixed with the meat or be served to the puppies with milk, fresh or canned. It may be necessary to immerse their noses into such a mixture to teach them to eat it. Calcium phosphate and a small amount of cod-liver oil should be added to such a mixture, both of which substances the puppies should have every day until their maturity. At the fourth week, while they are still at the dam's breast, they may be fed three or four times a day upon this extra ration, or something similar, such as cottage cheese or soft boiled egg. By the sixth week their dam will be trying to wean them, and they may have four or five meals daily. One of these may be finely broken dog biscuit thoroughly soaked in milk. One or two of the meals should consist largely or entirely of meat with liver.

The old advice about feeding puppies "little and often" should be altered to "much and often." Each puppy at each meal should have all the food he will readily clean up. Food should not be left in front of the puppies. They should be fed and after two or three minutes the receptacle should be taken away. Young puppies should be roly-poly fat, and kept so up to at least five or six months of age. Thereafter they should be slightly on the fat side, but not pudgy, until maturity.

The varied diet of six-week-old puppies may be continued, but at eight or nine weeks the number of meals may be reduced to four, and at three months, to three large rations per day. After six months the meals may be safely reduced again to two a day, but they must be generous meals with meat, liver, milk, cod-liver oil, and calcium phosphate. At full maturity, one meal a day suffices, or two may be continued.

The secret of turning good puppies into fine, vigorous dogs is to keep them growing through the entire period of their maturation. The most important item in the rearing of puppies is adequate and frequent meals of highly nourishing foods. Growth requires two or three times as much food as maintenance. Time between meals should be allowed for digestion, but puppies should never be permitted to become really hungry. Water in a shallow dish should be available to puppies at all times after they are able to walk.

45

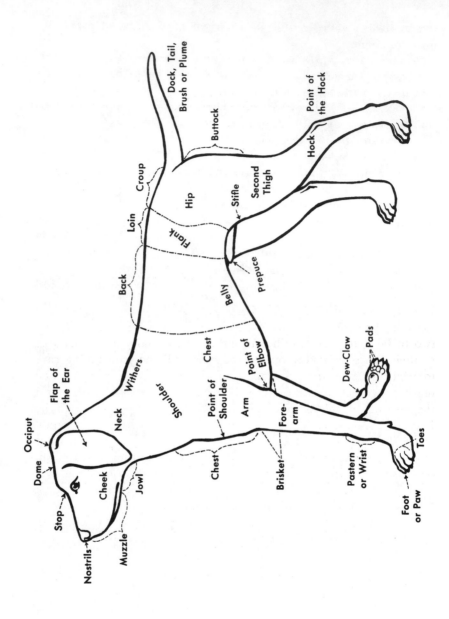

The Breeding
of Dogs

H ERE, if anywhere in the entire process of the care
and management of dogs, the exercise of good judgment is involved.
Upon the choice of the two dogs, male and female, to be mated
together depends the future success or failure of one's dogs. If the
two to be mated are ill chosen, either individually or as pertains
to their fitness as mates, one to the other, all the painstaking care
to feed and rear the resultant puppies correctly is wasted. The
mating together of two dogs is the drafting of the blueprints and
the writing of the specifications of what the puppies are to be
like. The plans, it is true, require to be executed; the puppies,
when they arrive, must be adequately fed and cared for in order
to develop them into the kinds of dogs they are in their germ plasm
designed to become. However, if the plans as determined in the
mating are defective, just so will the puppies that result from them
be defective, in spite of all the good raising one can give them.

The element of luck in the breeding of dogs cannot be discounted,
for it exists. The mating which on paper appears to be the best
possible may result in puppies that are poor and untypical of
their breed. Even less frequently, a good puppy may result from
a chance mating together of two ill chosen parents. These results
are fortuitous and unusual, however. The best dogs as a lot come
from parents carefully chosen as to their individual excellences and
as to their suitability as mates for each other. It is as unwise as

47

it is unnecessary to trust to luck in the breeding of dogs. Careful planning pays off in the long run, and few truly excellent dogs are produced without it.

Some breeders without any knowledge of genetics have been successful, without knowing exactly why they succeeded. Some of them have adhered to beliefs in old wives' tales and to traditional concepts that science has long since exploded and abandoned. Such as have succeeded have done so in spite of their lack of knowledge and not because of it.

There is insufficient space at our disposal in this book to discuss in detail the science of genetics and the application of that science to the breeding of dogs. Whole books have been written about the subject. One of the best, clearest, and easiest for the layman to understand is *The New Art of Breeding Better Dogs,* by Philip Onstott, which may be obtained from Howell Book House, the publisher. In it and in other books upon the subject of genetics will be found more data about the practical application of science to the breeding of livestock than can be included here.

The most that can be done here is to offer some advice soundly based upon the genetic laws. Every feature a dog may or can possess is determined by the genes carried in the two reproductive cells, one from each parent, from the union of which he was developed. There are thousands of pairs of these determiners in the life plan of every puppy, and often a complex of many genes is required to produce a single recognizable attribute of the dog.

These genes function in pairs, one member of each pair being contributed by the father and the other member of the pair coming from the mother. The parents obtained these genes they hand on from their parents, and it is merely fortuitous which half of any pair of genes present in a dog's or a bitch's germ plasm may be passed on to any one of the progeny. Of any pair of its own genes, a dog or a bitch may contribute one member to one puppy and the other member to another puppy in the same litter or in different litters. The unknown number of pairs of genes is so great that there is an infinite number of combinations of them, which accounts for the differences we find between two full brothers or two full sisters. In fact, it depends upon the genes received whether a dog be a male or a female.

We know that the male dog contributes one and the bitch the

48

other of every pair of genes that unite to determine what the puppy will be like and what he will grow into. Thus, the parents make exactly equal contributions to the germ plasm or zygote from which every puppy is developed. It was long believed that the male dog was so much more important than the bitch in any mating that the excellence or shortcomings of the bitch might be disregarded. This theory was subsequently reversed and breeders considered the bitch to be more important than the dog. We now know that their contribution in every mating and in every individual puppy is exactly equal, and neither is to be considered more than the other.

There are two kinds of genes—the recessive genes and the dominant. And there are three kinds of pairs of genes: a recessive from the sire plus a recessive from the dam; a dominant from the sire plus a dominant from the dam; and a dominant from one parent plus a recessive from the other. It is the last combination that is the source of our trouble in breeding. When both members of a pair of genes are recessive, the result is a recessive attribute in the animal that carries them; when both members of the pair are dominant, the result is a pure dominant attribute; but when one member of the pair is recessive and the other member dominant, the result will be a wholly or only partially dominant attribute, which will breed true only half of the time. This explains why a dog or a bitch may fail to produce progeny that looks at all like itself.

If all the pairs of a dog's genes were purely dominant, we could expect him to produce puppies that resembled himself in all particulars, no matter what kind of mate he was bred to. Or if all his genes were recessive and he were mated to a bitch with all recessive genes, the puppies might be expected to look quite like the parents. However, a dog with mixed pairs of genes bred to a bitch with mixed pairs of genes may produce anything at all, puppies that bear no resemblance to either parent.

Long before the Mendelian laws were discovered, some dogs were known to be "prepotent" to produce certain characters, that is the characters would show up in their puppies irrespective of what their mates might be like. For instance, some dogs, themselves with dark eyes, might be depended upon never to produce a puppy with light eyes, no matter how light eyed the mate to which he was bred. This was true despite the fact that the dog's litter brother which had equally dark eyes, when bred to a light eyed bitch might produce a large percentage of puppies with light eyes.

Before it is decided to breed a bitch, it is well to consider whether she is worth breeding, whether she is good enough as an individual and whether she came from a good enough family to warrant the expectations that she will produce puppies worth the expense and trouble of raising. It is to be remembered that the bitch contributes exactly half the genes to each of her puppies; if she has not good genes to contribute, the time and money involved in breeding her and rearing her puppies will be wasted.

It is conceded that a bad or mediocre bitch when bred to an excellent dog will probably produce puppies better than herself. But while one is "grading up" from mediocre stock, other breeders are also grading upward from better stock and they will keep just so far ahead of one's efforts that one can never catch up with them. A merely pretty good bitch is no good at all for breeding. It is better to dispose of a mediocre bitch or to relegate her to the position of a family pet than to breed from her. It is difficult enough, with all the care and judgment one is able to muster, to obtain superlative puppies even from a fine bitch, without cluttering the earth with inferior puppies from just any old bitch.

If one will go into the market and buy the best possible bitch from the best possible family one's purse can afford and breed her sensibly to the best and most suitable stud dog one can find, success is reasonably sure. Even if for economy's sake, the bitch is but a promising puppy backed up by the best possible pedigree, it will require only a few months until she is old enough to be bred. From such a bitch, one may expect first-rate puppies at the first try, whereas in starting with an inferior bitch one is merely lucky if in two or three generations he obtains a semblance of the kind of dog he is trying to produce.

Assuming it is decided that the bitch is adequate to serve as a brood bitch, it becomes necessary to choose for her a mate in collaboration with which she may realize the ultimate of her possibilities. It is never wise to utilize for stud the family pet or the neighbor's pet just because he happens to be registered in the studbook or because his service costs nothing. Any dog short of the best and most suitable (wherever he may be and whoever may own him) is an extravagance. If the bitch is worth breeding at all, she is worth shipping clear across the continent, if need be, to obtain for her a mate to enable her to realize her possibilities. Stud fees may range from fifty to one hundred dollars or even more. The average value of each puppy, if well reared, should at the time of weaning approximate the legitimate stud fee of its sire. With a good bitch it is therefore profitable to lay out as much as may be required to obtain the services of the best and most suitable stud dog—always assuming that he is worth the price asked. However, it is never wise to choose an inferior or unsuitable dog just because he is well ballyhooed and commands an exorbitant stud fee.

There are three considerations by which to evaluate the merits of a stud dog—his outstanding excellence as an individual, his pedigree and the family from which he derived, and the excellence or inferiority of the progeny he is known to have produced.

As an individual a good stud dog may be expected to be bold and aggressive (not vicious) and structurally typical of his breed, but without any freakish exaggerations of type. He must be sound, a free and true mover, possess fineness and quality, and be a gentleman of his own breed. Accidentally acquired scars or injuries such as broken legs should not be held against him, because he can transmit only his genes to his puppies and no such accidents impair his genes.

A dog's pedigree may mean much or little. One of two litter brothers, with pedigrees exactly alike, may prove to be a superlative show and stud dog, and the other worth exactly nothing for either purpose. The pedigree especially is not to be judged on its length, since three generations is at most all that is required, although further extension of the pedigree may prove interesting to a curious owner. No matter how well-bred his pedigree may show a dog to be, if he is not a good dog the ink required to write the pedigree was wasted.

The chief value of a pedigree is to enable us to know from which of a dog's parents, grandparents, or great-grandparents, he derived his merits, and from which his faults. In choosing a mate for him (or for her, as the case may be) one seeks to reinforce the one and to avoid the other. Let us assume that one of the grandmothers was upright in shoulder, whereas the shoulder should be well laid back; we can avoid as a mate for such a dog one with any

51

tendency to straight shoulders or one from straight shouldered ancestry. The same principle would apply to an uneven mouth, a light eye, a soft back, splayed feet, cowhocks, or to any other inherited fault. Suppose, on the other hand, that the dog himself, the parents, and all the grandparents are particularly nice in regard to their fronts; in a mate for such a dog, one desires as good a front as is obtainable, but if she, or some of her ancestors are not too good in respect to their fronts, one may take a chance anyway and trust to the good fronted dog with his good fronted ancestry to correct the fault. That then is the purpose of the pedigree as a guide to breeding.

A stud dog can best be judged, however, by the excellence of the progeny he is known to have produced, if it is possible to obtain all the data to enable the breeder to evaluate that record. A complete comparative evaluation is perhaps impossible to make, but one close enough to justify conclusions is available. Not only the number but the quality of the bitches to which the dog has been bred must enter into the consideration. A young dog may not have had the opportunity to prove his prowess in the stud. He may have been bred to few bitches and those few of indifferent merits, or his get may not be old enough as yet to hit the shows and establish a record for themselves or for their sire. Allowance may be made for such a dog.

On the other hand, a dog may have proved himself to be phenomenal in the show ring, or may have been made to seem phenomenal by means of the owner's ballyhoo and exploitation. Half of the top bitches in the entire country may have been bred to him upon the strength of his winning record. Merely from the laws of probability such a dog, if he is not too bad, will produce some creditable progeny. It is necessary to take into consideration the opportunities a dog has had in relation to the fine progeny he has produced.

That, however, is the chief criterion by which a good stud dog may be recognized. A dog which can sire two or three excellent puppies in every litter from a reasonably good bitch may be considered as an acceptable stud. If he has in his lifetime sired one or two champions each year, and especially if one or two of the lot are superlative champions, top members of their breed, he is a great stud dog. Ordinarily and without other considerations, such a dog is to be preferred to one of his unproved sons, even though the son be as good or better an individual. In this way one employs genes one knows to produce what one wants. The son may be only hybrid dominant for his excellent qualities.

In the choice of a stud dog no attention whatever need be paid to claims that he sires numerically big litters. Unless the sire is deficient in sperm, the number of puppies in the litter, provided there are any puppies at all, depends entirely upon the bitch. At one service, a dog deposits enough spermatozoa to produce a million puppies, if there were so many ova to be fertilized. In any event, the major purpose should be to obtain good puppies, not large numbers of them.

There are three methods of breeding employed by experienced breeders—outcrossing, inbreeding, and line breeding. By outcrossing is meant the breeding together of mates of which no blood relationship can be traced. It is much favored by novice breeders, who feel that the breeding together of blood relatives is likely to result in imbecility, constitutional weakness, or some other kind of degeneration. Inbreeding is the mating together of closely related animals—father to daughter, mother to son, brother to sister, half brother to half sister. Some of the best animals ever produced have been bred from some such incestuous mating, and the danger from such practices, if they are carried out by persons who know what they are about, is minimal. Line breeding is the mating together of animals related one to another, but less closely—such as first cousins, grandsire to granddaughter, granddam to grandson, uncle to niece, or aunt to nephew.

Absolute outcrossing is usually impossible, since all the good dogs in any breed are more or less related—descended from some common ancestor in the fifth or sixth or seventh generation of their pedigrees. In any event, it is seldom to be recommended, since the results from it in the first generation of progeny are usually not satisfactory. It may be undertaken by some far-sighted and experienced breeder for the purpose of bringing into his strain some particular merit lacking in it and present in the strain of the unrelated dog. While dogs so bred may obtain an added vigor from what is known in genetics as *heterosis,* they are likely to manifest a coarseness and a lack of uniformity in the litter which is not to be found in more closely bred puppies. Good breeders never outcross if it is possible to obtain the virtues they want by sticking to their own strain. And when they do outcross, it is for the purpose of utilizing the outcrossed product for further breeding. It is not an end in itself.

Inbreeding (or incest breeding, as it is sometimes called) involves no such hazards as are and in the past have been attributed to it. It produces some very excellent dogs when correctly employed, some very bad ones even when correctly employed, and all bad ones when carelessly used. All the standard breeds of dogs were established as uniform breeds through intense inbreeding and culling over many generations. Inbreeding brings into manifestation undesirable recessive genes, the bearers of which can be discarded and the strain can thus be purged of its bad recessives.

Dogs of great soundness and excellence, from excellent parents and grandparents, all of them much alike, may be safely mated together, no matter how closely they may be related, with reasonable hope that most of the progeny will be sound and typical with a close resemblance to all the members of their ancestry. However, two such superlative and well-bred dogs are seldom to be found. It is the way to make progress rapidly and to establish a strain of dogs much alike and which breeds true. The amateur with the boldness and courage to try such a mating in the belief that his dogs are good enough for it is not to be discouraged. But if his judgment is not justified by the results, let him not complain that he has not been warned.

Line breeding is the safest course between the Scylla of outcrossing and the Charybdis of inbreeding for the inexperienced navigator in the sea of breeding. It, too, is to be used with care, because when it succeeds it partakes much of the nature of inbreeding. At any rate, its purpose is the pairing of like genes.

Here the pedigrees come into use. We examine the pedigree of the bitch to be bred. We hope that all the dogs named in it are magnificent dogs, but we look them over and choose the best of the four grandparents. We check this grandparent's breeding and find it good, as it probably is if it is itself a dog or bitch of great excellence. We shall assume that this best dog in the bitch's pedigree is the maternal grandsire. Then our bitch may be bred back to this particular grandsire, to his full brother if he has one of equal excellence, to his best son or best grandson. In such a fashion we compound the genes of this grandsire, and hope to obtain some puppies with his excellences intensified.

The best name in the pedigree may be some other dog or bitch, in which case it is his or her germ plasm that is to be doubled to serve for the foundation of the pedigrees of the puppies of the projected litter.

In making a mating, it is never wise to employ two dogs with the same positive fault. It is wise to use two dogs with as many of the same positive virtues as it is possible to obtain. Neither should faults balance each other, as one with a front too wide, the other with a front too narrow; one with a sway back, the other roach backed. Rather, one member of the mating should be right where the other is wrong. We cannot trust to obtain the intermediate, if we overcompensate the fault of one mate with a fault of the other.

NEGOTIATIONS TO USE THE STUD DOG

Plans to use a stud dog should be laid far enough in advance to enable one to make sure that the services of the dog will be available when they are required. Most men with a dog at public stud publish "stud cards," on which are printed the dog's pedigree and pertinent data pertaining to its record. These should be requested for all the dogs one contemplates using. Most such owners reserve the right to refuse to breed their dogs to bitches they deem unsuitable for them; they wish to safeguard their dog's reputation as a producer of superior puppies, by choosing the bitches to which he shall be bred. Therefore, it is advisable to submit a description of the bitch, with or without a picture of her, and her pedigree to the stud dog's owner at the time the application to use him is made.

Notification should be sent to the owner of the dog as soon as the bitch begins to show in heat, and she should be taken or sent by air or by railway express to the dog's owner about the time she is first recognized to be in full heat and ready to breed. The stud dog's owner should be advised by telegram or telephone just how she has been sent and just when she may be expected, and instruction should be given about how she is to be returned.

Extreme care should be used in securely crating a bitch for shipment when she is in heat. Such bitches are prone to chew their way out of insecure boxes and escape to be bred by some vagrant mongrel. A card containing a statement of the bitch's condition should be attached to the crate as a warning to the carrier to assure her greater security.

MATING

The only time the bitch may become pregnant is during her period of oestruation, a time also variously referred to as the "oestrus," "the season," and as being in "heat." A bitch's first season usually occurs when she is between six and nine months of age, with the average age being eight months. In rare instances it may occur as early as five months or as late as thirteen months of age. After the first season, oestrus usually recurs at intervals of approximately six months, though this too is subject to variation. Also, the bitch's cycle may be influenced by factors such as a change of environment or a change of climate, and her cycle will, of course, be changed if it is interrupted by pregnancy. Most bitches again come in season four to six months after whelping.

There is a decided controversy among breeders as to the wisdom of breeding a bitch during her first season. Some believe a really fine bitch should be bred during her first season in order that she may produce as many puppies as possible during the fertile years of her life span. Others feel that definite physical harm results from breeding a bitch at her first season. Since a normal healthy bitch can safely produce puppies until she is about nine years old, she can comfortably yield eight to ten litters with rests between them in her life. Any breeder should be satisfied with this production from one animal. It seems wiser, therefore, to avoid the risk of any harm and pass her first season. Bitches vary in temperament and in the ages at which they reach sufficient maturity for motherhood and its responsibilities. As with the human animal, stability comes with age and a dam is much more likely to be a good mother if she is out of the puppy phase herself. If the bitch is of show quality, she might become a champion between her first and second heats if not bred.

Usually, oestruation continues for a period of approximately three weeks, but this too is subject to variation. Prior to the beginning of the oestrus, there may be changes in the bitch's actions and demeanor; she may appear restless, or she may become increasingly affectionate. Often there is increased frequency of urination and the bitch may be inclined to lick her external parts. The breeder should be alert for any signs of the approach of oestrus since the bitch must be confined and protected at this time in order to preclude the

57

possibility of the occurrence of a mating with any but the selected stud.

The first physical sign of oestrus is a bloody discharge of watery consistency. The mucous membrane lining the vulva becomes congested, enlarged, and reddened, and the external parts become puffy and swollen. The color of the discharge gradually deepens during the first day or two until it is a rich red color; then it gradually becomes lighter until by the tenth to twelfth day it has only a slightly reddish, or straw-colored, tinge. During the next day or so it becomes almost clear. During this same period, the swelling and hardness of the external parts gradually subside, and by the time the discharge has lost most of its color, the parts are softened and spongy. It is at this time that ovulation, the production of ripened ova (or eggs), takes place, although physical manifestations of oestrus may continue for another week.

A normal bitch has two ovaries which contain her ova. All the eggs she will produce during her lifetime are present in the ovaries at birth. Ordinarily, some of the ova ripen each time the bitch comes in season. Should a bitch fail to ovulate (produce ripened ova), she cannot, of course, become pregnant. Actually, only one ovary is necessary for ovulation, and loss of or damage to one ovary without impairment of the other will not prevent the bitch from producing puppies.

If fertilization does not occur, the ova (and this is also true of the sperm of the male) live only a short time—probably a couple of days at the most. Therefore, if mating takes place too long before or after ovulation, a bitch will not conceive, and the unfertilized ova will pass through the uterus into the vagina. Eventually they will either be absorbed or will pass out through the vulva by the same opening through which urination takes place. If fertilization does occur, the fertilized eggs become implanted on the inner surface of the uterus and grow to maturity.

Obviously, the breeder must exercise great care in determining when the dog and the bitch should be put together. Because the length of time between the beginning of the oestrus and the time of ovulation varies in different bitches, no hard and fast rule can be established, although the twelfth to fourteenth day is in most cases the correct time. The wise breeder will keep a daily record of the changes in the bitch's condition and will arrange to put the bitch and dog together when the discharge has become almost clear and the external parts are softened and spongy. If the bitch refuses the advances of the dog, it is preferable to separate the two, wait a day, then again permit the dog to approach the bitch.

Ordinarily, if the bitch is willing to accept the dog, fertilization of the ovum will take place. Usually one good service is sufficient, although two at intervals of twenty-four to forty-eight hours are often allowed.

Male dogs have glands on the penis which swell after passing the sphincter muscle of the vagina and "tie" the two animals together. The time may last for a period of a few minutes, a half hour, or occasionally up to an hour or more, but will end naturally when the locking glands have deflated the needful amount. While tying may increase the probability of success, in many cases no tie occurs, yet the bitches become pregnant.

Sperm are produced in the dog's testicles and are stored in the epididymis, a twisting tube at the side of the testicle. The occasional male dog whose testicles are not descended (a cryptorchid) is generally conceded to be sterile, although in a few instances it has been asserted that cryptorchids were capable of begetting progeny. The sterility in cryptorchids is believed to be due to the fact that the sperm are destroyed if the testicle remains within the abdominal cavity because the temperature is much higher there than in the normally descended testicle. Thus all sperm produced by the dog may be destroyed if both testicles are undescended. A monorchid (a dog with one testicle descended, the other undescended) may be fertile. Nevertheless, it is unwise to use a monorchid for stud purposes, because monorchidism is believed to be a heritable trait, and the monorchid, as well as the cryptorchid, is ineligible for the show ring.

After breeding, a bitch should be confined for a week to ten days to avoid mismating with another dog.

WHELPING CALENDAR

Find the month and date on which your bitch was bred in one of the left-hand columns. Directly opposite that date, in the right-hand column, is her expected date of whelping, bearing in mind that 61 days is as common as 63.

Bred Jan	Due Mar	Bred Feb	Due Apr	Bred Mar	Due May	Bred Apr	Due Jun	Bred May	Due Jul	Bred Jun	Due Aug	Bred Jul	Due Sep	Bred Aug	Due Oct	Bred Sep	Due Nov	Bred Oct	Due Dec	Bred Nov	Due Jan	Bred Dec	Due Feb
1	5	1	5	1	3	1	3	1	3	1	3	1	2	1	3	1	3	1	3	1	3	1	2
2	6	2	6	2	4	2	4	2	4	2	4	2	3	2	4	2	4	2	4	2	4	2	3
3	7	3	7	3	5	3	5	3	5	3	5	3	4	3	5	3	5	3	5	3	5	3	4
4	8	4	8	4	6	4	6	4	6	4	6	4	5	4	6	4	6	4	6	4	6	4	5
5	9	5	9	5	7	5	7	5	7	5	7	5	6	5	7	5	7	5	7	5	7	5	6
6	10	6	10	6	8	6	8	6	8	6	8	6	7	6	8	6	8	6	8	6	8	6	7
7	11	7	11	7	9	7	9	7	9	7	9	7	8	7	9	7	9	7	9	7	9	7	8
8	12	8	12	8	10	8	10	8	10	8	10	8	9	8	10	8	10	8	10	8	10	8	9
9	13	9	13	9	11	9	11	9	11	9	11	9	10	9	11	9	11	9	11	9	11	9	10
10	14	10	14	10	12	10	12	10	12	10	12	10	11	10	12	10	12	10	12	10	12	10	11
11	15	11	15	11	13	11	13	11	13	11	13	11	12	11	13	11	13	11	13	11	13	11	12
12	16	12	16	12	14	12	14	12	14	12	14	12	13	12	14	12	14	12	14	12	14	12	13
13	17	13	17	13	15	13	15	13	15	13	15	13	14	13	15	13	15	13	15	13	15	13	14
14	18	14	18	14	16	14	16	14	16	14	16	14	15	14	16	14	16	14	16	14	16	14	15
15	19	15	19	15	17	15	17	15	17	15	17	15	16	15	17	15	17	15	17	15	17	15	16
16	20	16	20	16	18	16	18	16	18	16	18	16	17	16	18	16	18	16	18	16	18	16	17
17	21	17	21	17	19	17	19	17	19	17	19	17	18	17	19	17	19	17	19	17	19	17	18
18	22	18	22	18	20	18	20	18	20	18	20	18	19	18	20	18	20	18	20	18	20	18	19
19	23	19	23	19	21	19	21	19	21	19	21	19	20	19	21	19	21	19	21	19	21	19	20
20	24	20	24	20	22	20	22	20	22	20	22	20	21	20	22	20	22	20	22	20	22	20	21
21	25	21	25	21	23	21	23	21	23	21	23	21	22	21	23	21	23	21	23	21	23	21	22
22	26	22	26	22	24	22	24	22	24	22	24	22	23	22	24	22	24	22	24	22	24	22	23
23	27	23	27	23	25	23	25	23	25	23	25	23	24	23	25	23	25	23	25	23	25	23	24
24	28	24	28	24	26	24	26	24	26	24	26	24	25	24	26	24	26	24	26	24	26	24	25
25	29	25	29	25	27	25	27	25	27	25	27	25	26	25	27	25	27	25	27	25	27	25	26
26	30	26	30	26	28	26	28	26	28	26	28	26	27	26	28	26	28	26	28	26	28	26	27
27	31	27	1 (May)	27	29	27	29	27	29	27	29	27	28	27	29	27	29	27	29	27	29	27	28
28	1 (Apr.)	28	2	28	30	28	30	28	30	28	30	28	29	28	30	28	30	28	30	28	30	28	1 (Mar.)
29	2			29	31	29	1 (July)	29	31	29	31	29	30	29	31	29	1 (Dec.)	29	31	29	31	29	2
30	3			30	1 (June)	30	2	30	1 (Aug.)	30	1 (Sep.)	30	1 (Oct.)	30	1 (Nov.)	30	2	30	1 (Jan.)	30	1 (Feb.)	30	3
31	4			31	2			31	2			31	2	31	2			31	2			31	4

THE PREGNANCY AND WHELPING
OF THE BITCH

The "period of gestation" of the bitch, by which is meant the duration of her pregnancy, is usually estimated at sixty-three days. Many bitches, especially young ones, have their puppies as early as sixty days after they are bred. Cases have occurred in which strong puppies were born after only fifty-seven days, and there have been cases that required as many as sixty-six days. However, if puppies do not arrive by the sixty-fourth day, it is time to consult a veterinarian.

For the first five to six weeks of her pregnancy, the bitch requires no more than normal good care and unrestricted exercise. For that period, she needs no additional quantity of food, although her diet must contain sufficient amounts of all the food factors, as is stated in the division of this book that pertains to food. After the fifth to sixth week, the ration must be increased and the violence of exercise restricted. Normal running and walking are likely to be better for the pregnant bitch than a sedentary existence but she should not be permitted to jump, hunt, or fight during the latter half of her gestation. Violent activity may cause her to abort her puppies.

About a week before she is due to whelp, a bed should be prepared for her and she be persuaded to use it for sleeping. This bed may be a box of generous size, big enough to accommodate her with room for activity. It should be high enough to permit her to stand upright, and is better for having a hinged cover. An opening in one side will afford her ingress and egress. This box should be placed in a secluded location, away from any possible molestation by other dogs, animals, or children. The bitch must be made confident of her security in her box.

A few hours, or perhaps a day or two, before her whelping, the bitch will probably begin arranging the bedding of the box to suit herself, tearing blankets or cushions and nosing the parts into the corners. Before the whelping actually starts, however, it is best to substitute burlap sacking, securely tacked to the floor of the box. This is to provide traction for the puppies to reach the dam's breast.

The whelping may take place at night without any assistance from the owner. The box may be opened in the morning to reveal

61

the happy bitch nursing a litter of complacent puppies. But she may need some assistance in her parturition. If whelping is recognized to be in process, it is best to help the bitch.

As the puppies arrive, one by one, the enveloping membranes should be removed as quickly as possible, lest the puppies suffocate. Having removed the membrane, the umbilical cord should be severed with clean scissors some three or four inches from the puppy's belly. (The part of the cord attached to the belly will dry up and drop off in a few days.) There is no need for any medicament or dressing of the cord after it is cut.

The bitch should be permitted to eat the afterbirth if she so desires, and she normally does. If she has no assistance, she will probably remove the membrane and sever the cord with her teeth. The only dangers are that she may delay too long or may bite the cord too short. Some bitches, few of them, eat their newborn puppies (especially bitches not adequately fed during pregnancy). This unlikelihood should be guarded against.

As they arrive, it is wise to remove all the puppies except one, placing them in a box or basket lined and covered by a woolen cloth, somewhere aside or away from the whelping bed, until all have come and the bitch's activity has ceased. The purpose of this is to prevent her from walking or lying on the whelps, and to keep her from being disturbed by the puppies' whining. A single puppy should be left with the bitch to ease her anxiety.

It is best that the "midwife" be somebody with whom the bitch is on intimate terms and in whom she has confidence. Some bitches exhibit a jealous fear and even viciousness while they are whelping. Such animals are few, and most appear grateful for gentle assistance through their ordeal.

The puppies arrive at intervals of a few minutes to an hour until all are delivered. It is wise to call a veterinarian if the interval is greater than one hour. Though such service is seldom needed, an experienced veterinarian can usually be depended upon to withdraw with obstetrical forceps an abnormally presented puppy. It is possible, but unlikely, that the veterinarian will recommend a Caesarian section. This surgery in the dog is not very grave, but it should be performed only by an expert veterinarian. It is unnecessary to describe the process here, or the subsequent management of the patient, since, if a Caesarian section should be necessary, the veterinarian will provide all the needed instructions.

Some bitches, at or immediately after their whelping period, go into a convulsive paralysis, which is called *eclampsia*. This is unlikely if the bitch throughout her pregnancy has had an adequate measure of calcium in her rations. The remedy for eclampsia is the intravenous or intramuscular administration of parenteral calcium. The bitch suspected of having eclampsia should be attended by a veterinarian.

Assuming that the whelping has been normal and without untoward incident, all of the puppies are returned to the bitch, and put, one by one, to the breast, which strong puppies will accept with alacrity. The less handling of puppies for the first four or five hours of their lives, the better. However, the litter should be looked over carefully for possible defectives and discards, which should be destroyed as soon as possible. There is no virtue in rearing hare-lipped, crippled, or mismarked puppies.

It is usually unwise to destroy sound, healthy puppies just to reduce the number in the litter, since it is impossible to sort young puppies for excellence and one may be destroying the best member of the litter, a future champion. Unless a litter is extraordinarily numerous, the dam, if well fed, can probably suckle them all. If it is found that her milk is insufficient, the litter may be artificially fed or may be divided, and the surplus placed on a foster mother if it is possible to obtain one. The foster mother need not be of the same breed as the puppies, a mongrel being as good as any. She should be approximately the same size as the actual mother of the puppies, clean, healthy, and her other puppies should be of as nearly the same age as the ones she is to take over as possible. She should be removed from her own puppies (which may well be destroyed) and her breasts be permitted to fill with milk until she is somewhat uncomfortable, at which time her foster puppies can be put to her breasts and will usually be accepted without difficulty. Unless the services of the foster mother are really required, it is better not to use her.

The whelping bitch may be grateful for a warm meal even between the arrivals of her puppies. As soon as her chore is over, she should be offered food in her box. This should be of cereal and milk or of meat and broth, something sloppy. She will probably not leave her puppies to eat and her meals must be brought to her.

63

It is wise to give a mild laxative for her bowels, also milk of magnesia. She will be reluctant to get out of her box even to relieve herself for about two days, but she should be urged, even forced, to do so regularly. A sensible bitch will soon settle down to care for her brood and will seldom give further trouble. She should be fed often and well, all that she can be induced to eat during her entire lactation.

As a preventive for infections sometimes occurring after whelping, some experienced breeders and veterinarians recommend injecting the bitch with penicillin or another antibiotic immediately following the birth of the last puppy. Oral doses of the same drug may be given daily thereafter for the first week. It is best to consult your veterinarian about this treatment.

ACID MILK

Occasionally a bitch produces early milk (colostrum) so acid that it disagrees with, sometimes kills, her puppies. The symptoms of the puppies are whining, disquiet, frequently refusal to nurse, frailty, and death. It is true that all milk is slightly acid, and it should be, turning blue litmus paper immersed in it a very light pink. However, milk harmfully on the acid side will readily turn litmus paper a vivid red. It seems that only the first two or three days milk is so affected. Milk problems come also from mastitis and other infections in the bitch.

This is not likely to occur with a bitch that throughout her pregnancy has received an adequate supply of calcium phosphate regularly in her daily ration. That is the best way to deal with the situation—to see to the bitch's correct nutrition in advance of her whelping. The owner has only himself to blame for the bitch's too acid milk, since adequate calcium in advance would have neutralized the acid.

If it is found too late that her milk is too acid, the puppies must be taken from her breast and either given to a foster mother or artificially fed from bottle or by medicine dropper. Artificial feeding of very young puppies seldom is successful. Sometimes the acidity of the dam's milk can be neutralized by giving her large doses of bicarbonate of soda (baking soda), but the puppies should not be restored to her breasts until her milk ceases to turn litmus paper red.

If it is necessary to feed the puppies artificially, "Esbilac," a commercial product, or the following orphan puppy formula, may be used.

7 oz. whole milk

1 oz. cream (top milk)

1 egg yolk

2 tbsp. corn syrup

2 tbsp. lime water

REARING THE PUPPIES

Puppies are born blind and open their eyes at approximately the ninth day thereafter. If they were whelped earlier than the full sixty-three days after the breeding from which they resulted, the difference should be added to the nine days of anticipated blindness. The early eye color of young puppies is no criterion of the color to which the eyes are likely to change, and the breeder's anxiety about his puppies' having light eyes is premature.

In breeds that require the docking of the tail, this should be done on the third day and is a surgical job for the veterinarian. Many a dog has had his tail cut off by an inexperienced person, ruining his good looks and his possibility for a win in the show ring. Dew claws should be removed at the same time. There is little else to do with normal puppies except to let them alone and permit them to grow. The most important thing about their management is their nutrition, which is discussed in another chapter. The first two or three weeks, they will thrive and grow rapidly on their mother's milk, after which they should have additional food as described.

Puppies sleep much of the time, as do other babies, and they should not be frequently awakened to be played with. They grow more and more playful as they mature.

After the second week their nails begin to grow long and sharp. The mother will be grateful if the puppies' nails are blunted with scissors from time to time so that in their pawing of the breast they do not lacerate it. Sharp nails tend to prompt the mother to wean the whelps early, and she should be encouraged to keep them with her as long as she will tolerate them. Even the small amount of milk they can drain from her after the weaning process is begun is the best food they can obtain. It supplements and makes digestible the remainder of their ration.

Many bitches, after their puppies are about four weeks of age, eat and regurgitate food, which is eaten by the puppies. This food is warmed and partly digested in the bitch's stomach. This practice, while it may appear digusting to the novice keeper of dogs, is perfectly normal and should not be discouraged. However, it renders it all the more necessary that the food of the bitch be sound, clean, and nutritious.

It is all but impossible to rear a litter of puppies without their becoming infested with roundworms. Of course, the bitch should be wormed, if she harbors such parasites, before she is bred, and her teats should be thoroughly washed with mild soap just before she whelps to free them from the eggs of roundworms. Every precaution must be taken to reduce the infestation of the puppies to a minimum. But, in spite of all it is possible to do, puppies will have roundworms. These pests hamper growth, reduce the puppies' normal resistance to disease, and may kill them outright unless the worms are eliminated. The worming of puppies is discussed in the chapter entitled "Intestinal Parasites and Their Control."

External Vermin
and Parasites

UNDER this heading the most common external parasites will be given consideration. Fleas, lice, ticks, and flies are those most commonly encountered and causing the most concern. The external parasite does not pose the problem that it used to before we had the new "miracle" insecticides. Today, with DDT, lindane, and chlordane, the course of extermination and prevention is much easier to follow. Many of the insecticide sprays have a four to six weeks residual effect. Thus the premises can be sprayed and the insect pests can be quite readily controlled.

FLEAS

Neglected dogs are too often beset by hundreds of blood-thirsty fleas, which do not always confine their attacks to the dogs but also sometimes feast upon their masters. Unchecked, they overrun kennels, homes, and playgrounds. Moreover, they are the intermediate hosts for the development of the kind of tapeworm most frequently found in dogs, as will be more fully discussed under the subject of *Intestinal Parasites*. Fleas are all-round bad actors and nuisances. Although it need hardly concern us in America, where the disease is not known to exist, fleas are the recognized and only vectors of bubonic plague.

67

There are numerous kinds and varieties of fleas, of which we shall discuss here only the three species often found on dogs. These are the human flea (*Pulex irritans*), the dog flea (*Ctenocephalides canis*), and the so-called chicken flea or sticktight flea (*Echidnophaga gallinacea*).

Of these the human flea prefers the blood of man to that of the dog, and unless humans are also bothered, are not likely to be found on the dog. They are small, nearly black insects, and occur mostly in the Mississippi Valley and in California. Their control is the same as for the dog flea.

The dog flea is much larger than his human counterpart, is dark brown in color and seldom bites mankind. On an infested dog these dog fleas may be found buried in the coat of any part of the anatomy, but their choicest habitat is the area of the back just forward from the tail and over the loins. On that part of a badly neglected dog, especially in summer, fleas by the hundreds will be found intermixed with their dung and with dried blood. They may cause the dog some discomfort or none. It must not be credited that because a dog is not kept in a constant or frequent agitation of scratching that he harbors no fleas. The coats of pet animals are soiled and roughened by the fleas and torn by the scratching that they sometimes induce. Fleas also appear to be connected with summer eczema of dogs; at least the diseased condition of the skin often clears up after fleas are eradicated.

Although the adults seldom remain long away from the dog's body, fleas do not reproduce themselves on the dog. Rather, their breeding haunts are the debris, dust, and sand of the kennel floor, and especially the accumulations of dropped hair, sand, and loose soil of unclean sleeping boxes. Nooks and cracks and crannies of the kennel may harbor the eggs or maggot-like larvae of immature fleas.

This debris and accumulation must be eliminated—preferably by incineration—after which all possible breeding areas should be thoroughly sprayed with a residual effect spray.

The adult dog may be combed well, then bathed in a detergent solution, rinsed thoroughly in warm water, and allowed to drip fairly dry. A solution of Pine Oil (1 oz. to a quart of water) is then used as a final rinse. This method of ridding the dog of its fleas is ideal in warm weather. The Pine Oil imparts a pleasant odor to the dog's coat and the animal will enjoy being bathed and groomed.

The same procedure may be followed for young puppies except that the Pine Oil solution should be rinsed off. When bathing is not feasible, then a good flea powder—one containing lindane—should be used.

Sticktight fleas are minute, but are to be found, if at all, in patches on the dog's head and especially on the ears. They remain quiescent and do not jump, as the dog fleas and human fleas do. Their tiny heads are buried in the dog's flesh. To force them loose from the area decapitates them and the heads remain in the skin which is prone to fester from the irritation. They may be dislodged by placing a cotton pad or thick cloth well soaked in ether or alcohol over the flea patch, which causes them immediately to relinquish their hold, after which they can be easily combed loose and destroyed.

These sticktights abound in neglected, dirty, and abandoned chicken houses, which, if the dogs have access to them, should be cleaned out thoroughly and sprayed with DDT.

Fleas, while a nuisance, are only a minor problem. They should be eliminated not only from the dog but from all the premises he inhabits. Dogs frequently are reinfested with fleas from other dogs with which they play or come in contact. Every dog should be occasionally inspected for the presence of fleas, and, if any are found, immediate means should be taken to eradicate them.

LICE

There are even more kinds of lice than of fleas, although as they pertain to dogs there is no reason to differentiate them. They do not infest dogs, except in the events of gross neglect or of unforeseen accident. Lice reproduce themselves on the body of the dog. To rid him of the adult lice is easy. The standard Pine Oil solution used to kill fleas will also kill lice. However, the eggs or "nits" are harder to remove. Weather permitting, it is sometimes best to have the dog clipped of all its hair. In heavily infested dogs this is the only sure way to cope with the situation. When the hair is clipped, most of the "nits" are removed automatically. A good commercial flea and louse powder applied to the skin will then keep the situation under control.

Rare as the occurrence of lice upon dogs may be, they must be promptly treated and eradicated. Having a dog with lice can prove to be embarrassing, for people just do not like to be around anything lousy. Furthermore, the louse may serve as the intermediate host of the tapeworm in dogs.

The dog's quarters should be thoroughly sprayed with a residual spray of the same type recommended for use in the control of fleas. The problem of disinfecting kennel and quarters is not as great as it is in the case of fleas, for the louse tends to stay on its host, not leaving the dog as the flea does.

TICKS

The terms "wood ticks" and "dog ticks," as usually employed, refer to at least eight different species, whose appearances and habits are so similar that none but entomologists are likely to know them apart. It is useless to attempt to differentiate between these various species here, except to warn the reader that the Rocky Mountain spotted fever tick (*Dermacentor andersoni*) is a vector of the human disease for which it is named, as well as of rabbit fever (tularemia), and care must be employed in removing it from dogs lest the hands be infected. Some one or more of these numerous species are to be found in well nigh every state in the Union, although there exist wide areas where wood ticks are seldom seen and are not a menace to dogs.

All the ticks must feed on blood in order to reproduce themselves. The eggs are always deposited on the ground or elsewhere after the female, engorged with blood, has dropped from the dog or other animal upon which she has fed. The eggs are laid in masses in protected places on the ground, particularly in thick clumps of grass. Each female lays only one such mass, which contains 2500 to 5000 eggs. The development of the American dog tick embraces four stages: the egg, the larva or seed tick, the nymph, and the adult. The two intermediate stages in the growth of the tick are spent on rodents, and only in the adult stage does it attach itself to the dog. Both sexes affix themselves to dogs and to other animals and feed on their blood; the males do not increase in size, although the female is tremendously enlarged as she gorges. Mating occurs while the female is feeding. After some five to thirteen days, she drops

70

from her host, lays her eggs and dies. At no time do ticks feed on anything except the blood of animals.

The longevity and hardihood of the tick are amazing. The larvae and nymphs may live for a full year without feeding, and the adults survive for more than two years if they fail to encounter a host to which they may attach. In the Northern United States the adults are most active in the spring and summer, few being found after July. But in the warmer Southern states they may be active the year around.

Although most of the tick species require a vegetative cover and wild animal hosts to complete their development, at least one species, the brown tick (*Rhipicephalus sanguinius*), is adapted to life in the dryer environment of kennels, sheds, and houses, with the dog as its only necessary host. This tick is the vector of canine piroplasmosis, although this disease is at this time almot negligible in the United States.

This brown dog tick often infests houses in large numbers, both immature and adult ticks lurking around baseboards, window casings, furniture, the folds of curtains, and elsewhere. Thus, even dogs kept in houses are sometimes infested with hundreds of larvae, nymphs, and adults of this tick. Because of its ability to live in heated buildings, the species has become established in many Northern areas. Unlike the other tick species, the adult of the brown dog tick does not bite human beings. However, also unlike the other ticks, it is necessary not only to rid the dogs of this particular tick but also to eliminate the pests from their habitat, especially the dogs' beds and sleeping boxes. A spray with a 10% solution of DDT suffices for this purpose. Fumigation of premises seldom suffices, since not only are brown dog ticks very resistant to mere fumigation, but the ticks are prone to lurk around entry ways, porches and outbuildings, where they cannot be reached with a fumigant. The spraying with DDT may not penetrate to spots where some ticks are in hiding, and it must be repeated at intervals until all the pests are believed to be completely eradicated.

Dogs should not be permitted to run in brushy areas known to be infested with ticks, and upon their return from exercise in a place believed to harbor ticks, dogs should be carefully inspected for their presence.

If a dog's infestation is light, the ticks may be picked individually

71

from his skin. To make tick release its grip, dab with alcohol or a drop of ammonia. If the infestation is heavy, it is easier and quicker to saturate his coat with a derris solution (one ounce of soap and two ounces of derris powder dissolved in one gallon of water). The derris should be of an excellent grade containing at least 3% of rotenone. The mixture may be used and reused, since it retains its strength for about three weeks if it is kept in a dark place.

If possible, the dip should be permitted to dry on the dog's coat. It should not get into a dog's eyes. The dip will not only kill the ticks that are attached to the dog, but the powder drying in the hair will repel further infestation for two or three days and kill most if not all the boarders. These materials act slowly, requiring sometimes as much as twenty-four hours to complete the kill.

If the weather is cold or the use of the dip should be otherwise inconvenient, derris powder may be applied as a dust, care being taken that it penetrates the hair and reaches the skin. Breathing or swallowing derris may cause a dog to vomit, but he will not be harmed by it. The dust and liquid should be kept from his eyes.

Since the dog is the principal host on which the adult tick feeds and since each female lays several thousand eggs after feeding, treating the dog regularly will not only bring him immediate relief but will limit the reproduction of the ticks. Keeping underbrush, weeds, and grass closely cut tends to remove protection favorable to the ticks. Burning vegetation accomplishes the same results.

Many of the ticks in an infested area may be killed by the thorough application of a spray made as follows: Four tablespoonfuls of nicotine sulphate (40% nicotine) in three gallons of water. More permanent results may be obtained by adding to this solution four ounces of sodium fluorides, but this will injure the vegetation.

Besides the ticks that attach themselves to all parts of the dog, there is another species that infests the ear specifically. This pest, the spinose ear tick, penetrates deep into the convolutions of the ear and often causes irritation and pain, as evidenced by the dog's scratching its ears, shaking its head or holding it on one side. One part derris powder (5% rotenone) mixed with ten parts medicinal mineral oil and dropped into the ear will kill spinose ear ticks. Only a few drops of the material is required, but it is best to massage the base of the ear to make sure the remedy penetrates to the deepest part of the ear to reach all the ticks.

72

FLIES

Flies can play havoc with dogs in outdoor kennels, stinging them and biting the ears until they are raw. Until recently the only protection against them was the screening of the entire kennel. The breeding places of flies, which are damp filth and stagnant garbage, are in most areas now happily abated, but the chief agent for control of the pest is DDT.

A spray of a 10% solution of DDT over all surfaces of the kennel property may be trusted to destroy all the flies that light on those surfaces for from two weeks to one month. It must, of course, be repeated from time to time when it is seen that the efficacy of the former treatment begins to diminish.

Intestinal Parasites and Their Control

THE varieties of worms that may inhabit the alimentary tract of the dog are numerous. Much misapprehension exists, even among experienced dog keepers, about the harm these parasites may cause and about the methods of getting rid of them. Some dog keepers live in terror of these worms and continually treat their dogs for them whether they are known to be present or not; others ignore the presence of worms and do nothing about them. Neither policy is justified.

Promiscuous dosing, without the certainty that the dog harbors worms or what kind he may have, is a practice fraught with danger for the well-being of the animal. All drugs for the expulsion or destruction of parasites are poisonous or irritant to a certain degree and should be administered only when it is known that the dog is infested by parasites and what kind. It is hardly necessary to say that when a dog is known to harbor worms he should be cleared of them, but in most instances there is no such urgency as is sometimes manifested.

It may be assumed that puppies at weaning time are more or less infested with intestinal roundworms or ascarids (*Toxocara canis*) and that such puppies need to be treated for worms. It is all but impossible to rear a litter of puppies to weaning age free from those parasites. Once the puppies are purged of them, it is amazing to see the spurt of their growth and the renewal of their thriftiness.

74

Many neglected puppies surmount the handicap of their worms and at least some of them survive. This, however, is no reason that good puppies—puppies that are worth saving—should go unwormed and neglected.

The ways to find out that a dog actually has worms are to see some of the worms themselves in the dog's droppings or to submit a sample of his feces to a veterinarian or to a biological laboratory for microscopic examination. From a report of such an examination, it is possible to know whether or not a dog is a host to intestinal parasites at all and intelligently to undertake the treatment and control of the specific kind he may harbor.

All of the vermifuges, vermicides, and anthelmintic remedies tend to expel other worms besides the kind for which they are specifically intended, but it is better to employ the remedy particularly effective against the individual kind of parasite the dog is known to have, and to refrain from worm treatment unless or until it is known to be needed.

ROUNDWORMS

The ascarids, or large intestinal roundworms, are the largest of the worm parasites occurring in the digestive tract of the dog, varying in length from 1 to 8 inches, the females being larger than the males. The name "spool worms," which is sometimes applied to them, is derived from their tendency to coil in a springlike spiral when they are expelled, either from the bowel or vomited, by their hosts. There are at least two species of them which frequently parasitize dogs: *Toxocara canis* and *Toxascaris leonina,* but they are so much alike except for some minor details in the life histories of their development that it is not practically necessary for the dog keeper to seek to distinguish between them.

Neither specie requires an intermediate host for its development. Numerous eggs are deposited in the intestinal tract of the host animal; these eggs are passed out by the dog in his feces and are swallowed by the same or another animal, and hatching takes place in its small intestine. Their development requires from twelve to sixteen days under favorable circumstances.

It has been shown that puppies before their birth may be infested by roundworms from their mother. This accounts for the occasional finding of mature or nearly mature worms in very young puppies. It cannot occur if the mother is entirely free from worms, as she should be.

These roundworms are particularly injurious to young puppies. The commonest symptoms of roundworm infestation are general unthriftiness, digestive disturbances, and bloat after feeding. The hair grows dead and lusterless, and the breath may have a peculiar sweetish odor. Large numbers of roundworms may obstruct the intestine, and many have been known to penetrate the intestinal wall. In heavy infestations the worms may wander into the bile ducts, stomach, and even into the lungs and upper respiratory passages where they may cause pneumonia, especially in very young animals.

The control of intestinal roundworms depends primarily upon prompt disposal of feces, keeping the animals in clean quarters and on clean ground, and using only clean utensils for feed and water. Dampness of the ground favors the survival of worm eggs and larvae. There is no known chemical treatment feasible for the destruction of eggs in contaminated soil, but prolonged exposure to sunlight and drying has proved effective.

Numerous remedies have been in successful use for roundworms, including turpentine, which has a recognized deleterious effect upon the kidneys; santonin, an old standby; freshly powdered betel nut and its derivative, arecoline, both of which tend to purge and sicken the patient; oil of chenopodium, made from American wormseed; carbon tetrachloride, widely used as a cleaning agent; tetrachlorethylene, closely related chemically to the former, but less toxic; and numerous other medicaments. While all of them are effective as vermifuges or vermicides, if rightly employed, to each of them some valid objection can be interposed.

In addition to the foregoing, there are other vermifuges available for treatment of roundworms. Some may be purchased without a prescription, whereas others may be procured only when prescribed by a veterinarian.

HOOKWORMS

Hookworms are the most destructive of all the parasites of dogs. There are three species of them—*Ancylostoma caninum, A. braziliense,* and *Uncinaria stenocephalia*—all to be found in dogs in some parts of the United States. The first named is the most widespread; the second found only in the warmer parts of the South and Southwest; the last named, in the North and in Canada. All are similar one to another and to the hookworm that infests mankind (*Ancylostoma uncinariasis*). For purposes of their eradication, no distinction need be made between them.

It is possible to keep dogs for many years in a dry and well drained area without an infestation with hookworms, which are contracted only on infested soils. However, unthrifty dogs shipped from infested areas are suspect until it is proved that hookworm is not the cause of their unthriftiness.

Hookworm males seldom are longer than half an inch, the females somewhat larger. The head end is curved upward, and is equipped with cutting implements, which may be called teeth, by which they attach themselves to the lining of the dog's intestine and suck his blood.

The females produce numerous eggs which pass out in the dog's feces. In two weeks or a little more these eggs hatch, the worms pass through various larval stages, and reach their infective stage. Infection of the dog may take place through his swallowing the organism, or by its penetration of his skin through some lesion. In the latter case the worms enter the circulation, reach the lungs, are coughed up, swallowed, and reach the intestine where their final development occurs. Eggs appear in the dog's feces from three to six weeks after infestation.

Puppies are sometimes born with hookworms already well developed in their intestines, the infection taking place before their birth. Eggs of the hookworm are sometimes found in the feces of puppies only thirteen days old. Assumption is not to be made that all puppies are born with hookworms or even that they are likely to become infested, but in hookworm areas the possibility of either justifies precautions that neither shall happen.

Hookworm infestation in puppies and young dogs brings about a condition often called kennel anemia. There may be digestive disturbances and blood streaked diarrhea. In severe cases the feces may be almost pure blood. Infested puppies fail to grow, often lose weight, and the eyes are sunken and dull. The loss of blood results in an anemia with pale mucous membranes of the mouth and eyes. This anemia is caused by the consumption of the dog's blood by the worms and the bleeding that follows the bites. The worms are not believed to secrete a poison or to cause damage to the dog except loss of blood.

There is an admitted risk in worming young puppies before weaning time, but it is risk that must be run if the puppies are known to harbor hookworms. The worms, if permitted to persist, will ruin the puppies and likely kill them. No such immediacy is needful for the treatment of older puppies and adult dogs, although hookworm infestation will grow steadily worse until it is curbed. It should not be delayed and neglected in the belief or hope that the dog can cure himself.

If treatment is attempted at home, there are available three fairly efficacious and safe drugs that may be used: normal butyl chloride, hexaresorcinal, and methyl benzine.

If a dog is visibly sick and a diagnosis of hookworm infestation has been made, treatment had best be under professional guidance.

Brine made by stirring common salt (sodium chloride) into boiling water, a pound and a half of salt to the gallon of water, will destroy hookworm infestation in the soil. A gallon of brine should be sufficient to treat eight square feet of soil surface. One treatment of the soil is sufficient unless it is reinfested.

TAPEWORMS

The numerous species of tapeworm which infest the dog may, for practical purposes, be divided into two general groups, the armed forms and the unarmed forms. Species of both groups resemble each other in their possession of a head and neck and a chain of segments. They are, however, different in their life histories, and the best manner to deal with each type varies. This is unfortunately not well understood, since to most persons a tapeworm is a tapeworm.

The armed varieties are again divided into the single pored forms of the genera *Taenia, Multiceps,* and *Echinococcus,* and the double pored tapeworm, of which the most widespread and prevalent among dogs in the United States is the so-called dog tapeworm, *Dipylidium caninum.* This is the variety with segments shaped like cucumber-seeds. The adult rarely exceeds a foot in length, and the head is armed with four or five tiny hooks. For the person with well cared for and protected dogs, this is the only tapeworm of which it is necessary to take particular cognizance.

The dog tapeworm requires but a single intermediate host for its development, which in most cases is the dog flea or the biting louse. Thus, by keeping dogs free from fleas and lice the major danger of tapeworm infestation is obviated.

The tapeworm is bi-sexual and requires the intermediate host in order to complete its life cycle. Segments containing the eggs of the tapeworm pass out with the stool, or the detached proglottid may emerge by its own motile power and attach itself to the contiguous hair. The flea then lays its eggs on this segment, thus affording sustenance for the larva. The head of the tapeworm develops in the lung chamber of the baby flea. Thus, such a flea, when it develops and finds its way back to a dog, is the potential carrier of tapeworm. Of course, the cycle is complete when the flea bites the dog and the dog, in biting the area to relieve the itching sensation, swallows the flea.

Since the egg of the tapeworm is secreted in the segment that breaks off and passes with the stool, microscopic examination of the feces is of no avail in attempting to determine whether tapeworms infest a dog. It is well to be suspicious of a finicky eater— a dog that refuses all but the choicest meat and shows very little

80

appetite. The injury produced by this armed tapeworm to the dog that harbors it is not well understood. Frequently it produces no symptoms at all, and it is likely that it is not the actual cause of many of the symptoms attributed to it. At least, it is known that a dog may have one or many of these worms over a long period of time and apparently be no worse for their presence. Nervous symptoms or skin eruptions, or both, are often charged to the presence of tapeworm, which may or may not be the cause of the morbid condition.

Tapeworm-infested dogs sometimes involuntarily pass segments of worms and so soil floors, rugs, furniture, or bedding. The passage by dogs of a segment or a chain of segments via the anus is a frequent cause of the dog's itching, which he seeks to allay by sitting and dragging himself on the floor by his haunches. The segments or chains are sometimes mistakenly called pinworms, but pinworms are a kind of roundworm to which dogs are not subject.

Despite that they may do no harm, few dogs owners care to tolerate tapeworms in their dogs. These worms, it has been definitely established, are not transmissible from dog to dog or to man. Without the flea or the louse, it is impossible for the adult dog tapeworm to reproduce itself, and by keeping dogs free from fleas and lice it is possible to keep them also free from dog tapeworm.

The various unarmed species of tapeworm find their intermediate hosts in the flesh and other parts of various animals, fish, crustacians and crayfish. Dogs not permitted to eat raw meats which have not been officially inspected, never have these worms, and it is needless here to discuss them at length. Hares and rabbits are the intermediate hosts to some of these worms and dogs should not be encouraged to feed upon those animals.

Little is known of the effects upon dogs of infestations of the unarmed tapeworms, but they are believed to be similar to the effects (if any) of the armed species.

The prevention of tapeworm infestation may be epitomized by saying: Do not permit dogs to swallow fleas or lice nor to feed upon uninspected raw meats. It is difficult to protect dogs from such contacts if they are permitted to run at large, but it is to be presumed that persons interested enough in caring for dogs to read this book will keep their dogs at home and protect them.

The several species of tapeworm occurring in dogs are not all removable by the same treatment. The most effective treatment for the removal of the armed species, which is the one most frequently found in the dogs, is arecoline hydrobromide. This drug is a drastic purgative and acts from fifteen to forty-five minutes after its administration. The treatment should be given in the morning after the dog has fasted overnight, and food should be withheld for some three hours after dosing.

Arecoline is not so effective against the double-pored tapeworm as against the other armed species, and it may be necessary to repeat the dose after a few days waiting, since some of the tapeworm heads may not be removed by the first treatment and regeneration of the tapeworm may occur in a few weeks. The estimatedly correct dosage is not stated here, since the drug is so toxic that the dosage should be estimated for the individual dog by a competent veterinarian, and it is better that he should be permitted to administer the remedy and control the treatment.

WHIPWORMS

The dog whipworm (*Trichuris vulpis*) is so called from its fancied resemblance to a tiny blacksnake whip, the front part being slender and hairlike and the hinder part relatively thick. It rarely exceeds three inches in its total length. Whipworms in dogs exist more or less generally throughout the world, but few dogs in the United States are known to harbor them. They are for the most part confined to the caecum, from which they are hard to dislodge, but sometimes spill over into the colon, whence they are easy to dislodge.

The complete life history of the whipworm is not well established, but it is known that no intermediate host is required for its development. The eggs appear to develop in much the same way as the eggs of the large roundworm, but slower, requiring from two weeks to several months for the organisms to reach maturity.

It has not as yet been definitely established that whipworms are the true causes of all the ills of which they are accused. In many instances they appear to cause little damage, even in heavy infestations. A great variety of symptoms of an indefinite sort have been ascribed to whipworms, including digestive disturbances, diarrhea, loss of weight, nervousness, convulsions, and general unthriftiness, but it remains to be proved that whipworms were responsible.

To be effective in its removal of whipworms, a drug must enter the caecum and come into direct contact with them; but the entry of the drug into this organ is somewhat fortuitous, and to increase the chances of its happening, large doses of a drug essentially harmless to the dog must be used. Normal butyl chloride meets this requirement, but it must be given in large doses. Even then, complete clearance of whipworms from the caecum may not be expected; the best to be hoped is that their numbers will be reduced and the morbid symptoms will subside.

Before treatment the dog should be fasted for some eighteen hours, although he may be fed two hours after being treated. It is wise to follow the normal butyl chloride in one hour with a purgative dose of castor oil. This treatment, since it is not expected to be wholly effective, may be repeated at monthly intervals.

The only known means of the complete clearance of whipworms from the dog is the surgical removal of the caecum, which of course should be undertaken only by a veterinary surgeon.

HEART WORMS

Heart worms (*Dirofilaria immitis*) in dogs are rare. They occur largely in the South and Southeast, but their incidence appears to be increasing and cases have been reported along the Atlantic Seaboard as far north as New York. The various species of mosquitoes are known to be vectors of heart worms, although the flea is also accused of spreading them.

The symptoms of heart worm infestation are somewhat vague, and include coughing, shortness of breath and collapse. In advanced cases, dropsy may develop. Nervous symptoms, fixity of vision, fear of light, and convulsions may develop. However, all such symptoms may occur from other causes and it must not be assumed because a dog manifests some of these conditions that he has heart worms. The only way to be sure is a microscopic examination of the blood and the presence or absence of the larvae. Even in some cases where larvae have been found in the blood, post mortem examinations have failed to reveal heart worms in the heart.

Both the diagnosis and treatment of heart worm are functions of the veterinarian. They are beyond the province of the amateur. The drug used is a derivative from antimony known as fuadin, and many dogs are peculiarly susceptible to antimony poisoning. If proper treatment is used by a trained veterinarian, a large preponderance of cases make a complete recovery. But even the most expert of veterinarians may be expected to fail in the successful treatment of a percentage of heart worm infestations. The death of some of the victims is to be anticipated.

LESS FREQUENTLY FOUND WORMS

Besides the intestinal worms that have been enumerated, there exist in some dogs numerous other varieties and species of worms which are of so infrequent occurrence that they require no discussion in a book for the general dog keeper. These include, esophageal worms, lungworms, kidney worms, and eye worms. They are in North America, indeed, so rare as to be negligible.

COCCIDIA

Coccidia are protozoic, microscopic organisms. The forms to which the dog is a host are *Isospora rivolta, I. bigeminia* and *I. felis.* Coccidia eggs, called *oocysts,* can be carried by flies and are picked up by dogs as they lick themselves or eat their stools.

These parasides attack the intestinal wall and cause diarrhea. They are particularly harmful to younger puppies that have been weaned, bringing on fever, running eyes, poor appetite and debilitation as well as the loose stools.

The best prevention is scrupulous cleanliness of the puppy or dog, its surroundings and its playmates whether canine or human Flies should be eliminated as described in the preceding chapter and stools removed promptly where the dog cannot touch it.

Infection can be confirmed by microscopic examination of the stool. Treatment consists of providing nourishing food, which should be force-fed if necessary, and whatever drug the veterinarian recommends. Puppies usually recover, though occasionally their teeth may be pitted as in distemper.

A dog infected once by one form develops immunity to that form but may be infected by another form.

Skin Troubles

THERE is a tendency on the part of the amateur dog keeper to consider any lesion of the dog's skin to be mange. Mange is an unusual condition in clean, well fed, and well cared for dogs. Eczema occurs much more frequently and is often more difficult to control.

MANGE OR SCABIES

There are at least two kinds of mange that effect dogs—sarcoptic mange and demodectic or red mange, the latter rare indeed and difficult to cure.

Sarcoptic mange is caused by a tiny spider-like mite (*Sarcoptes scabiei canis*) which is similar to the mite that causes human scabies or "itch." Indeed, the mange is almost identical with scabies and is transmissible from dog to man. The mite is approximately 1/100th of an inch in length and without magnification is just visible to acute human sight.

Only the female mites are the cause of the skin irritation. They burrow into the upper layers of the skin, where each lays twenty to forty eggs, which in three to seven days hatch into larvae. These larvae in turn develop into nymphs which later grow into adults. The entire life cycle requires from fourteen to twenty-one days for completion. The larvae, nymphs, and males do not burrow into the skin, but live under crusts and scabs on the surface.

86

The disease may make its first appearance on any part of the dog's body, although it is usually first seen on the head and muzzle, around the eyes, or at the base of the ears. Sometimes it is first noticed in the armpits, the inner parts of the thighs, the lower abdomen or on the front of the chest. If not promptly treated it may cover the whole body and an extremely bad infestation may cause the death of the dog after a few months.

Red points which soon develop into small blisters are the first signs of the disease. These are most easily seen on the unpigmented parts of the skin, such as the abdomen. As the female mites burrow into the skin, there is an exudation of serum which dries and scabs. The affected parts soon are covered with bran-like scales followed with grayish crusts. The itching is intense, especially in hot weather or after exercise. The rubbing and scratching favor secondary bacterial infections and the formation of sores. The hair may grow matted and fall out, leaving bare spots. The exuded serum decomposes and gives rise to a peculiar mousy odor which increases as the disease develops and which is especially characteristic.

Sarcoptic mange is often confused with demodectic (red) mange, ringworm, or with simple eczema. If there is any doubt about the diagnosis, a microscopic examination of the scrapings of the lesions will reveal the true facts.

It is easy to control sarcoptic mange if it is recognized in its earlier stages and treatment is begun immediately. Neglected, it may be very difficult to eradicate. If it is considered how rapidly the causative mites reproduce themselves, the necessity for early treatment becomes apparent. That treatment consists not only of medication of the dog but also of sterilization of his bedding, all tools and implements used on him, and the whole premises upon which he has been confined. Sarcoptic mange is easily and quickly transmissible from dog to dog, from area to area on the same dog, and even from dog to human.

In some manner which is not entirely understood, an inadequate or unbalanced diet appears to predispose a dog to sarcoptic mange, and few dogs adequately fed and cared for ever contract it. Once a dog has contracted mange, however, improvement in the amount of quality of his food seems not to hasten his recovery.

There are various medications recommended for sarcoptic mange, sulphur ointment being the old standby. However, it is messy, difficult to use, and not always effective. For the treatment of sarcoptic mange, there are available today such insecticides as lindane, chlordane, and DDT. The use of these chemicals greatly facilitates treatment and cure of the dogs affected with mange and those exposed to it.

A bath made by dissolving four ounces of derris powder (containing at least 5% rotenone) and one ounce of soap in one gallon of water has proved effective, especially if large areas of the surface of the dog's skin are involved. All crusts and scabs should be removed before its application. The solution must be well scrubbed into the skin with a moderately stiff brush and the whole animal thoroughly soaked. Only the surplus liquid should be taken off with a towel and the remainder must be permitted to dry on the dog. This bath should be repeated at intervals of five days until all signs of mange have disappeared. Three such baths will usually suffice.

The advantage of such all over treatment is that it protects uninfected areas from infection. It is also a precautionary measure to bathe in this solution uninfected dogs which have been in contact with the infected one.

Isolated mange spots may be treated with oil of lavender. Roll a woolen cloth into a swab with which the oil of lavender can be applied and rubbed in thoroughly for about five minutes. This destroys all mites with which the oil of lavender comes into contact.

Even after a cure is believed to be accomplished, vigilance must be maintained to prevent fresh infestations and to treat new spots immediately if they appear.

DEMODECTIC OR RED MANGE

Demodectic mange, caused by the wormlike mite *Demodex canis,* which lives in the hair follicles and the sebaceous glands of the skin, is difficult to cure. It is a baffling malady of which the prognosis is not favorable. The life cycle of the causative organism is not well understood, the time required from the egg to maturity being so far unknown. The female lays eggs which hatch into young of appearance similar to that of the adult, except that they are smaller and have but three pairs of legs instead of four.

One peculiar feature about demodectic mange is that some dogs appear to be genetically predisposed to it while others do not contract it whatever their contact with infected animals may be. Young animals seem to be especially prone to it, particularly those with short hair. The first evidence of its presence is the falling out of the hair on certain areas of the dog. The spots may be somewhat reddened, and they commonly occur near the eyes, on the hocks, elbows, or toes, although they may be on any part of the dog's body. No itching occurs at the malady's inception, and it never grows so intense as in sarcoptic mange.

In the course of time, the hairless areas enlarge, and the skin attains a copper hue; in severe cases it may appear blue or leadish gray. During this period the mites multiply and small pustules develop. Secondary invasions may occur to complicate the situation. Poisons are formed by the bacteria in the pustules, and the absorption of toxic materials deranges the body functions and eventually affects the whole general health of the dog, leading to emaciation, weakness, and the development of an acrid, unpleasant odor.

This disease is slow and subtle in its development, runs a casual course, and frequently extends over a period of two or even three years. Unless it is treated, it usually terminates in death, although spontaneous recovery occasionally occurs, especially if the dog has been kept on a nourishing diet. As in other skin diseases, correct nutrition plays a major part in recovery from demodectic mange, as it plays an even larger part in its prevention.

It is possible to confuse demodectic mange with sarcoptic mange, fungus infection, acne, or eczema. A definite diagnosis is possible only from microscopic examination of skin scrapings and of material from the pustules. The possibility of demodectic mange, partic-

89

ularly in its earlier stages, is not negated by the failure to find the mites under the microscope, and several examinations may be necessary to arrive at a definite diagnosis.

The prognosis is not entirely favorable. It may appear that the mange is cured and a new and healthy coat may be re-established only to have the disease manifest itself in a new area, and the whole process of treatment must be undertaken afresh.

In the treatment of demodectic mange, the best results have been obtained by the persistent use of benzine hexachloride, chlordane, rotenone, and 2-mercapto benzothiazole. Perseverance is necessary, but even then failure is possible.

EAR MITES OR EAR MANGE

The mites responsible for ear mange (*Ododectes cynotis*) are considerably larger than the ones which cause sarcoptic mange. They inhabit the external auditory canal and are visible to the unaided eye as minute, slowly moving, white objects. Their life history is not known, but is probably similar to that of the mite that causes sarcoptic mange.

These mites do not burrow into the skin, but are found deep in the ear canal, near the eardrum. Considerable irritation results from their presence, and the normal secretions of the ear are interfered with. The ear canal is filled with inflammatory products, modified ear wax, and mites, causing the dog to scratch and rub its ears and to shake its head. While ear mange is not caused by incomplete washing or inefficient drying of the ears, it is encouraged by such negligence.

The ear mange infestation is purely local and is no cause for anxiety. An ointment containing benzine hexachloride is very effective in correcting this condition. The ear should be treated every third or fourth day.

90

ECZEMA

Eczema is probably the most common of all ailments seen in the dog. Oftentimes it is mistaken for mange or ringworm, although there is no actual relationship between the conditions. Eczema is variously referred to by such names as "hot spots," "fungitch," and "kennel itch."

Some years ago there was near-unanimity of opinion among dog people that the food of the animal was the major contributing factor of eczema. Needless to say, the manufacturers of commercial dog foods were besieged with complaints. Some research on the cause of eczema placed most of the blame on outside environmental factors, and with some help from other sources it was found that a vegetative organism was the causative agent in a great majority of the cases.

Some dogs do show an allergic skin reaction to certain types of protein given to them as food, but this is generally referred to as the "foreign protein" type of dermatitis. It manifests itself by raising numerous welts on the skin, and occasionally the head, face, and ears will become alarmingly swollen. This condition can be controlled by the injection of antihistamine products and subsequent dosage with antihistaminic tablets or capsules such as chlortrimenton or benedryl. Whether "foreign protein" dermatitis is due to an allergy or whether it is due to some toxin manufactured and elaborated by the individual dog is a disputed point.

Most cases of eczema start with reddening of the skin in certain parts. The areas most affected seem to be the region along the spine and at the base of the tail. In house dogs this may have its inception from enlarged and plugged anal glands. The glands when full and not naturally expressed are a source of irritation. The dog will rub his hind parts on the grass in order to alleviate the itching sensation. Fleas, lice, and ticks may be inciting factors, causing the dog to rub and roll in the grass in an attempt to scratch the itchy parts.

In hunting dogs, it is believed that the vegetative cover through which the dogs hunt causes the dermatitis. In this class of dogs the skin becomes irritated and inflamed in the armpits, the inner surfaces of the thighs, and along the belly. Some hunting dogs are bedded down in straw or hay, and such dogs invariably show a

91

general reddening of the skin and a tendency to scratch.

As a general rule, the difference between moist and dry eczema lies in the degree to which the dog scratches the skin with his feet or chews it with his teeth. The inflammation ranges from a simple reddening of the skin to the development of papules, vesicles, and pustules with a discharge. Crusts and scabs like dandruff may form, and if the condition is not treated, it will become chronic and then next to impossible to treat with any success. In such cases the skin becomes thickened and may be pigmented. The hair follicles become infected, and the lesions are constantly inflamed and exuding pus.

When inflammation occurs between the toes and on the pads of the feet, it closely resembles "athletes foot" in the human. Such inflammation generally causes the hair in the region to turn a reddish brown. The ears, when they are affected, emit a peculiar moldy odor and exude a brownish black substance. It is thought that most cases of canker of the ear are due to a primary invasion of the ear canal by a vegetative fungus. If there is a pustular discharge, it is due to the secondary pus-forming bacteria that gain a foothold after the resistance of the parts is lowered by the fungi.

Some breeds of dogs are more susceptible to skin ailments than are others. However, all breeds of dogs are likely to show some degree of dermatitis if they are exposed to causative factors.

Most cases of dermatitis are seen in the summer time, which probably accounts for their being referred to as "summer itch" or "hot spots." The warm moist days of summer seem to promote the growth and development of both fleas and fungi. When the fleas bite the dog, the resulting irritation causes the dog to scratch or bite to alleviate the itch. The area thus becomes moist and makes a perfect place for fungi spores to propagate. That the fungi are the cause of the trouble seems evident, because most cases respond when treated externally with a good fungicide. Moreover, the use of a powder containing both an insecticide and a fungicide tends to prevent skin irritation. Simply dusting the dog once or twice a week with a good powder of the type mentioned is sound procedure in the practice of preventive medicine.

(Editor's note: I have had some success with hydrogen peroxide in treating mild skin troubles. Saturate a cotton pad with a mixture of 2 parts 3% hydrogen peroxide to 1 part boiled water. Apply,

92

but do NOT rub, to affected skin. Let dry naturally and when *completely* dry apply an antiseptic talcum powder like Johnson & Johnson's Medicated Powder. When this treatment was suggested to my veterinarian, he confirmed that he had had success with it. If the skin irritation is not noticeably better after two of these treatments, once daily, the case should be referred to a veterinarian.)

RINGWORM

Ringworm is a communicable disease of the skin of dogs, readily transmissible to man and to other dogs and animals. The disease is caused by specific fungi, which are somewhat similar to ordinary molds. The lesions caused by ringworm usually first appear on the face, head, or legs of the dog, but they may occur on any part of the surface of his body.

The disease in dogs is characterized by small, circular areas of dirty gray or brownish-yellow crusts or scabs partially devoid of hair, the size of a dime. As the disease progresses, the lesions increase both in size and in number and merge to form larger patches covered with crusts containing broken off hair. A raw, bleeding surface may appear when crusts are broken or removed by scratching or rubbing to relieve itching. In some cases, however, little or no itching is manifested. Microscopic examination and culture tests are necessary for accurate diagnosis.

If treatment of affected dogs is started early, the progress of the disease can be immediately arrested. Treatment consists of clipping the hair from around the infected spots, removing the scabs and painting the spots with tincture of iodine, five percent salicylic acid solution, or other fungicide two or three times weekly until recovery takes place. In applying these remedies it is well to cover the periphery of the circular lesion as well as its center, since the spots tend to expand outward from their centers. Scabs, hair, and debris removed from the dog during his treatments should be burned to destroy the causative organisms and to prevent reinfection. Precautions in the handling of animals affected with ringworm should be observed to preclude transmission to man and other animals. Isolation of affected dogs is not necessary if the treatment is thorough.

COAT CARE

Skin troubles can often be checked and materially alleviated by proper grooming. Every dog is entitled to the minimum of weekly attention to coat, skin and ears; ideally, a daily stint with brush and comb is highly recommended. Frequent examination may catch skin disease in its early stages and provide a better chance for a quick cure.

The outer or "guard" hairs of a dog's coat should glint in the sunlight. There should be no mats or dead hair in the coat. Wax in the outer ear should be kept at a minimum.

It is helpful to stand the dog on a flat, rigid surface off the floor at a height convenient to the groomer. Start at the head and ears brushing briskly *with* the lay of short hair, *against* the lay of long hair at first then with it. After brushing, use a fine comb with short teeth on fine, short hair and a coarse comb with long teeth on coarse or long hair. If mats cannot be readily removed with brush or comb, use barber's thinning shears and cut into the matted area several times until mat pulls free easily. Some mats can be removed with the fingers if one has the patience to separate the hair a bit at a time.

After brushing and combing, run your palms over the dog's coat from head to tail. Natural oils in your skin will impart sheen to your dog's coat.

The ears of some dogs secrete and exude great amounts of wax. Frequent examination will determine when your dog's ears need cleaning. A thin coating of clean, clear wax is not harmful. But a heavy accumulation of dirty, dark wax needs removal by cotton pads soaked in diluted hydrogen peroxide (3% cut in half with boiled water), or alcohol or plain boiled water if wax is not too thick.

There are sprays, "dry" bath preparations and other commercial products for maintaining your dog's coat health. Test them first, and if they are successful, you may find them beneficial time-savers in managing your dog's coat.

First Aid

JOHN STEINBECK, the Nobel Prize winning author, in *Travels with Charley in Search of America* bemoans the lack of a good, comprehensive book of home dog medicine. Charley is the aged Poodle that accompanies his illustrious author-owner on a motor tour of the U.S.A.

As in human medicine, most treatment and dosing of dogs are better left in the experienced, trained hands and mind of a professional—in this case, the veterinarian. However, there are times and situations when professional aid is not immediately available and an owner's prompt action may save a life or avoid permanent injury. To this purpose, the following suggestions are given.

The First Aid Kit

For instruments keep on hand a pair of tweezers, a pair of pliers, straight scissors, a rectal thermometer, a teaspoon, a tablespoon, and swabs for cotton.

For dressings, buy a container of cotton balls, a roll of cotton and a roll of 2″ gauze. Strips of clean, old sheets may come in handy.

For medicines, stock ammonia, aspirin, brandy, 3% hydrogen peroxide, bicarbonate of soda, milk of bismuth, mineral oil, salt, tea, vaseline, kaopectate, baby oil and baby talcum powder.

Handling the Dog for Treatment

Approach any injured or sick dog calmly with reassuring voice and gentle, steady hands. If the dog is in pain, slip a gauze or sheet strip noose over its muzzle tying the ends first under the throat and then back of the neck. Make sure the dog's lips are not caught between his teeth, but make noose around muzzle *tight*.

If the dog needs to be moved, grasp the loose skin on the back of the neck with one hand and support chest with the other hand. If the dog is too large to move in this manner, slide him on a large towel, blanket or folded sheet which may serve as a stretcher for two to carry.

If a pill or liquid is to be administered, back the dog in a corner in a sitting position. For a pill, pry back of jaws apart with thumb and forefinger of one hand and with the same fingers of your other hand place pill as far back in dog's throat as possible; close and hold jaws, rubbing throat to cause swallowing. If dog does not gulp, hold one hand over nostrils briefly; he will gulp for air and swallow pill. For liquids, lift the back of the upper lip and tip spoon into the natural pocket formed in the rear of the lower lip; it may be necessary to pull this pocket out with forefinger. Do not give liquids by pouring directly down the dog's throat; this might choke him or make the fluid go down the wrong way.

After treatment keep dog quiet, preferably in his bed or a room where he cannot injure himself or objects.

Bites and Wounds

Clip hair from area. Wash gently with pure soap and water or hydrogen peroxide. If profuse bleeding continues, apply sheet strip or gauze tourniquet between wound and heart but nearest the wound. Release tourniquet briefly at ten-minute intervals. Cold water compresses may stop milder bleeding.

For insect bites and stings, try to remove stinger with tweezers or a dab of cotton, and apply a few drops of ammonia. If dog is in pain, give aspirin at one grain per 10 pounds. (An aspirin tablet is usually 5 grains.)

Burns

Clip hair from area. Apply strong, lukewarm tea (for its tannic acid content) on a sheet strip compress. Vaseline may be used for slight burns. Give aspirin as recommended if dog is in pain. Keep him warm if he seems to be in shock.

Constipation

Give mineral oil: one-quarter teaspoon up to 10 pounds; half teaspoon from 10 to 25 pounds; full teaspoon from 25 to 75 pounds; three-quarters tablespoon over 75 pounds.

Diarrhea

Give kaopectate in same doses by size as indicated for mineral oil above, but repeat within four and eight hours.

Fighting

Do not try forcibly to separate dogs. If available throw a pail of cold water on them. A sharp rap on the rump of each combatant with a strap or stick may help. A heavy towel or blanket dropped over the head of the aggressor, or a newspaper twisted into a torch, lighted and held near them, may discourage the fighters. If a lighted newspaper is used, be careful that sparks do not fall or blow on dogs.

Fits

Try to get the dog into a room where he cannot injure himself. If possible, cover him with a towel or blanket. When the fit ends, give aspirin one grain for every 10 pounds.

Nervousness

Remove cause or remove the dog from the site of the cause. Give the recommended dose of aspirin. Aspirin acts as a tranquilizer.

97

Poisoning

If container of the poison is handy, use recommended antidote printed thereon. Otherwise, make a strong solution of household salt in water and force as much as possible into the dog's throat using the lip pocket method. Minutes count with several poisons; if veterinarian cannot be reached immediately, try to get dog to an MD or registered nurse.

Shock

If dog has chewed electric cord, protect hand with rubber glove or thick dry towel and pull cord from socket. If dog has collapsed, hold ammonia under its nose or apply artificial respiration as follows: place dog on side with its head low, press on abdomen and rib cage, releasing pressure at one- or two-second intervals. Keep dog warm.

Stomach Upsets

For mild stomach disorders, milk of bismuth in same doses as recommended for mineral oil under *Constipation* will be effective. For more severe cases brandy in the same doses but diluted with an equal volume of water may be helpful.

Swallowing Foreign Objects

If object is still in mouth or throat, reach in and remove it. If swallowed, give strong salt solution as for *Poisoning*. Some objects that are small, smooth or soft may not give trouble.

Porcupines and Skunks

Using tweezers or pliers, twist quills one full turn and pull out. Apply hydrogen peroxide to bleeding wounds. For skunk spray, wash dog in tomato juice.

WARNING! Get your dog to a veterinarian *soonest* for severe bites, wounds, burns, poisoning, fits and shock.

Internal Canine Diseases
and Their Management

THE word *management* is employed in this chapter heading rather than *treatment,* since the treatment of disease in the dog is the function of the veterinarian, and the best counsel it is possible to give the solicitous owner of a sick dog is to submit the case to the best veterinarian available and to follow his instructions implicitly. In general, it may be said, the earlier in any disease the veterinarian is consulted, the more rapid is the sick animal's recovery and the lower the outlay of money for the services of the veterinarian and for the medicine he prescribes.

Herein are presented some hints for the prevention of the various canine maladies and for their recognition when they occur. In kennel husbandry, disease is a minor problem, and, if preventive methods are employed, it is one that need not be anticipated.

DISTEMPER

Distemper, the traditional bugbear of keeping dogs, the veritable scourge of dog-kind, has at long last been well conquered. Compared with some years ago when "over distemper" was one of the best recommendations for the purchase of a dog, the incidence of distemper in well-bred and adequately cared for dogs is now minimal.

The difference between then and now is that we now have available preventive sera, vaccines, and viruses, which may be employed to forestall distemper before it ever appears. There are valid differences of opinion about which of these measures is best to use and at what age of the dog they are variously indicated. About the choice of preventive measures and the technique of administering them, the reader is advised to consult his veterinarian and to accept his advice. There can be no doubt, however, that any person with a valued or loved young dog should have him immunized.

For many years most veterinarians used the so-called "three-shot" method of serum, vaccine and virus, spaced two weeks apart after the puppy was three or four months old, for permanent immunization. For temporary immunization lasting up to a year, some veterinarians used only vaccine; this was repeated annually if the owner wished, though since a dog was considered most susceptible to distemper in the first year of his life, the annual injection was often discontinued. Under both these methods, serum was used at two-week intervals from weaning to the age when permanent or annual immunization was given.

Until 1950 living virus, produced by the methods then known to and used by laboratories, was considered too dangerous to inject without the preparation of the dog for it by prior use of serum or vaccine (killed virus). Then, researchers in distemper developed an attenuated or weakened live virus by injecting strong virus into egg embryos and other intermediate hosts. The weakened virus is now often used for permanent, one-shot distemper immunization of puppies as young as eight weeks.

Today certain researchers believe that the temporary immunity given by the bitch to her young depends on her own degree of immunity. If she has none, her puppies have none; if she has maximum immunity, her puppies may be immune up to the age of 12 weeks or more. By testing the degree of the bitch's immunity early in her pregnancy, these researchers believe they can determine the proper age at which her puppies should receive their shots.

The veterinarian is best qualified to determine the method of distemper immunization and the age to give it.

Canine distemper is an acute, highly contagious, febrile disease caused by a filterable virus. It is characterized by a catarrhal inflammation of all the mucous membranes of the body, frequently

100

accompanied by nervous symptoms and pustular eruptions of the skin. Its human counterpart is influenza, which, though not identical with distemper, is very similar to it in many respects. Distemper is so serious and complicated a disease as to require expert attention; when a dog is suspected of having it, a veterinarian should be consulted immediately. It is the purpose of this discussion of the malady rather to describe it that its recognition may be possible than to suggest medication for it or means of treating it.

Distemper is known in all countries and all parts of the United States in all seasons of the year, but it is most prevalent during the winter months and in the cold, damp weather of early spring and late autumn. No breed of dogs is immune. Puppies of low constitutional vigor, pampered, overfed, unexercised dogs, and those kept in overheated, unventilated quarters contract the infection more readily and suffer more from it than hardy animals, properly fed and living in a more natural environment. Devitalizing influences which decrease the resistance of the dog, such as rickets, parasitic infestations, unsanitary quarters, and especially an insufficient or unbalanced diet, are factors predisposing to distemper.

While puppies as young as ten days or two weeks have been known to have true cases of distemper, and very old dogs in rare instances, the usual subjects of distemper are between two months (after weaning) and full maturity at about eighteen months. The teething period of four to six months is highly critical. It is believed that some degree of temporary protection from distemper is passed on to a nursing litter through the milk of the mother.

As was first demonstrated by Carré in 1905 and finally established by Laidlaw and Duncan in their work for the Field Distemper Fund in 1926 to 1928, the primary causative agent of distemper is a filterable virus. The clinical course of the disease may be divided into two parts, produced respectively by the primary Carré filterable virus and by a secondary invasion of bacterial organisms which produce serious complicating conditions usually associated with the disease. It is seldom true that uncomplicated Carré distemper would cause more than a fever with malaise and indisposition if the secondary bacterial invasion could be avoided. The primary disease but prepares the ground for the secondary invasion which produces the havoc and all too often kills the patient.

Although it is often impossible to ascertain the source of infection

101

in outbreaks of distemper, it is known that the infection may spread from affected to susceptible dogs by either direct or indirect contact. The disease, while highly infectious throughout its course, is especially easy to communicate in its earliest stages, even before clinical symptoms are manifested. The virus is readily destroyed by heat and by most of the common disinfectants in a few hours, but it resists drying and low temperatures for several days, and has been known to survive freezing for months.

The period of incubation (the time between exposure to infection and the development of the first symptoms) is variable. It has been reported to be as short as three days and as long as two weeks. The usual period is approximately one week. The usual course of the disease is about four weeks, but seriously complicated cases may prolong themselves to twelve weeks.

The early symptoms of distemper, as a rule, are so mild and subtle as to escape the notice of any but the most acute observer. These first symptoms may be a rise in temperature, a watery discharge from the eyes and nose, an impaired appetite, a throat-clearing cough, and a general sluggishness. In about a week's time the symptoms become well marked, with a discharge of mucus or pus from the eyes and nose, and complications of a more or less serious nature, such as broncho-pneumonia, hemorrhagic inflammation of the gastro-intestinal tract, and disturbances of the brain and spinal cord, which may cause convulsions. In the early stages of distemper the body temperature may suddenly rise from the normal 101°F. to 103°. Shivering, dryness of the nostrils, a slight dry cough, increased thirst, a drowsy look, reluctance to eat, and a desire to sleep may follow. Later, diarrhea (frequently streaked with blood or wholly of blood), pneumonia, convulsions, paralysis, or chorea (a persistent twitching condition) may develop. An inflammation of the membranes of the eye may ensue; this may impair or destroy the sight through ulceration or opacity of the cornea. Extreme weakness and great loss of body weight occur in advanced stages.

All, any, or none of these symptoms may be noticeable. It is believed that many dogs experience distemper in so mild a form as to escape the owner's observation. Because of its protean and obscure nature and its strong similarity to other catarrhal affections, the diagnosis of distemper, especially in its early stages, is difficult. In young dogs that are known to have been exposed to the disease, a rise of body temperature, together with shivering, sneezing, loss of appetite, eye and nasal discharge, sluggishness, and diarrhea (all or any of these symptoms), are indicative of trouble.

There is little specific that can be done for a dog with primary distemper. The treatment is largely concerned with alleviating the symptoms. No drug or combination of drugs is known at this time that has any specific action on the disease. Distemper runs a definite course, no matter what is done to try to cure it.

Homologous anti-distemper serum, administered subcutaneously or intravenously by the veterinarian, is of value in lessening the severity of the attack. The veterinarian may see fit to treat the secondary pneumonia with penicillin or one of the sulpha drugs, or to allay the secondary intestinal infection with medication. It is best to permit him to manage the case in his own way. The dog is more prone to respond to care in his own home and with his own people, if suitable quarters and adequate nursing are available to him. Otherwise, he is best off in a veterinary hospital.

The dog affected with distemper should be provided with clean, dry, warm but not hot, well ventilated quarters. It should be given moderate quantities of nourishing, easily digested food—milk, soft boiled eggs, cottage cheese, and scraped lean beef. The sick dog should not be disturbed by children or other dogs. Discharges from eyes and nose should be wiped away. The eyes may be bathed with boric acid solution, and irritation of the nose allayed with greasy substances such as petrolatum. The dog should not be permitted to get wet or chilled, and he should have such medication as the veterinarian prescribes and no other.

When signs of improvement are apparent, the dog must not be given an undue amount of food at one meal, although he may be fed at frequent intervals. The convalescing dog should be permitted to exercise only very moderately until complete recovery is assured.

In the control of distemper, affected animals should be promptly isolated from susceptible dogs. After the disease has run its course, whether it end in recovery or death, the premises where the patient has been kept during the illness should be thoroughly cleaned and disinfected, as should all combs, brushes, or other utensils used on the dog, before other susceptible dogs are brought in. After an apparent recovery has been made in the patient, the germs are present for about four weeks and can be transmitted to susceptible dogs.

103

CHOREA OR ST. VITUS DANCE

A frequent sequela of distemper is chorea, which is characterized by a more or less pronounced and frequent twitching of a muscle or muscles. There is no known remedy for the condition. It does not impair the usefulness of a good dog for breeding, and having a litter of puppies often betters or cures chorea in the bitch. Chorea is considered a form of unsoundness and is penalized in the show ring. The condition generally becomes worse.

ECLAMPSIA OR WHELPING TETANY

Convulsions of bitches before, during, or shortly after their whelping are called eclampsia. It seldom occurs to a bitch receiving a sufficient amount of calcium and vitamin D in her diet during her pregnancy. The symptoms vary in their severity for nervousness and mild convulsions to severe attacks which may terminate in coma and death. The demands of the nursing litter for calcium frequently depletes the supply in the bitch's system.

Eclampsia can be controlled by the hypodermic administration of calcium gluconate. Its recurrence is prevented by the addition to the bitch's ration of readily utilized calcium and vitamin D.

RICKETS, OR RACHITIS

The failure of the bones of puppies to calcify normally is termed rickets, or more technically rachitis. Perhaps more otherwise excellent puppies are killed or ruined by rickets than by any other disease. It is essentially a disease of puppies, but the malformation of the skeleton produced by rickets persists through the life of the dog.

The symptoms of rickets include lethargy, arched neck, crouched stance, knobby and deformed joints, bowed legs, and flabby muscles. The changes characteristic of defective calcification in the puppy are most marked in the growth of the long bones of the leg, and at the cartilaginous junction of the ribs. In the more advanced stages of rickets the entire bone becomes soft and easily deformed or broken. The development of the teeth is also retarded.

Rickets results from a deficiency in the diet of calcium, phosphorus, or vitamin D. It may be prevented by the inclusion of sufficient amounts of those substances in the puppy's diet. It may also be cured, if not too far advanced, by the same means, although distortions in the skeleton that have already occurred are seldom rectified. The requirements of vitamin D to be artificially supplied are greater for puppies raised indoors and with limited exposure to sunlight or to sunlight filtered through window glass.

(It is possible to give a dog too much vitamin D, but very unlikely without deliberate intent.)

Adult dogs that have had rickets in puppyhood and whose recovery is complete may be bred from without fear of their transmission to their puppies of the malformations of their skeletons produced by the disease. The same imbalance or absence from their diet that produced rickets in the parent may produce it in the progeny, but the disease in such case is reproduced and not inherited.

The requirements of adult dogs for calcium, phosphorus, and vitamin D are much less than for puppies and young dogs, but a condition called osteomalacia, or late rickets, is sometimes seen in grown dogs as the result of the same kind of nutritional deficiency that causes rickets in puppies. In such cases a softening of the bones leads to lameness and deformity. The remedy is the same as in the rickets of puppyhood, namely the addition of calcium, phosphorus, and vitamin D to the diet. It is especially essential that bitches during pregnancy and lactation have included in their diets ample amounts of these elements, both for their own nutrition and for the adequate skeletal formations of their fetuses and the development of their puppies.

BLACKTONGUE

Blacktongue (the canine analogue of pellagra in the human) is no longer to be feared in dogs fed upon an adequate diet. For many years, it was a recognized scourge among dogs, and its cause and treatment were unknown. It is now known to be caused solely by the insufficiency in the ration of vitamin B complex and specifically by an insufficiency of nicotinic acid. (Nicotinic acid is vitamin B_2, formerly known as vitamin G.)

Blacktongue may require a considerable time for its full development. It usually begins with a degree of lethargy, a lack of appetite for the kind of food the dog has been receiving, constipation, often with spells of vomiting, and particularly with a foul odor from the mouth. As the disease develops, the mucous membranes of the mouth, gums, and tongue grow red and become inflamed, with purple splotches of greater or lesser extent, especially upon the front part of the tongue, and with ulcers and pustules on the lips and the lining of the cheeks. Constipation may give way to diarrhea as the disease develops. Blacktongue is an insidious malady, since its development is so gradual.

This disease is unlikely to occur except among dogs whose owners are so unenlightened, careless, or stingy as to feed their dogs exclusively on a diet of cornmeal mush, salt pork, cowpeas, sweet potatoes, or other foodstuffs that are known to be responsible for the development of pellagra in mankind. Blacktongue is not infectious or contagious, although the same deficiency in the diet of dogs may produce the malady in all the inmates throughout a kennel.

Correct treatment involves no medication as such, but consists wholly in the alteration of the diet to include foods which are good sources of the vitamin B complex, including nicotinic acid; such food as the muscles of beef, mutton, or horse, dried yeast, wheat germ, milk, eggs, and especially fresh liver. As an emergency treatment, the hypodermic injection of nicotinic acid may be indicated. Local treatments of the mouth, its cleansing and disinfection, are usually included, although they will avail nothing without the alteration in the diet.

LEPTOSPIROSIS OR CANINE TYPHUS

Leptospirosis, often referred to as canine typhus, is believed to be identical with Weil's disease (infectious jaundice) in the human species. It is not to be confused with non-infectious jaundice in the dog, which is a mere obstruction in the bile duct which occurs in some liver and gastric disorders. Leptospirosis is a comparatively rare disease as yet, but its incidence is growing and it is becoming more widespread.

It is caused by either of two spirocheates, *Leptospira canicola* or *Leptospira icterohenorrhagiae*. These causative organisms are found

in the feces or urine of infected rats, and the disease is transmitted
to dogs by their ingestion of food fouled by those rodents. It is
therefore wise in rat infested houses to keep all dog food in covered
metal containers to which it is impossible for rats to gain access.
It is also possible for an ill dog to transmit the infection to a well
one, and, it is believed, to man. Such cases, however, are rare.

Symptoms of leptospirosis include a variable temperature, vomiting, loss of appetite, gastroenteritis, diarrhea, jaundice and depression. Analysis of blood and urine may be helpful toward diagnosis.
The disease is one for immediate reference to the veterinarian
whenever suspected.

Prognosis is not entirely favorable, especially if the disease is
neglected in its earlier stages. Taken in its incipience, treatment
with penicillin has produced excellent results, as has antileptospiral
serum and vaccine.

Control measures include the extermination of rats in areas where
the disease is known to exist, and the cleaning and disinfection of
premises where infected dogs have been kept.

INFECTIOUS HEPATITIS

This is a virus disease attacking the liver. Apparently it is not
the same virus that causes hepatitis in humans. Symptoms include
an unusual thirst, loss of appetite, vomiting, diarrhea, pain causing
the dog to moan, anemia and fever. The afflicted dog may try to
hide.

The disease runs a fast course and is often fatal. A dog recover-
ing from it may carry the virus in his urine for a long period, thus
infecting other dogs months later.

Serum and vaccine are available to offer protection. A combination for distemper and hepatitis is now offered.

TURNED-IN OR TURNED-OUT EYELIDS

When the eyelid is inverted, or turned-in, it is technically termed
entropion. When the eyelid is turned-out, it is referred to as ex-
tropion. Both conditions seem to be found in certain strains of
dogs and are classified as being heritable. Both conditions may be
corrected by competent surgery. It is possible to operate on such

cases and have complete recovery without scar formation. However, cognizance should be taken of either defect in a dog to be used for breeding purposes.

CONJUNCTIVITIS OR INFLAMMATION OF THE EYE

Certain irritants, injuries or infections, and many febrile diseases, such as distemper, produce conjunctivitis, an inflammation of the membranes lining the lids of the dog's eyes. At first there is a slight reddening of the membranes and a watery discharge. As the condition progresses, the conjunctivae become more inflamed looking and the color darkens. The discharge changes consistency and color, becoming muco-purulent in character and yellow in color. The eyelids may be pasted shut and granulation of the lids may follow.

When eye infection persists for an extended period of time, the cornea sometimes becomes involved. Ulcers may develop, eventually penetrating the eyeball. When this happens, the condition becomes very painful and, even worse, often leads to the loss of vision.

Home treatment, to be used only until professional care may be had, consists of regular cleaning of the eye with a 2% boric acid solution and the application of one of the antibiotic eye ointments.

When anything happens to the dog's eye, it is always best to seek professional help and advice.

RABIES

This disease, caused by a virus, is transmissible to all warm blooded animals, and the dog seems to be the number one disseminator of the virus. However, outbreaks of rabies have been traced to wild animals—the wolf, coyote, or fox biting a dog which in turn bites people, other dogs, or other species of animals.

The virus, which is found in the saliva of the rabid animal, enters the body only through broken skin. This usually is brought about by biting and breaking the skin, or through licking an open cut on the skin. The disease manifests itself clinically in two distinct forms. One is called the "furious type" and the other the "dumb type." Both types are produced by the same strain of virus.

The disease works rather peculiarly on the dog's disposition and character. The kindly old dog may suddenly become ferocious; just the reverse may also occur, the mean, vicious dog becoming gentle and biddable. At first the infected dog wants to be near his master, wants to lick his hand or his boots; his appetite undergoes a sudden change, becoming voracious, and the animal will eat anything— stones, bits of wood, even metal. Soon there develops a sense of wanderlust, and the dog seems to wish to get as far away as possible from his owner.

In all rabid animals there is an accentuation of the defense mechanisms. In other words, the dog will bite, the cat will hiss and claw, the horse will bite and kick, and the cow will attack anything that moves.

An animal afflicted with rabies cannot swallow because there is usually a paralysis of the muscles of deglutinition. The animal, famished for a drink, tries to bite the water or whatever fluid he may be attempting to drink. The constant champing of the jaws causes the saliva to become mixed and churned with air, making it appear whipped and foamy. In the old days when a dog "frothed at the mouth," he was considered "mad." There is no doubt but what some uninfected dogs have been suspected of being rabid and shot to death simply because they exhibited these symptoms.

One of the early signs of rabies in the dog is the dropping of the lower jaw. This is a sign of rabies of the so-called "dumb type." The animal has a "faraway" look in his eyes, and his voice or bark has an odd pitch. Manifesting these symptoms, the dog is often taken to the clinic by the owner, who is sure the dog has a bone in the throat. The hind legs, and eventually the whole hindquarters, subsequently become paralyzed, and death ensues.

Many commonwealths have passed laws requiring that all dogs be vaccinated against rabies, and usually, a vaccination certificate must be presented before a dog license may be issued. The general enforcement of this law alone would go a long way toward the eradication of rabies.

Some will ask why a dog must be impounded as a biter when he has taken a little "nip" at someone and merely broken the skin— if this must be done, they cannot understand the "good" of the vaccination. But the vaccination does not give the dog the right to bite. Statistics show that rabies vaccination is effective in about 88% of the cases. All health authorities wish it were 100% effective,

109

thus eliminating a good deal of worry from their minds. Because the vaccination is not 100% effective, we cannot take a chance on the vaccine alone. The animal must be impounded and under the daily supervision of a qualified observer, generally for a period of fourteen days. It is pretty well recognized that if the bite was provocated by rabies, the biting animal will develop clinical symptoms in that length of time; otherwise, he will be released as "clinically normal."

THE SPAYING OF BITCHES

The spaying operation, technically known as an ovariectomy, is the subject of a good deal of controversy. It is an operation that has its good and its bad points.

Spayed bitches cannot be entered in the show ring, and of course can never reproduce their kind. However, under certain circumstances, the operation is recommended by veterinarians. If the operation is to be performed, the bitch should preferably be six to eight months of age. At this age, she has pretty well reached the adolescent period; time enough has been allowed for the endocrine balance to become established and the secondary sex organs to develop.

Mechanical difficulties sometimes arise in the urinary systems of bitches that have been operated on at three or four months of age. In a very small percentage of the cases, loss of control of the sphincter muscles of the bladder is observed. But this can readily be corrected by an injection of the female hormone stilbestrol.

There are many erroneous ideas as to what may happen to the female if she is spayed. Some people argue that the disposition will be changed, that the timid dog may become ferocious, and, strangely enough, that the aggressive animal will become docile. Some breeders say that the spayed bitch will become fat, lazy, and lethargic. According to the records that have been kept on bitches following the spaying operation, such is not the case. It is unjust to accuse the spaying operation when really the dog's owner is at fault—he just feeds the dog too much.

THE CASTRATION OF DOGS

This operation consists of the complete removal of the testes. Ordinarily the operation is not encouraged. Circumstances may attenuate the judgment, however. Castration may be necessary to correct certain pathological conditions such as a tumor, chronic prostatitis, and types of perineal troubles. Promiscuous wetting is sometimes an excuse for desexing.

It must be remembered that as with the spayed bitch, the castrated dog is barred from the show ring.

ANAL GLANDS

On either side of the anus of the dog is situated an anal gland, which secretes a lubricant that better enables the dog to expel the contents of the rectum. These glands are subject to being clogged, and in them accumulates a fetid mass. This accumulation is not, strictly speaking, a disease—unless it becomes infected and purulent. Almost all dogs have it, and most of them are neglected without serious consequences. However, they are better if they are relieved. Their spirits improve, their eyes brighten, and even their coats gradually grow more lively if the putrid mass is occasionally squeezed out of the anus.

This is accomplished by seizing the tail with the left hand, encircling its base with the thumb and forefinger of the right hand, and pressing the anus firmly between thumb and finger. The process results in momentary pain to the dog and often causes him to flinch, which may be disregarded. A semi-liquid of vile odor is extruded from the anus. The operation should be repeated at intervals of from one week to one month, depending on the rapidity of glandular accumulation. No harm results from the frequency of such relief, although there may be no apparent results if the anal glands are kept free of their accumulations.

If this process of squeezing out of the glands is neglected, the glands sometimes become infected and surgery becomes necessary. This is seldom the case, but, if needful at all, it must be entrusted to a skillful veterinary surgeon.

METRITIS

Metritis is the acute or chronic inflammation of the uterus of the bitch and may result from any one of a number of things. Perhaps the most common factor, especially in eight- to twelve-year-old bitches, is pseudocyesis, or false pregnancy. Metritis often follows whelping; it may be the result of a retained placenta, or of infection of the uterus following the manual or instrument removal of a puppy.

The term pyometria is generally restricted to cases where the uterus is greatly enlarged and filled with pus. In most such cases surgery must be resorted to in order to effect a cure.

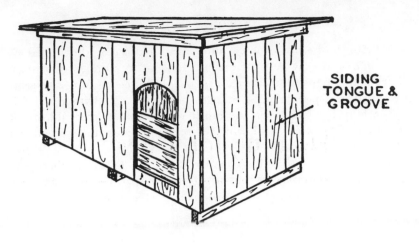

SIDING
TONGUE &
GROOVE

ASSEMBLED VIEW

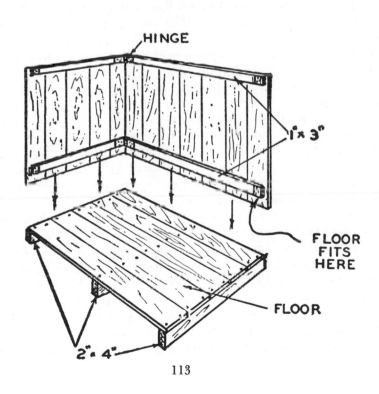

HINGE

1" x 3"

FLOOR
FITS
HERE

FLOOR

2" x 4"

Housing for Dogs

EVERY owner will have, and will have to solve, his own problems about providing his dog or dogs with quarters best suited to the dog's convenience. The special circumstances of each particular owner will determine what kind of home he will provide for his dogs. Here it is impossible to provide more than a few generalities upon the subject.

Little more need be said than that fit quarters for dogs must be secure, clean, dry, and warm. Consideration must be given to convenience in the care of kennel inmates by owners of a large number of dogs, but by the time one's activities enlarge to such proportions one will have formulated one's own concept of how best to house one's dogs. Here, advice will be predicated upon the maintenance of not more than three or four adult dogs with accommodations for an occasional litter of puppies.

First, let it be noted that dogs are not sensitive to aesthetic considerations in the place they are kept; they have no appreciation of the beauty of their surroundings. They do like soft beds of sufficient thickness to protect them from the coldness of the floors. These beds should be secluded and covered to conserve body heat. A box or crate of adequate size to permit the dog to lie full length in it will suffice. The cushion may be a burlap bag stuffed with shredded paper, *not straw, hay, or grass*. Paper is recommended, for its use will reduce the possibility of the dog's developing skin trouble.

114

Most dogs are allergic to fungi found on vegetative matter such as straw, hay, and grass. Wood shavings and excelsior may be used with impunity.

The kennel should be light, except for a retiring place; if sunshine is available at least part of the day, so much the better. Boxes in a shed or garage with secure wire runs to which the dogs have ready access suffice very well, are very inexpensive, and are easy to plan and to arrange. The runs should be made of wire fencing strong enough that the dogs are unable to tear it with their teeth and high enough that the dogs are unable to jump or climb over it. In-turning flanges of wire netting at the tops of the fences tend to obviate jumping. Boards, rocks, or cement buried around the fences forestall burrowing to freedom.

These pens need not be large, if the dogs are given frequent respites from their captivity and an opportunity to obtain needed exercise. However, they should be large enough to relieve them of the aspect of cages. Concrete floors for such pens are admittedly easy to keep clean and sanitary. However, they have no resilience, and the feet of dogs confined for long periods on concrete floors are prone to spread and their shoulders to loosen. A further objection to concrete is that it grows hot in the summer sunshine and is very cold in winter. If it is used for flooring at all, a low platform of wood, large enough to enable the dogs to sprawl out on it full length, should be provided in each pen.

A well drained soil is to be preferred to concrete, if it is available; but it must be dug out to the depth of three inches and renewed occasionally, if it is used. Otherwise, the accumulation of urine will make it sour and offensive. Agricultural limestone, applied monthly and liberally, will "sweeten" the soil.

Gates, hinges, latches, and other hardware must be trustworthy. The purpose of such quarters is to confine the dogs and to keep them from running at large; unless they serve such a purpose they are useless. One wants to know when one puts a dog in his kennel, the dog will be there when one returns. An improvised kennel of old chicken wire will not suffice for one never knows whether it will hold one's dogs or not.

Frequently two friendly bitches may be housed together, or a dog housed with a bitch. Unless one is sure of male friendships, it is seldom safe to house two adult male dogs together. It is better, if possible, to provide a separate kennel for each mature dog. But, if the dogs can be housed side by side with only a wire fence between them, they can have companionship without rancor. Night barking can be controlled by confining the dogs indoors or by shutting them up in their boxes.

Adult dogs require artificial heat in only the coldest of climates, if they are provided with tight boxes placed under shelter. Puppies need heat in cold weather up until weaning time, and even thereafter if they are not permitted to sleep together. Snuggled together in a tight box with shredded paper, they can withstand much cold without discomfort. All dogs in winter without artificial heat should have an increase of their rations—especially as pertains to fat content.

Whatever artificial heat is provided for dogs should be safe, foolproof, and dog-proof. Caution should be exercised that electric wiring is not exposed, that stoves cannot be tipped over, and that it is impossible for sparks from them to ignite the premises. Many fires in kennels, the results of defective heating apparatus or careless handling of it, have brought about the deaths of the inmates. It is because of them that this seemingly unnecessary warning is given.

No better place for a dog to live can be found than the home of its owner, sharing even his bed if permitted. So is the dog happiest. There is a limit, however, to the number of dogs that can be tolerated in the house. The keeper of a small kennel can be expected to alternate his favorite dogs in his own house, thus giving them a respite to confinement in a kennel. Provision must be made for a place of exercise and relief at frequent intervals for dogs kept in the house. An enclosed dooryard will serve such a purpose, or the dog may be exercised on a lead with as much benefit to the owner as to the dog.

That the quarters of the dog shall be dry is even more important than that they shall be warm. A damp, drafty kennel is the cause of much kennel disease and indisposition. It is harmless to permit a dog to go out into inclement weather of his own choice, if he is provided with a sheltered bed to which he may retire to dry himself.

By cleanness, sanitation is meant—freedom from vermin and bacteria. A little coat of dust or a degree of disorder does not discommode the dog or impair his welfare, but the best dog keepers are orderly persons. They at least do not permit bedding and old

116

bones to accumulate in a dog's bed, and they take the trouble to spray with antiseptic or wash with soap and water their dog's house at frequent intervals. The feces in the kennel runs should be picked up and destroyed at least once, and better twice, daily. Persistent filth in kennels can be counted on as a source of illness sooner or later. This warning appears superfluous, but it isn't; the number of ailing dogs kept in dirty, unsanitary kennels is amazing. It is one of the axioms of keeping dogs that their quarters must be sanitary or disease is sure to ensue.

GOOD DOG KEEPING PRACTICES

Pride of ownership is greatly enhanced when the owner takes care to maintain his dog in the best possible condition at all times. And meticulous grooming not only will make the dog look better but also will make him feel better. As part of the regular, daily routine, the grooming of the dog will prove neither arduous nor time consuming; it will also obviate the necessity for indulging in a rigorous program designed to correct the unkempt state in which too many owners permit their dogs to appear. Certainly, spending a few minutes each day will be well worth while, for the result will be a healthier, happier, and more desirable canine companion.

THAT DOGGY ODOR

Many persons are disgusted to the point of refusal to keep a dog by what they fancy is a "doggy odor." Of course, almost everything has a characteristic odor everyone is familiar with the smell of the rose. No one would want the dog to smell like a rose, and, conversely, the world wouldn't like it very well if the rose smelled doggy. The dog must emit a certain amount of characteristic odor or he woudn't be a dog. That seems to be his God-given grant. However, when the odor becomes too strong and obnoxious, then it is time to look for the reason. In most cases it is the result of clogged anal glands. If this be the case, all one must do to rid the pet of his odor is to express the contents of these glands and apply to the anal region a little soap and water.

If the odor is one of putrefaction, look to his mouth for the trouble. The teeth may need scaling, or a diseased root of some one or two teeth that need to be treated may be the source of the odor. In some dogs there is a fold or a crease in the lower lip near the lower canine tooth, and this may need attention. This spot is favored by fungi that cause considerable damage to the part. The smell here is somewhat akin to the odor of human feet that have been attacked by the fungus of athlete's foot.

The odor may be coming from the coat if the dog is heavily infested with fleas or lice. Too, dogs seem to enjoy the odor of dead fish and often roll on a foul smelling fish that has been cast up on the beach. The dog with a bad case of otitis can fairly "drive you out of the room" with this peculiar odor. Obviously, the way to rid the dog of odor is to find from whence it comes and then take steps to eliminate it. Some dogs have a tendency toward excessive flatulence (gas). These animals should have a complete change of diet and with the reducing of the carbohydrate content, a teaspoon of granular charcoal should be added to each feeding.

BATHING THE DOG

There is little to say about giving a bath to a dog, except that he shall be placed in a tub of warm (not hot) water and thoroughly scrubbed. He may, like a spoiled child, object to the ordeal, but if handled gently and firmly he will submit to what he knows to be inevitable.

The water must be only tepid, so as not to shock or chill the dog. A bland, unmedicated soap is best, for such soaps do not irritate the skin or dry out the hair. Even better than soap is one of the powdered detergents marketed especially for this purpose. They rinse away better and more easily than soap and do not leave the coat gummy or sticky.

It is best to begin with the face, which should be thoroughly and briskly washed with a cloth. Care should be taken that the cleaning solvent does not get into the dog's eyes, not because of the likelihood of causing permanent harm, but because such an experience is unpleasant to the dog and prone to prejudice him against future baths. The interior of the ear canals should be thoroughly cleansed until they not only look clean but also until no unpleasant odor comes from them. The head may then be rinsed and dried before proceeding to the body. Especial attention should be given to the drying of the ears, inside and outside. Many ear infections arise from failure to dry the canals completely.

With the head bathed and the surplus water removed from that part, the body must be soaked thoroughly with water, either with a hose or by dipping the water from the bath and pouring it over the dog's back until he is totally wetted. Thereafter, the soap or detergent should be applied and rubbed until it lathers freely. A stiff brush is useful in penetrating the coat and cleansing the skin. It is not sufficient to wash only the back and sides—the belly, neck, legs, feet, and tail must all be scrubbed thoroughly.

If the dog is very dirty, it may be well to rinse him lightly and repeat the soaping process and scrub again. Thereafter, the dog must be rinsed with warm (tepid) water until all suds and soil come away. If a bath spray is available, the rinsing is an easy matter. If the dog must be rinsed in standing water, it will be needful to renew it two or three times.

When he is thoroughly rinsed, it is well to remove such surplus water as may be squeezed with the hand, after which he is enveloped with a turkish towel, lifted from the tub, and rubbed until he is dry. This will probably require two or three dry towels. In the process of drying the dog, it is well to return again and again to the interior of the ears.

THE DOG'S TEETH

The dog, like the human being, has two successive sets of teeth, the so-called milk teeth or baby teeth, which are shed and replaced later by the permanent teeth. The temporary teeth, which begin to emerge when the puppy is two and a half to three weeks of age, offer no difficulty. The full set of milk teeth (consisting usually of six incisors and two canines in each jaw, with four molars in the upper jaw and six molars in the lower jaw) is completed usually just before weaning time. Except for some obvious malformation, the milk teeth may be ignored and forgotten about.

At about the fourth month the baby teeth are shed and gradually replaced by the permanent teeth. This shedding and replacement process may consume some three or four months. This is about the most critical period of the dog's life—his adolescence. Some constitutionally vigorous dogs go through their teething easily, with no

119

seeming awareness that the change is taking place. Others, less vigorous, may suffer from soreness of the gums, go off in flesh, and require pampering. While they are teething, puppies should be particularly protected from exposure to infectious diseases and should be fed on nutritious foods, especially meat and milk.

The permanent teeth normally consist of 42—six incisors and two canines (fangs) in each jaw, with twelve molars in the upper jaw and fourteen in the lower jaw. Occasionally the front molars fail to emerge; this deficiency is considered by most judges to be only a minor fault, if the absence is noticed at all.

Dentition is a heritable factor in the dog, and some dogs have soft, brittle and defective permanent teeth, no matter how excellent the diet and the care given them. The teeth of those dogs which are predisposed to have excellent sound ones, however, can be ruined by an inferior diet prior to and during the period of their eruption. At this time, for the teeth to develop properly, a dog must have an adequate supply of calcium phosphate and vitamin D, besides all the protein he can consume.

Often the permanent teeth emerge before the shedding of the milk teeth, in which case the dog may have parts of both sets at the same time. The milk teeth will eventually drop out, but as long as they remain they may deflect or displace the second teeth in the process of their growth. The incisors are the teeth in which a malformation may result from the late dropping of the baby teeth. When it is realized just how important a correct "bite" may be deemed in the show ring, the hazards of permitting the baby teeth to deflect the permanent set will be understood.

The baby teeth in such a case must be dislodged and removed. The roots of the baby teeth are resorbed in the gums, and the teeth can usually be extracted by firm pressure of thumb and finger, although it may be necessary to employ forceps or to take the puppy to the veterinarian.

The permanent teeth of the puppy are usually somewhat overshot, by which is meant that the upper incisors protrude over and do not play upon the lower incisors. Maturity may be trusted to remedy this apparent defect unless it is too pronounced.

An undershot mouth in a puppy, on the other hand, tends to grow worse as the dog matures. Whether or not it has been caused by the displacement of the permanent teeth by the persistence of

120

the milk teeth, it can sometimes be remedied (or at least bettered) by frequent hard pressure of the thumb on the lower jaw, forcing the lower teeth backward to meet the upper ones. Braces on dog teeth have seldom proved efficacious, but pressure and massage are worth trying on the bad mouth of an otherwise excellent puppy.

High and persistent fevers, especially from the fourth to the ninth month, sometimes result in discolored, pitted, and defective teeth, commonly called "distemper teeth." They often result from maladies other than distemper. There is little that can be done for them. They are unpleasant to see and are subject to penalty in the show ring, but are serviceable to the dog. Distemper teeth are not in themselves heritable, but the predisposition for their development appears to be. At least, at the teething age, the offspring from distemper toothed ancestors seem to be especially prone to fevers which impair their dentition.

Older dogs, especially those fed largely upon carbohydrates, tend to accumulate more or less tartar upon their teeth. The tartar generally starts at the gum line on the molars and extends gradually to the cusp. To rectify this condition, the dog's teeth should be scaled by a veterinarian.

The cleanliness of a dog's mouth may be brought about and the formation of tartar discouraged by the scouring of the teeth with a moist cloth dipped in a mixture of equal parts of table salt and baking soda.

A large bone given the dog to chew on or play with tends to prevent tartar from forming on the teeth. If tartar is present, the chewing and gnawing on the bone will help to remove the deposit mechanically. A bone given to puppies will act as a teething ring and aid in the cutting of the permanent teeth. So will beef hide strips you can buy in pet shops.

CARE OF THE NAILS

The nails of the dog should be kept shortened and blunted right down to the quick—never into the quick. If this is not done, the toes may spread and the foot may splay into a veritable pancake. Some dogs have naturally flat feet, which they have inherited. No pretense is made that the shortening of the nails of such a foot will obviate the fault entirely and make the foot beautiful or serviceable.

It will only improve the appearance and make the best of an obvious fault. Short nails do, however, emphasize the excellence of a good foot.

Some dogs keep their nails short by digging and friction. Their nails require little attention, but it is a rare dog whose foot cannot be bettered by artificially shortening the nails.

Nail clippers are available, made especially for the purpose. After using them, the sides of the nail should be filed away as much as is possible without touching the quick. Carefully done, it causes the dog no discomfort. But, once the quick of a dog's nail has been injured, he may forever afterward resent and fight having his feet treated or even having them examined.

The obvious horn of the nail can be removed, after which the quick will recede to permit the removal of more horn the following week. This process may be kept up until the nail is as short and blunt as it can be made, after which nails will need attention only at intervals of six weeks or two months.

Some persons clip the nails right back to the toes in one fell swoop, disregarding injury to the quick and pain of the dog. The nails bleed and the dog limps for a day or two, but infection seldom develops. Such a procedure should not be undertaken without a general anesthetic. If an anesthetic is used, this forthright method does not prejudice the dog against having his feet handled.

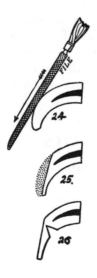

NAIL TRIMMING
ILLUSTRATED

The method here illustrated is to take a sharp file and stroke the nail downwards in the direction of the arrow, as in Figure 24, until it assumes the shape in Figure 25, the shaded portion being the part removed, a three-cornered file should then be used on the underside just missing the quick, as in Figure 26, and the operation is then complete, the dog running about quickly wears the nail to the proper shape.

Care for
the Old Dog

FIRST, how old is old, in a dog? Some breeds live longer than others, as a general rule. The only regularity about dog ages at death is their irregularity breed to breed and dog to dog.

The dog owner can best determine senility in his canine friend by the dog's appearance and behavior. Old dogs "slow down" much as humans do. The stairs are a little steeper, the breath a little shorter, the eye dimmer, the hearing usually a little harder.

As prevention is always better than cure, a dog's life may be happily and healthfully extended if certain precautionary steps are taken. As the aging process becomes quite evident, the owner should become more considerate of his dog's weaknesses, procrastinations and lapses. A softer, drier, warmer bed may be advisable; a foam rubber mattress will be appreciated. If a kennel dog has been able to endure record-breaking hot or cold, torrential or desert-dry days, he may in his old age appreciate spending his nights at least in a warm, comfy human house. And if the weather outside is frightful during the day, he should—for minimum comfort and safety—be brought inside before pneumonia sets in.

The old dog should NOT be required or expected to chase a ball, or a pheasant, or one of his species of different sex. The old bitch should not continue motherhood.

123

If many teeth are gone or going, foods should be softer. The diet should be blander—delete sweet or spicy or heavy tidbits—and there should be less of it, usually. The older dog needs less fat, less carbohydrate and less minerals unless disease and convalescence dictate otherwise. DON'T PERMIT AN OLD DOG TO GET FAT! It's cruel. The special diet known as PD or KD may be in order, if the dog has dietary troubles or a disease concomitant with old age. The veterinarian should be asked about PD or KD diets. Vitamin B-12 and other vitamin reinforcements may help.

The dog diseases of old age parallel many of the human illnesses. Senior male dogs suffer from prostate trouble, kidney disease and cancer. Senior bitches suffer from metritis and cancer. Both sexes suffer blindness, deafness and paralysis. Dogs suffer from heart disease; I know one old dog that is living an especially happy old age through the courtesy of digitalis. If the symptoms of any disease manifest themselves in an old dog the veterinarian MUST be consulted.

Many dog owners are selfish about old dogs. In their reluctance to lose faithful friends, they try to keep their canine companions alive in terminal illnesses, such as galloping cancer. If the veterinarian holds little or no promise for recovery of a pet from an illness associated with old age, or if the pet suffers, the kindest act the owner can perform is to request euthanasia. In this sad event, the kindest step the owner may take in *his* interest is to acquire a puppy or young dog of the same breed immediately. Puppies have a wonderful way of absorbing grief!

Glossary of Dog Terms

Achilles tendon: The large tendon attaching the muscle of the calf in the second thigh to the bone below the hock; the hamstring.

A.K.C.: The American Kennel Club.

Albino: An animal having a congenital deficiency of pigment in the skin, hair, and eyes.

American Kennel Club: A federation of member show-giving and specialty clubs which maintains a stud book, and formulates and enforces rules under which dog shows and other canine activities in the United States are conducted. Its address is 51 Madison Ave., New York, N. Y. 10010.

Angulation: The angles of the bony structure at the joints, particularly of the shoulder with the upper arm (front angulation), or the angles at the stifle and the hock (rear angulation).

Anus: The posterior opening of the alimentary canal through which the feces are discharged.

Apple head: A rounded or domed skull.

Balance: A nice adjustment of the parts one to another; no part too big or too small for the whole organism; symmetry.

Barrel: The ribs and body.

Bitch: The female of the dog species.

Blaze: A white line or marking extending from the top of the skull (often from the occiput), between the eyes, and over the muzzle.

Brisket: The breast or lower part of the chest in front of and between the forelegs, sometimes including the part extending back some distance behind the forelegs.

Burr: The visible, irregular inside formation of the ear.

Butterfly nose: A nose spotted or speckled with flesh color.

Canine: (Noun) Any animal of the family *Canidae*, including dogs, wolves, jackals, and foxes.
(Adjective) Of or pertaining to such animals; having the nature and qualities of a dog.

Canine tooth: The long tooth next behind the incisors in each side of each jaw; the fang.

Castrate: (Verb) Surgically to remove the gonads of either sex, usually said of the testes of the male.

Character: A combination of points of appearance, behavior, and disposition contributing to the whole dog and distinctive of the individual dog or of its particular breed.

Cheeky: Having rounded muscular padding on sides of the skull.

Chiseled: (Said of the muzzle) modeled or delicately cut away in front of the eyes to conform to breed type.

Chops: The mouth, jaws, lips, and cushion.

Close-coupled: Short in the loins.

Cobby: Stout, stocky, short-bodied; compactly made; like a cob (horse).

Coupling: The part of the body joining the hindquarters to the parts of the body in front; the loin; the flank.

Cowhocks: Hocks turned inward and converging like the presumed hocks of a cow.

Croup: The rear of the back above the hind limbs; the line from the pelvis to the set-on of the tail.

Cryptorchid: A male animal in which the testicles are not externally apparent, having failed to descend normally, not to be confused with a castrated dog.

Dentition: The number, kind, form, and arrangement of the teeth.

Dewclaws: Additional toes on the inside of the leg above the foot; the ones on the rear legs usually removed in puppyhood in most breeds.

Dewlap: The pendulous fold of skin under the neck.

Distemper teeth: The discolored and pitted teeth which result from some febrile disease.

Down in (or on) pastern: With forelegs more or less bent at the pastern joint.

Dry: Free from surplus skin or flesh about mouth, lips, or throat.

Dudley nose: A brown or flesh-colored nose, usually accompanied by eye-rims of the same shade and light eyes.

Ewe-neck: A thin sheep-like neck, having insufficient, faulty, or concave arch.

Expression: The combination of various features of the head and face, particularly the size, shape, placement and color of eyes, to produce a certain impression, the outlook.

Femur: The heavy bone of the true thigh.

Fetlock or Fetlock joint: The joint between the pastern and the lower arm; sometimes called the "knee," although it does not correspond to the human knee.

Fiddle front: A crooked front with bandy legs, out at elbow, converging at pastern joints, and turned out pasterns and feet, with or without bent bones of forearms.

Flews: The chops; pendulous lateral parts of the upper lips.

Forearm: The part of the front leg between the elbow and pastern.

Front: The entire aspect of a dog, except the head, when seen from the front; the forehand.

Guard hairs: The longer, smoother, stiffer hairs which grow through the undercoat and normally conceal it.

Hackney action: The high lifting of the front feet, like that of a Hackney horse, a waste of effort.

Hare-foot: A long, narrow, and close-toed foot, like that of the hare or rabbit.

Haw: The third eyelid, or nictitating membrane, especially when inflamed.

Height: The vertical distance from withers at top of shoulder blades to floor.

Hock: The lower joint in the hind leg, corresponding to the human ankle; sometimes, incorrectly, the part of the hind leg, from the hock joint to the foot.

Humerus: The bone of the upper arm.

Incisors: The teeth adapted for cutting; specifically, the six small front teeth in each jaw between the canines or fangs.

126

Knuckling over: Projecting or bulging forward of the front legs at the pastern joint; incorrectly called knuckle knees.

Leather: Pendant ears.

Lippy: With lips longer or fuller than desirable in the breed under consideration.

Loaded: Padded with superfluous muscle (said of such shoulders).

Loins: That part on either side of the spinal column between the hipbone and the false ribs.

Molar tooth: A rear, cheek tooth adapted for grinding food.

Monorchid: A male animal having but one testicle in the scrotum; monorchids may be potent and fertile.

Muzzle: The part of the face in front of the eyes.

Nictitating membrane: A thin membrane at the inner angle of the eye or beneath the lower lid, capable of being drawn across the eyeball. This membrane is frequently surgically excised in some breeds to improve the expression.

Occiput or occipital protuberance: The bony knob at the top of the skull between the ears.

Occlusion: The bringing together of the opposing surfaces of the two jaws; the relation between those surfaces when in contact.

Olfactory: Of or pertaining to the sense of smell.

Out at elbow: With elbows turned outward from body due to faulty joint and front formation, usually accompanied by pigeon-toes; loose-fronted.

Out at shoulder: With shoulder blades loosely attached to the body, leaving the shoulders jutting out in relief and increasing the breadth of the front.

Overshot: Having the lower jaw so short that the upper and lower incisors fail to meet; pig-jawed.

Pace: A gait in which the legs move in lateral pairs, the animal supported alternatively by the right and left legs.

Pad: The cushion-like, tough sole of the foot.

Pastern: That part of the foreleg between the fetlock or pastern joint and the foot; sometimes incorrectly used for pastern joint or fetlock.

Period of gestation: The duration of pregnancy, about 63 days in the dog.

Puppy: Technically, a dog under a year in age.

Quarters: The two hind legs taken together.

Roach-back: An arched or convex spine, the curvature rising gently behind the withers and carrying over the loins; wheel-back.

Roman nose: The convex curved top line of the muzzle.

Scapula: The shoulder blade.

Scissors bite: A bite in which the incisors of the upper jaw just overlap and play upon those of the lower jaw.

Slab sides: Flat sides with insufficient spring of ribs.

Snipey: Snipe-nosed, said of a muzzle too sharply pointed, narrow, or weak.

Spay: To render a bitch sterile by the surgical removal of her ovaries; to castrate a bitch.

Specialty club: An organization to sponsor and forward the interests of a single breed.

Specialty show: A dog show confined to a single breed.

Spring: The roundness of ribs.

Stifle or stifle joint: The joint next above the hock, and near the flank, in the hind leg; the joint corresponding to the knee in man.

Stop: The depression or step between the forehead and the muzzle between the eyes.

Straight hocks: Hocks lacking bend or angulation.

127

Straight shoulders: Shoulder formation with blades too upright, with angle greater than 90° with bone of upper arm.

Substance: Strength of skeleton, and weight of solid musculature.

Sway-back: A spine with sagging, concave curvature from withers to pelvis.

Thorax: The part of the body between the neck and the abdomen, and supported by the ribs and sternum.

Throaty: Possessing a superfluous amount of skin under the throat.

Undercoat: A growth of short, fine hair, or pile, partly or entirely concealed by the coarser top coat which grows through it.

Undershot: Having the lower incisor teeth projecting beyond the upper ones when the mouth is closed; the opposite to overshot; prognathous; underhung.

Upper arm: The part of the dog between the elbow and point of shoulder.

Weaving: Crossing the front legs one over the other in action.

Withers: The part between the shoulder bones at the base of the neck; the point from which the height of a dog is usually measured.

(End of Part II. Please see Contents page for total number of pages in book.)